To Jay Walljasper —
Thank you for your leadership,
inspiration, and good editing for a
better world!
with best wishes,
Barbara Brandt
5/31/95

WHOLE LIFE ECONOMICS
Revaluing Daily Life

Barbara Brandt

New Society Publishers
Philadelphia, PA   Gabriola Island, BC

Library of Congress Cataloging-in-Publication Data

Brandt, Barbara.
    Whole life economics : revaluing daily life / Barbara Brandt.
       p. cm.
    Includes bibliographic references and index.
    ISBN 0-86571-265-4 — ISBN 0-86571-266-2 (pbk.)
    1. Sustainable development. 2. Women in development. 3. Sex discrimination in
employment. 4. Ecofeminism. 5. Human ecology. I. Title.
HC79.E5B72 1995   338.9—dc20   94-24071

Inquiries regarding requests to reprint all or part of *Whole Life Economics: Revaluing Daily Life* should be addressed to New Society Publishers, 4527 Springfield Avenue, Philadelphia, PA, 19143.
    ISBN Hardcover   USA 0-86571-265-4   CAN 1-55092-208-4
    ISBN Paperback   USA 0-86571-266-2   CAN 1-55092-209-2

Cover by Parallel Design, Inc. Book design by Martin Kelley. Index by Do Mi Stauber. Printed on partially-recycled paper using soy-based ink by Capital City Press of Montpelier, Vermont.

To order directly from the publisher, add $3.00 to the price for the first copy, and add 75¢ for each additional copy. Send check or money order to:

In the United States:
New Society Publishers
4527 Springfield Avenue
Philadelphia, PA 19143

In Canada:
New Society Publishers
PO Box 189
Gabriola Island, BC VOR 1XO

New Society Publishers is a project of the New Society Educational Foundation, a nonprofit, tax-exempt, public foundation in the United States, and of the Catalyst Education Society, a nonprofit society in Canada. Opinions expressed in this book do not necessarily represent positions of the New Society Educational Foundation, nor the Catalyst Education Society.

The author and publisher gratefully acknowledge the following for permission to reproduce material: Ann Oakley, for excerpts from *Woman's Work* (Vintage, 1974); excerpts from Gita Sen and Caren Grown, *Development, Crises, and Alternative Visions* (Monthly Review Press, 1987), © 1987 by Sen and Grown, reprinted by permission of Monthly Review Foundation; Hazel Henderson, for the diagram "Interactive Prodcutive System of an Industrial Society," from *Paradigms in Progress* (Knowledge Systems, 1991); Scott Burns, for excerpts from *Home, Inc.* (Doubleday, 1975); Andrew Kimbrell, for excerpts from "A Time for Men to Pull Together," originally published in *Utne Reader*; Vanier Institute of the Family, for excerpts from William M. Nicholls and William A. Dyson, *The Informal Economy* (VIF, 1983); David Morris, for excerpts from "Good Stewardship Encourages Local Self-Reliance," originally published in *Co-op America Quarterly*; Western Canada Wilderness Society, for excerpts from Wade Davis, *The Penan* (WCWS, 1990); Stillpoint Institute, for excerpts from an interview with Helena Norberg-Hodge; Gene Logsdon, for excerpts from *At Nature's Pace* (Pantheon, 1994); Doubleday, for excerpts from Helen Augur, *Zapotec* (Doubleday, 1954).

TABLE OF CONTENTS

ACKNOWLEDGMENTS

I'd like to thank some of the new-economics visionaries and activists I have had the honor of meeting, whose pioneering work educated and inspired me to write this book: Hazel Henderson, for her ground breaking work; Paul Ekins, Susan Hunt, Joan Gussow, and the many other people of TOES (The Other Economic Summit), for bringing so much together and opening so many new doors; Mark Lutz, for his critical history of economic thought; Michael Linton, who taught me a new way of understanding money; Boston-area educator-activists Mel King and Severyn Bruyn, for their broad visions of and lifelong work for a more socially just economy; Susan Witt and Bob Swann of the E. F. Schumacher Society, tireless advocates for and innovators of an environmentally sustainable, community-based economics; Barbara Neely, Roz Feldberg, Laurie Sheridan, and the other members of the Shorter Work-Time Group and Women for Economic Justice, for their dedication to a multiclass, multiracial, multicultural feminism that makes a real difference in women's lives; and the members of the International Association for Feminist Economics, for broadening my understanding of economic invisibility and affirming the value of women's economic voices.

My deepest thanks also to the following people, who took the time to read and comment on parts or all of the manuscript in its various incarnations, for their intelligent, informed, and sometimes impassioned responses, both critical and encouraging:

Diane Balser, Joanne Brandt, Laurie Brandt, Barbara Carter, Jane Elioseff, Bob Erickson, Roz Feldberg, Lenore Finn, Joan Gussow, Deborah Holder, "D. L.," Larry Martin, Diana McCourt, Kim Mitchell, Tova Muller, Julie Nelson, Jessica Nembhard, Walter N., Bobbie Patrick, Judith Plant, Roger Pritchard, Jon Rosales, Naomi Rose, Deirdre Shea, Laurie Sheridan, Terri Small, Gerald Alonzo Smith, Jeff Snyder, Ellen Steese, Janet Stone, Andrea Szmyt, Bob Swann, Emily Tan, Laurie Taymor-Berry, Lisa Tiemann, and "M. Z."

I'd like to thank Anne Wilson Schaef for teaching us that addiction is not just an individual problem but also an institutionally and societally generated phenomenon.

And finally, thanks to my editor at New Society Publishers, Barbara Hirshkowitz, for insisting that I express myself more clearly and eloquently, to Dawn Ripley for efficient copy-editing, and to all at NSP for having faith in this book.

FOREWORD

When Barbara Brandt contacted me and asked if I would be willing to write a foreword to this book, I had my usual hesitation. I am honored to have many more requests of this kind than I can possibly do, and since I believe in doing a thorough job of studying the manuscript before I say anything, an undertaking of this kind involves a significant amount of time and effort. Yet, even though I have avoided reading books on economics and politics as I consider them both to be unreal constructs of an addictive society, I was intrigued. I am very glad that I accepted the offer.

The process of reading *Whole Life Economics* was for me the process of coming home. I can see that I have not avoided economics. I have avoided the prevailing modernist economic paradigm. That it is a creation of Western culture, mechanistic science and a progressively addictive society comes as no surprise to me. What does come as a surprise to me is that I did not see this clearly until I read this book. Of course this Western mechanistic scientific paradigm that has evoked a culture that not only supports addictions but *demands* them in order to be able to tolerate what we have created would also create an approach to economics that is mechanistic, denies wholeness, and follows the progressive deterioration of the disease of addiction. I would never have done the research to document this knowing, and I applaud Barbara Brandt for her research, her synthesis of the material, and her excellent lists of sources and resources. It is a relief to see the documentation for my suspicions and to have salient relationships so carefully demonstrated.

Secondly, there is the relief of no longer feeling crazy and having my experience validated. Some years ago, I had the horrific and enlightening experience of being sued. While it was painfully unpleasant, it has turned out to be one of the most powerful learning and spiritual experiences of my life.

During the "inquisition" I discovered that any part of my life was fair game. My diaries, personal letters, financial dealings both professional and private, and whatever else, were all open to scrutiny. Thank goodness I had nothing to hide. At one point, I was being interrogated about how I "ran" my office-corporation. My response was that I did not "run" my office. The two women who run my office run my office. The opposing attorneys then asked, "Who supervises your office manager?" I responded, "No one." They then said, "Don't you supervise her?" "No," I replied, "Why would I supervise her when she knows more about running an office than I do?" They were incredulous. "Then who supervises the other woman in your office?" "No one," I said, "She does a completely different job than the other woman, and they cooperate on joint tasks that they determine."

Needless to say, the opposing lawyers were shocked. They clearly communicated to me and to each other that I was either lying or crazy or both. It was clear to me that we were dealing with a "systems issue" coming from very different systems. I knew that their system asked us to be not dead and not alive and killed the spirit and spirituality long before it kills the body and the planet. Unfortunately, the addictive system is the dominant system, and it is not possible to see it as an addictive system or even as a system until one gets out of it. When one is in it, it is perceived as "reality." Even though I had left it, I remembered it. And, I also know the system I am living out of now and which I choose to call a Living Process System. They thought their system was "reality" and knew of no other systems. Often, persons who believe that their system is reality when they are faced with other realities feel that they have no other choice than to call those who differ "crazy" or say that they do not understand reality. For those of us pioneering new and ancient "realities" there is always the invitation to accept the judgment of "crazy" or "unrealistic."

I remembered this experience as I read *Whole Life Economics* and was grateful to have myself and the Wilson Schaef Corporation validated on every page. We have experimented with a corporation that is ever-changing and evolving to meet the needs of those who work there and those we serve. We have evolved a wholistic, participatory model and have done well. It is a corporation that does healthy things for people and is a good place to work. We operate out of a post-modernist paradigm.

This made me think of another corporation in which I am involved which is also evolving new models. A group of us have gone together and bought a 110-ten-year-old hot springs hotel in Montana. It is a place where people have come for healing for hundreds of years. The Indians called it Peace Valley and would never fight there as they felt the healing should be available to everyone. We feel the same way and have tried to restore it and run it on a community model as a place for healing and renewal. Most of us who have put money into this effort feel that the owners meetings themselves are more than enough "return" on our investment. We are operating with respect, integrity, openness, honesty, and a value system that supports our diverse spiritualities. We are not perfect, and we practice what we preach as a way of life, not as an abstract concept. I am grateful to be a part of this adventure. Again, I found support for what we are doing in *Whole Life Economics*. I will recommend this book to all the owners of Boulder Hot Springs as well as the people who are training with me. I am glad to have it to recommend.

The author of *Serpent in the Sky* suggested that culture came to an important juncture some time ago. One road led to the Egyptian culture and its belief systems and the other to the Greco-Roman belief systems. It seems that Western culture chose the Greco-Roman. This is known history. What leapt out at me from that book was not the facts but the statement that in the Greco-Roman system, the purpose of government is regulation and control while the purpose of government in the Egyptian system was the spiritual growth of the individual and the system. I pondered that for some time. It was almost twenty years ago when I read that book, and I tried to imagine what a system would be like that was based upon spirituality.

All dominant modern systems are based upon modernist economics. In fact, we have evolved a worldview that teaches that economics as measured by the GNP/GDP is the basis of the social system. I have long said that any system that is based upon economics is destined to fail. It does not matter whether it is capitalism, communism or socialism. It will fail. Economics is not the center of human existence. Only social systems that are based upon spirituality will meet the needs of humans, nature and the planet.

For the last several years, I have been spending a large amount of my time with Native elders throughout the world. This has been one of the most enriching experiences of my life. And as I have listened to the wisdom of these elders and explored my own Native American heritage, I have come to see that the systems that they are teaching are based in spirituality, the spiritual growth of each individual and the spirituality of all nature and of all the planet. We have models of *Whole Life Economics* all around us if we are not too arrogant to see them. Barbara Brandt and the elders are saying many of the same things. Tribal peoples know about participation and cooperation, living with the Earth and caring for the Earth, having and sharing, and using and preserving. We have much to learn.

Whole Life Economics opens new doors and reminds us of our ancient memories. It gives support for trying new things and valuing what we are doing while learning our wholeness. It is a book well-timed and badly needed. I applaud it and recommend it.

—Anne Wilson Schaef, Ph.D., DHL

Author of *Women's Reality, When Society Becomes an Addict, Beyond Therapy, Beyond Science*, and forthcoming, *Like Water on Sandstone: Native Wisdom for White Minds*.

INTRODUCTION

THE ECONOMY—
FROM A NONECONOMIC PERSPECTIVE

This book describes a new economics emerging in the world today, an economics that more fully meets human needs, supports personal and community relationships, promotes justice and empowerment, and is more respectful of the natural environment than our officially recognized economic systems. It explains why this new economics is now emerging, and how you can make it more a reality, in your own life and in the larger community.

Many of my friends were surprised to hear that I was writing this book, because I'm not an economist. It's commonly assumed that only highly trained professionals have the ability to understand the issues, the right to think about economic problems or to come up with new solutions. As a result, many people feel powerless regarding the economy. This is reinforced by the fact that when experts talk about economics they use esoteric technical jargon and complicated mathematical models. And most business and government leaders and media spokespeople talk about the health or weakness of the economy as if it were some abstract entity far removed from our daily lives.

But the economy is not something "out there," understandable only to the experts. You and I create the economy every day, in the course of our daily lives, with our minds and bodies, our hearts and souls, our skills and dreams and values. We create the economy out of the feelings we have about ourselves and our own worth, through our relationships with each other and through our connections to the natural world. And if we create the economy, this also means that we can change it, through the activities of our daily lives, so that it more fully meets our real needs and expresses our deepest values.

WHY MODERN ECONOMIES MUST CHANGE

Most books about far-reaching economic changes focus on the so-called undeveloped nations, the Third World. It is commonly assumed that modern industrialized societies, such as the United States, Canada, the Western European nations, and Japan, have arrived at the ultimate stage of economic evolution, and that the rest of the world wants to be like us. The recent fall of the former Soviet empire has only confirmed the apparent triumph of modern capitalism and the free-market approach to economic progress.

But modern nations are increasingly beset by their own economic, social, and environmental crises: the crumbling of long-established corporations; falling wages and rising unemployment; increasing physical and emotional stress, both on and off the job; continued discrimination based on gender, race, ethnicity, and other harmful criteria; increasing violence; serious youth problems, such as vandalism and teen suicides, and other expressions of social and cultural breakdown; drug use and other forms of addiction; growing poverty, hunger, and homelessness; and continued environmental degradation.

In response to the mounting personal, social, political, economic, environmental, and spiritual problems of modern nations, a new economics is now being developed by a diverse range of people throughout the world. A major reason behind this new economics is people's concern that those activities considered most successful according to conventional economic standards are at the same time harming our mental and physical health, destroying the natural environment, running counter to our deepest values, and actually may be undermining our economic viability. Growing numbers of people today are realizing that what we need is not more economic success, but a new definition of what a successful economy can be.

TOWARD A NEW KIND OF ECONOMICS

These days all kinds of people—business and government leaders, professional economists, and even people at the grassroots level—are wondering where our economies are going, and what we can do—as individuals, through businesses and other organizations, and through government policy—to get us where we need to go. These concerns are usually phrased in such terms as: How can we raise productivity? Improve efficiency? Increase competitiveness? Develop new high-tech industries and take advantage of emerging new markets? How can we increase employment? Adjust from a manufacturing to a service and information economy? How can we best stimulate investment? Restore consumer confidence? Increase economic growth?

But such questions are based on the same old assumptions about what the economy is, what constitutes economic success, and what leads to individual and societal well-being. That's why they are inadequate for helping us resolve the current crisis. Only by starting from different kinds of questions can we come up with real solutions.

Many people these days have started raising the kinds of questions we now need to be asking, for example:

— How can we rear children without giving in to overly materialistic values?

— Why do we have to save companies by laying off employees, closing down local branches, and devastating communities?

— Can we meet our material needs and create jobs without destroying the natural environment?

— Why does the effort to make a living leave so little time and energy for personal, family, or social life?

If you have ever wondered about such things, then you, too, have begun to redefine the problem and are paving the way for new solutions.

ECONOMIC ADDICTION AND ECONOMIC INVISIBILITY

In order to understand why the old answers can no longer help us, this book explores two dynamics central to modern economies: economic addiction and economic invisibility. We must recognize and move beyond both of them in order to create a more personally fulfilling, socially just, and environmentally sustainable economy.

Economic addiction refers to the inability to set limits on or say no to our economic activities. Modern economies are characterized by many economic addictions—work addiction, job addiction, money addiction, and the addiction to constantly increasing production—all of them justified by the belief that more is better. A key example is the addiction to constantly increasing sales and consumption. It doesn't matter that our children are learning to measure their self-worth by how many designer jeans, sneakers, and video games they own, or that in order to keep this vast production-consumption mechanism going, the natural environment is being depleted and destroyed faster than we can repair it, and the resulting pollutants further threaten human and environmental health. If we stopped selling and consuming ever more, businesses would lose money, employees would have to be laid off, and the economy would eventually collapse. So any attempt to bring about a more humane, fulfilling, and environmentally supportive economy must improve our well-being while it frees us from the vicious cycle of economic addictions.

Economic invisibility refers to the fact that many activities essential for human well-being are not officially considered part of the economy. Entire groups of people—women, children, or the unemployed—can become economically invisible. For example, the economy is conventionally assumed to include such things as jobs, the activities of businesses, and the accumulation of money. Women's characteristic activities, such as giving birth to and raising children and caring for other family members, are often categorized as biological or emotional functions, not part of the economy. Many other crucial economic functions, such as the self-generating processes of the natural environment, are also not considered to be part of the economy. Any attempt to bring about a more just, humane, and personally fulfilling economy must begin with recognition of the far-reaching extent and implications of economic invisibility.

I became interested in these two dynamics, economic addiction and economic invisibility, because of my work as a community organizer and social-change activist in low- and moderate-income urban neighborhoods in the Boston area, communities such as the place where I live. For over twenty years I've been bringing people of many ages and backgrounds together to participate as volunteers in a variety of community-improvement, cultural, educational, political, and environmental projects.

I became aware of economic addiction because I kept running into the problem of jobs vs. the environment, the economy vs. the environment. Over and over again, construction projects were being proposed in the Boston area that threatened local ecosystems but were justified on the grounds that they would create jobs and stimulate economic development. As a resident of and activist in a poorer community, I was well aware of the need for better economic opportunities. But most of these construction projects were get-rich schemes for their developers, or would have resulted in more amenities for rich people, often at the expense of poorer people who would be displaced. No one was thinking seriously about what poor and unemployed people really needed.

Gradually I concluded that the supposed conflict between jobs and the environment is often no more than an excuse to sacrifice nature to the illusion of economic improvement, while in fact few people who really need help ever benefit. And in the long run, as the environment becomes more polluted, everyone comes out worse. It seems to me that society's eagerness to accept any kind of destructive project, as long as the magic words "jobs" or "economic development" are invoked, constitutes a form of addiction.

I learned about economic invisibility after I had spent many years as a community activist, often as a volunteer myself, working with other volunteers. It never occurred to me that our activities could be considered noneconomic. After all, the women and men with whom I planned and carried out these projects were doing exactly the same things in a volunteer capacity that other people get paid for: They were growing food; leading physical-fitness workshops; doing research on political and economic issues; educating people about energy, the environment, and other scientific topics through lectures, tours, and newsletters; even insulating people's homes and building solar-heated greenhouses.

But they did all those things in their free time, without pay. And they often carried out these volunteer projects with considerably more energy, enthusiasm, commitment, and creativity than many people display in their paying jobs.

Furthermore, unlike many large corporations or public bureaucracies, which often waste vast amounts of money and time with few positive results, these volunteers—in community gardening, energy-conservation education, community cultural festivals, campaigns for environmental restoration, or neighborhood improvement—were getting things done. We were learning new skills, improving our lives and the lives of the people we cared about, and having a good time.

Imagine my surprise when I discovered that according to conventional practice, such volunteer activities, being unpaid, are not considered part of the economy!

If you are aware of the amazing creativity, dedication, and effectiveness that can characterize people's activities in the voluntary sector, then you too might agree that this omission seems extremely strange and unfair. I began to wonder if perhaps other important activities which may also be just as significant and productive, if not more so, than the activities of the conventionally valued economy are also left out. So I was excited when I began to meet other people who talked about the need to redefine the economy and the meaning of economic success. Many of these people said that we need—and are now experiencing the birth of—a new economic paradigm.

ABOUT PARADIGMS

The word "paradigm" is not unique to economics. It was first brought to public attention during the 1960s by the U.S. scientist and historian Thomas S. Kuhn, in his influential and controversial book *The Structure of Scientific Revolutions*.

Kuhn observed that throughout the course of history, commonly accepted perceptions of reality developed by scientists are eventually displaced by new perceptions of how the world works. He defined a paradigm as a group of "universally recognized scientific achievements that for a time provide model problems and solutions to a community of practitioners," that is, the shared beliefs about the nature of reality held for a time by the scientific community.

As scientists conduct experiments, they regularly encounter surprise results that don't fit the assumptions of the prevailing paradigm. Kuhn called such exceptions "anomalies." As anomalies turn up, he said, scientists either have to find ways to explain them in terms of the prevailing paradigm — or, if enough anomalies appear, they eventually have to construct a new paradigm.[1]

Kuhn's description of changing paradigms seized the popular imagination, and the word began to be used in a much broader context to mean such things as a popularly accepted model for how the world works, or an underlying framework for looking at the world in general.

THE PASSING OF THE MODERN ERA

The last decades of the twentieth century have brought massive and rapid changes in every aspect of our lives. As we seek to make sense of these countless unprecedented developments, many people speak of a larger paradigm shift now taking place. The world has changed so much that we are now moving into the "postmodern" era.

Theologian David Ray Griffin, who has studied the emerging postmodern paradigm in the sciences and in other areas of society, explains:

> The rapid spread of the term *postmodern* in recent years witnesses to a growing dissatisfaction with modernity and to an increasing sense that the modern age not only had a beginning but can have an end as well. Whereas the word *modern* was almost always used until quite recently as a word of praise and as a synonym for *contemporary,* a growing sense is now evidenced that we can and should leave modernity behind—in fact, that we *must* if we are to avoid destroying ourselves and most of the life on our planet.
>
> *Modernity,* rather than being regarded as the norm for human society toward which all history has been aiming and into which all societies should be ushered—forcibly if necessary—is instead increasingly seen as an aberration . . . *modernism* as a worldview is less and less seen as The Final Truth, in comparison with which all divergent worldviews are automatically regarded as "superstitious." The modern worldview is increasingly relativized to the status of one among many, useful for some purposes, inadequate for others.[2]

So while it might sound strange at first, this means that the modern paradigm is actually the *old* system. Although still powerful in many areas of life, it is gradually falling away, being challenged by newly emerging postmodern structures, relationships, values, and paradigms.

But simply describing this new era as postmodern does not tell us much. What specific characteristics distinguish the postmodern from the modern world?

For many people, postmodernism is a depressing turn of events. It means the end of long-held beliefs and values that shaped the society they knew. It means social breakdown, the decline of traditional systems of authority, a loss of standards, a belief that everything is relative and anything goes.

But other people believe that the turmoil we are now going through actually represents a transition period. The old ways are breaking down as new, more just, humane, and healthful values and ways of doing things are being created. Of course this transition to a more humane, balanced, and loving world will not just happen by itself, and there is no guarantee that it will happen at all. But many people believe that it can be brought into being as more of us realize that this is not just a time of despair. As we recognize the potential of the times, we can take steps in our own lives to help realize this potential more fully.

MODERNISM:
A FRAGMENTED, HIERARCHICAL CONCEPTION OF REALITY

It is not easy to recognize the assumptions—and limitations—of a prevailing paradigm until one has started to move beyond it. Now that we are moving into a postmodern world, individuals from a wide variety of fields are attempting to articulate the essential differences between modern and postmodern worldviews.

The following books helped me understand the larger transitions taking place today as we move from the modern to the postmodern world: Fritjof Capra's *The Turning Point*, about overall changes in science and society; Riane Eisler's *The Chalice and the Blade*, about alternatives to destructive hierarchies and new models of gender relationships; *Spirituality and Society* and *The Reenchantment of Science*, edited by David Ray Griffin, about more holistic scientific models and positive social implications of postmodernism; John Naisbitt's *Megatrends*, about social, economic, and business changes; Anne Wilson Schaef's *Women's Reality*, about the emerging female perspective in society, and *Beyond Therapy, Beyond Science*, about a more holistic therapeutic process; and Linda Jean Shepherd's *Lifting The Veil*, on the emergence of the feminine in science.[3] I have also drawn on comments from friends and acquaintances about what they see happening around us, and made my own observations.

These sources helped me understand that the following five aspects of modernism were most important in shaping the old economic paradigm.

The Triumph of Science and Technology over Nature

In Europe during the sixteenth and seventeenth centuries, the work of scientists and philosophers such as Galileo, Francis Bacon, and René Descartes challenged the traditional veneration of nature and led to the radically new worldview of modern science. Among its assumptions: The world is a machine, made up of isolated pieces of physical matter; human beings are separate from and superior to the rest of the natural world; and the purpose of human intelligence is to subdue and control nature.[4] In the following centuries, inspired by these principles, numerous new inventions not only enabled scientists to pierce the long-hidden secrets of nature but gave people the power to manipulate, alter, and destroy the natural world at a rate and scale never before possible.

The Triumph of Numerical Measurement

Modern science broke the world up into myriads of distinct, numerically quantifiable characteristics. If something could be counted, it could be measured and studied. If it could not be turned into numbers, it did not exist. This obsession with numbers led to the worship of quantity over quality, and to the belief that more is better. It also led to the belief that even morality could be quantified, that values can be translated into dollars, and that monetary calculations can be used to determine individual or societal goals.

The Triumph of Bigness

Modern societies demonstrated their prowess through accomplishments of ever larger size: the world's tallest building, giant corporations employing hundreds of thousands of people, the world's largest gross national product and highest standard of living. Small buildings were torn down to make way for skyscrapers; small communities became megacities; small businesses were engulfed by multinational corporate empires. And with each new triumph, the only way to go was up, to supersede it with something even bigger. More is better. Bigger is better.

The Triumph of the Masculine

According to its own ideology, the modern world was created by the tireless efforts of idealized male figures: the pioneer, the adventurer, the entrepreneur, the scientist, the inventor. It was men who had the requisite characteristics for success: independence; an active, driving nature; bold visions and capacity for leadership; an ability for precise calculation and unbiased, rational thought. In the modern world, women—considered weak, passive, dependent, nurturing, and emotional by nature—were relegated to the home and the care of children, their purpose being to provide a quiet, reliable, undifferentiated backdrop for the achievements of individual males.

The Triumph of the White, Western Nations

Modernism, with its dominating technologies, acceptance of exclusively numerical standards, worship of bigness, and idolization of the active, striving male, came from Europe and North America—the West. And these societies used their economic, political, and technological power to subdue the non-white, non-Western peoples of the world, not just materially but also culturally. Defining itself as superior, modernism brought its standards to the entire world, creating a global hierarchy with white, Western nations and culture on top and so-called primitives—people of color and non-Western cultures—on the bottom.

Modernism breaks the world up into hierarchical structures. The five hierarchical principles described above are central to the modern economic paradigm—the old system, which is now passing.

THE BIRTH OF A NEW ECONOMICS

During the 1980s, new ways of thinking about and participating in the economy blossomed and began to enter the wider public consciousness. This growing consciousness is exemplified by the spread of many new kinds of economic institutions and activities, such as community-based economic development, socially responsible investing, and socially responsible business. And it has been advanced by a constantly growing stream of publications that describe such new concepts and practices as human economics, green economics, or social economics.[5] Many of these innovations had their origins in the 1970s or earlier, but in the 1980s they seemed to reach critical mass, became more formally organized, and began reaching a wider public.

Because of my growing interest in new economic approaches, I enthusiastically sought out these economic pioneers, attended many of their conferences, read their books and articles. I also did volunteer work for two groups—The Other Economic Summit (TOES), an international network of advocates and activists for a more socially just and sustainable economics, and the Industrial Cooperative Association, which organizes worker-owned businesses—in order to learn more about their fields of activity.[6] As I became familiar with the scope of this emerging new economics, I began to realize how many important and exciting things are happening, most of which are still almost completely unrecognized by our mainstream leaders, professional economists, and the media.

There are several reasons why this emerging new economy is still largely overlooked. For one thing, it is characterized by numerous scattered, small-scale, local innovations. Its projects are often developed in response to some very specific issue such as the humiliation of women on welfare, the closing of a long-running factory, the poverty of a specific ethnic community, or the decline of a particular inner-city neighborhood or rural small town. The small size, extreme diversity, and wide geographical dispersion of these new models make it difficult to recognize the emergence of a larger pattern.

Second, many of the new models being developed are aimed at or undertaken by "marginal" groups of people—inner-city African-Americans or Hispanics, lower-income mothers, hippies, or people from non-modernized, non-Western societies. Thus, it can easily be assumed that even if such projects meet these people's specific needs, they hardly have much applicability to the majority of the mainstream middle class in modern economies, or to the larger problems, such as unemployment and foreign competition, that beset entire nations.

Third, many aspects of this new economy would not be considered economic in conventional terms. Some of these new models involve using money for goals other than the maximization of production or monetary return. Others represent what might be called the invisible economy, numerous everyday activities through which ordinary people create and distribute necessary goods and services without buying, selling, or using money. For both reasons, many extremely important economic innovations now appearing in the world today remain unrecognized by those who adhere to the conventional definitions of what constitutes an economy. It is likely that even many people who are actually helping to create this new economy are not aware of the economic significance of their actions.

I decided to write this book because I wanted to let more people know about the numerous positive developments now taking place. And I wanted to emphasize the value of supposedly noneconomic activities in the creation of this new economic paradigm. Even many writings about postmodern economics are limited because they focus on changes in institutions and activities conventionally recognized as being part of the economy, while they overlook the importance of women's unpaid work and other aspects of the invisible economy. The fact that women's traditional roles, people's caring work for their families, community volunteer work, social change work, and the processes of the natural environment are conventionally considered outside the economy underscores why the prevailing economic paradigm must change.

THE OLD—MODERN—ECONOMIC PARADIGM

The modern economic paradigm refers to the conventionally accepted economic assumptions and practices that have dominated Western Europe and North America over the last few centuries and which these societies have recently been attempting to extend into the rest of the world.

The modern economic paradigm developed slowly, starting about five hundred years ago, and became more fully established with the Industrial Revolution, which originated in England in the late 1700s. It was made explicit by the Scottish philosopher Adam Smith, who articulated the principles of modern market economies in his classic work, *The Wealth Of Nations*, published in 1776.

In the late 1800s, formal mathematical models were applied to Smith's concepts in order to make his ideas more scientific, an approach called "neo-classical economics," which still dominates the study of economics to this day.[7] Over the years, these theories and models have been used to explain and justify modern capitalist economies and the market system. Meanwhile, the values of industrial capitalism—including the belief that more is better, and that we can and should continue to have more of everything—have spread through the educational system and the media, shaping popular culture and people's everyday beliefs and actions.

I suggest that the central assumption of the modern economic paradigm is the belief that money represents value. According to this belief, the more money one has, the more things of value one can buy, leading to greater well-being.

That's why the modern economic paradigm defines economics in terms of such issues as the success of businesses in producing and selling goods and services in order to make money and the ways in which individuals make money (from investments or paid employment). The operations of the market—that is, the rising and falling of prices in response to changes in supply and demand—are also among its central concerns. In the modern economic paradigm, the economy is defined by the movement and behavior of money, and any activity that increases the amount of money gained by an individual, business, or nation is considered economically successful.

WHOLE LIFE ECONOMICS AND THE POSTMODERN ECONOMIC PARADIGM

While there is a range of writings describing the new economics, this book explores the emerging postmodern economic paradigm in terms of a combination of values and perspectives that I call whole life economics.

The goal of whole life economics is to empower people and create a better balance between our economic activities and the rest of life.

Whole life economics recognizes that human well-being comes from treating individuals as whole people, integrating body, mind, emotions, social needs, and spiritual values. It follows that a good economic system is one that promotes such integration in all our activities. For this reason, the primary focus of whole life economics is not on money, business, interest rates, productivity, or other conventional economic concepts. Instead, whole life economics starts from such values as our physical well-being and mental and emotional health, our social relationships, our ability to meet our needs and the needs of those we care about, our connection to the natural environment, and our need for spiritual meaning. And the new paradigm is characterized by economic institutions that honor, rather than ignore or negate, these crucial sources of human well-being.

The old economic paradigm was characterized by economic invisibility and economic addictions. The values and institutions of the emerging paradigm are acknowledging that what was invisible provides a key to the new solutions we seek. This new paradigm of whole life economics is helping us recognize and learn from the many valuable contributions of formerly invisible actors and activities. This postmodern economic paradigm is also demonstrating ways for individuals and institutions to recover from economic addictions, so that we can meet our needs and improve our quality of life while simultaneously creating a more economically and socially just society that honors, rather than destroys, the Earth. The following five transitions are among the most important aspects of the new economic paradigm.

A New Relationship between People and the Earth

Central to the modern economic paradigm is the belief that the natural world should be subdued by man, controlled by science and technology, and turned into products and money. Modern economics devotes considerable energy to calculating how to extract and process natural resources most cheaply—without any regard for further consequences—and assumes that jobs and people's economic well-being can only be achieved through the destruction of nature.

By contrast, the new paradigm recognizes that nature is not merely a collection of passive physical materials mutely waiting around to be dug up or chopped down, but is a dynamic, living system of plants, animals, soils, waters, weather, and numerous other processes that constitute the ultimate source of all our economic activities. And it assumes that an economic system that honors the Earth is also one that enhances human quality of life. Whole life economics perceives human beings and the Earth not as competitors but as participants in a mutually sustaining relationship.

A New Role for Business

Businesses in modern nations are now changing radically. Many are becoming smaller, while others are reaching new heights of international power. Some companies are becoming leaner and meaner, while others are becoming more worker-friendly and more socially responsible. While all these changes are important, and the move of many businesses to greater social awareness is especially desirable, whole life economics nevertheless helps us recognize that businesses are only one aspect of the total economy. Many new economic forms that are clearly not businesses are also being developed and growing in importance. Besides, even with the best intentions and most admirable values, there is only so far that good businesses can go within the modern economic paradigm. The new paradigm recognizes the many changes needed in the larger society that can allow businesses to become even more humane, as well as socially and environmentally responsible.

A New Relationship beween Women and Men

Women's achievement of better jobs, higher pay, and greater respect in the paid workforce is an essential aspect of a more just economy. Nevertheless, the organization of paid work under the modern paradigm is often physically, emotionally, and economically harmful to jobholders in general, whether women or men. In the new paradigm, assumptions about jobs are changing, leading to more economically just and personally fulfilling work opportunities for both women and men.

The new whole life economics also helps us understand why the modern economy has typically been identified with masculine activities, while women's role has been idealized as being outside the economy. Furthermore, people are now recognizing how the old paradigm has kept men, as well as women, from becoming whole people. The new paradigm suggests what an economic system more fully shaped by traditionally female activities and concerns might look like, and how both women and men can implement such empowering changes in their lives.

New Assumptions about Jobs, Work, and Time

The continued generation of large numbers of jobs, long taken for granted in modern economies, is now being wiped out by corporate downsizing, automated production and service technologies, business flight to the Third World, and other recent trends. As the numbers of available jobs continue to shrink, work and time in modern economies are becoming ever more badly distributed, with continued widespread unemployment for many and overwork a common problem for those still lucky enough to have jobs.

Both unemployment and overwork corrode the quality of modern life. Unemployment brings about poverty and despair and destroys people's self-esteem. Overwork causes physical and emotional stress and takes away time for personal development, family life, and community involvement. So in the new paradigm, people are realizing that a more humane and just economy would provide not only better paid work opportunities for those who need them, but also would provide the opportunity for everyone to spend less time working.[8]

A New Relationship between
the United States and the Rest of the World

The United States of America has often been called the most modern of modern nations because it has most eagerly abandoned other values and traditions while making the expansion of the visible economy its leading goal. In no other culture is business so highly regarded as the source of society's wealth and well-being, the production and consumption of business output equated with the measure of well-being, the accumulation of money equated with social good, and one's paid work (or lack thereof) accepted as the basis of one's identity and self-esteem. Furthermore, the economic goals, values, and the institutions of the United States shape not only the lives of this nation's inhabitants but also affect millions of other people around the world.[9]

This book gives examples of the new economic paradigm now emerging in industrialized nations around the world, in the United States, Canada, Western Europe, and Japan. However, I emphasize that the United States is changing. Not only is it essential for people in the United States to know that they can help make their own society more humane, just, and environmentally responsible, both internally and internationally, but it's also important that people in other parts of the world know that the United States is changing. This can help people committed to greater justice, compassion, and environmental respect build supportive alliances, not just within their own communities but across national borders.

I should also clarify that although I emphasize changes taking place in the United States, the inspiration for such changes often comes from other nations, both modern and nonindustrialized. At this time in history it's especially necessary for the United States to relinquish its long-standing sense of self-importance and participate in the world more humbly, as would a student seeking to learn from other cultures and sources.

IN CONCLUSION

The first half of this book develops the perspectives of whole life economics to help explain why the modern economic paradigm and modern economies are increasingly destructive and dysfunctional. It explores invisibility in mainstream economies, especially the devaluation of caring activities, women and nature, and the invisibility of many of the system's costs and harmful consequences. And it explains the means by which the modern economy became an addictive system and examines the implications of economic addictions for our personal lives and the goals and activities of our institutions.

The second half describes many specific examples of the newly emerging economy, the lessons they teach us about how the economy really operates, and the new models they offer for a more fulfilling, equitable, and environmentally supportive society. It explores models that can help us move beyond economic addictions and suggests actions you can take to become more economically empowered. You will also find references to many organizations, publications, and other resources to help you follow up on new directions of most interest to you.

I hope that by making visible what has long been invisible, and by bringing long-hidden alternatives to light, this book will encourage you to recognize the value of your own contributions to the economy, whether they are paid or unpaid. It may help you discover that you are already modeling new economic alternatives, perhaps without realizing it. Most of all, I hope it encourages you to recognize and use the power you have to participate even further in creating a more fulfilling economy for yourself and others.

NOTES

1. Thomas S. Kuhn, *The Structure of Scientific Revolutions*, 2d ed, (Chicago: University of Chicago Press, 1970).

2. David Ray Griffin, *Spirituality and Society: Postmodern Visions* (Albany, N.Y.: State University of New York Press, 1988), ix. For a summary of various meanings of "postmodernism," see pp. ix–xii. By Griffin's definition, my approach would be classified as "constructive postmodernism."

3. On the postmodern paradigm, see Fritjof Capra, *The Turning Point: Science, Society, and the Rising Culture* (New York: Bantam, 1983); Riane Eisler, *The Chalice and The Blade: Our History, Our Future* (San Francisco: Harper & Row, 1987); David Ray Griffin, ed., *Spirituality and Society: Postmodern Visions* (Albany, N.Y.: State University of New York Press, 1988); David Ray Griffin, ed., *The Reenchantment of Science: Postmodern Proposals* (Albany, N.Y.: State University of New York Press, 1988); John Naisbitt, *Megatrends: Ten New Directions Transforming Our Lives* (New York: Warner Books, 1982); Anne Wilson Schaef, *Women's Reality: An Emerging Female System in White Male Society* (New York: Harper & Row, 1985), and Anne Wilson Schaef, *Beyond Therapy, Beyond Science: A New Model for Healing the Whole Person* (San Francisco: HarperSanFrancisco, 1992); Linda Jean Shepherd, *Lifting The Veil: The Feminine Face of Science* (Boston: Shambhala, 1993).

4. On the origins of the modern scientific worldview, see Capra, *The Turning Point*, chaps. 2 and 4.

5. Recent publications that indicate the growing interest in creating a new economics are included in the Bibliography.

6. The Other Economic Summit (TOES) is an informal network of individuals and organizations around the world who organize citizens' counter-summits each year in the nation where the leaders of the seven major industrialized nations (the G-7) are holding their annual international economic summit. For more information about TOES contacts and events, contact the New Economics Foundation, Universal House, 2d floor, 88–94 Wentworth St., London E17SA, England, phone (071) 377-5696. The Industrial Cooperative Association (now called the ICA Group), which provides technical assistance to worker-owned businesses, can be reached at 20 Park Plaza, Suite 1127, Boston, MA 02116, (617) 338-0010.

7. For a critical summary of the development of modern economic thought, see Mark A. Lutz and Kenneth Lux, *Humanistic Economics: The New Challenge* (New York: Bootstrap Press, 1988), chap. 3.

8. On the global influence of the United States today, see Walden Bello, with Shea Cunningham and Bill Rau, *Dark Victory: The United States, Structural Adjustment and Global Poverty* (Oakland, Calif.: Institute for Food and Development Policy, 1994).

PART ONE

The Problem of Economic Invisibility

Chapter 1

The Disappearance of Married Maids, Caring Communities, and Nature

The way the economy is conventionally defined and measured leads to the creation of economic invisibilty.

In the modern economic paradigm, the central measure of the economy is the gross domestic product (GDP). Up until a few years ago, most nations used a slightly different measure, the gross national product (GNP). Sometimes the media still refer to the GNP, although for most purposes the GDP has now become the official measure of the economy.[1]

The GDP is used not only to evaluate how well each nation is doing, but also to compare nations with each other. According to the conventional assumptions, when a nation's GDP rises, this is called "economic growth," and it means that the economy is improving and people are better off. When the GDP falls, the economy is in trouble. And the United States has the world's largest GDP, which—according to conventional assumptions—makes it the richest and most economically successful nation in the world.

The GDP is expressed in dollar values. Supposedly it represents the dollar value of all the wealth a society has produced over a specific time period (for example, during the last three months, or over the last year). But the way in which it is calculated tells us considerably more than that. By examining what the GDP actually includes, we can discover how modern economies define wealth, what kinds of activities they value, and, even more important, which wealth-producing activities they choose to devalue or ignore.

What the GDP actually measures is the dollar value of all the goods and services produced by the businesses within a nation. The GDP does not include the goods and services that people produce in their own homes, for their own use. Nor does it include the services that people freely give to others in their communities. In essence, the GDP equates the economy with the production of goods and services that are sold in order to make money. [2]

Is this a faulty definition of the economy? Are these omissions really important? Yes, for two reasons.

First, the GDP leaves out quite a large part of the total productive activity that takes place in modern economies (see chapter 4). It therefore gives us a highly inaccurate picture of the whole economy.

Second, most of the goods and services produced in the home, or freely given to others in the community, are produced by women. In other words, according to official measures of the economy, much of the productive work done by women is economically invisible.

THE STRANGE CASE OF THE DISAPPEARING MAID

Like any complicated, abstract measure of reality, the GDP has its flaws, as professional economists readily admit. However, its shortcomings and imperfections have not yet convinced enough experts and leaders that the GDP should be replaced with fairer and more accurate measures. This is because the biases of the GDP reflect the prevailing biases of modern society. A good example of this is what I call the Strange Case of the Disappearing Maid.

If a woman cooks and cleans in a man's home as a paid domestic servant, she is counted as part of the economy because her paid work is included in society's key economic measure, the GDP. However, if a man *marries* his maid, she no longer gets paid for her housework in his home, and her contribution to the GDP is suddenly eliminated from the official statistics. The now-married woman may still be doing exactly the same work she was doing before her nuptial ceremony—in fact, she may now be doing even more—but because she is no longer being paid for that work, she has in essence disappeared from the economy.

And just wait until she starts having children! Her day care providers, being paid for their specific and strictly limited services, will be included in measures of the economy. But the mother's 24-hour-a-day, seven-day-a-week commitment does not appear in the GDP.

Can a man's work also disappear from the economy as the result of marrying his former employer? Perhaps, if his formerly paid work was in an area commonly considered "women's" work, such as housecleaning, child care, or sexual services. On the other hand, consider a woman who hired a carpenter to remodel her kitchen, and then married him. While he might continue to do unpaid remodeling in his new home (work which would now also disappear from the GDP), it's unlikely that his wife would expect him to stop doing carpentry for other paying clients.

The Disappearing Maid is often mentioned in introductory economics textbooks as a cute example to show that the GDP is not perfect, and that even economists realize this. But of course, they then add, no abstract measure can be perfect, and the GDP overall is a pretty good basis for determining the state of the economy. Even many economists who realize that economic growth is not necessarily the same thing as social well-being or happiness still accept the basic worth of the GDP. "Yet, with all its shortcomings, GNP is still the simplest way we possess of summarizing the overall level of activity of the economy," say Robert L. Heilbroner and Lester C. Thurow.[3] So mainstream economists laugh good-humoredly at their own imperfections and rush on to study all those other familiar economic phenomena, such as interest rates, profits, employment trends, and international rates of exchange.

We shall not laugh at the Strange Case of the Disappearing Maid, nor forget her and rush on. Because far from being an embarrassing anomaly, the Disappearing Maid is just the tip of the iceberg. Many other crucial aspects of life are also omitted from official measures of the modern economy.

THE DISAPPEARANCE OF WOMEN AND NATURE

Marilyn Waring, a professional economist, international feminist, environmentalist, and peace activist from New Zealand, is one of the pioneers in publicly exposing the phenomenon of economic invisibility. In her passionate and impressively documented classic, *If Women Counted*, she demonstrates that not only the productive work of women but also the life-supporting services of nature are excluded from official measures of the economy. Waring makes five key observations:

1) Almost all women work. But women's most important work is often unpaid, from growing and processing food for their families, to hauling water and firewood, to homemaking. Women's constant bearing, birthing, and raising of children is another essential aspect of their unpaid work.

2) Governments and other political and economic institutions concerned about economic development (such as United Nations agencies and the World Bank) hire economists to provide them with information about the performance of national economies and the value of various economic activities. But economists are trained to recognize as productive and valuable only activities for which people are paid.

3) Since most of the work that women do is unpaid, the contribution and value of the large majority of women's work is omitted from most official economic assessments.

4) The natural environment is constantly renewing itself and providing us with wealth. However, since the natural world doesn't collect a salary, the contribution and value of nature's gifts and processes are also omitted from most conventional economic assessments.

5) Many traditionally male activities (especially the military) are blatantly nonproductive, even overtly destructive. Yet because men are paid to do them, economists must count them as productive and valuable.

Waring demonstrates how women in both industrialized and Third-World nations are made economically invisible, and why the conventional economic perceptions and standards that make women invisible are both inaccurate and inequitable. Her examples from the Third World are especially powerful. Consider the case of the Beti people, from southern Cameroon.

Beti men work about seven and a half hours a day, which includes raising cocoa for export, producing beer or palm-wine, building or repairing houses, producing simple commodities for the market, and part-time wage work. Beti women work eleven hours each day. This includes five hours on daily food production—four to meet family needs and one to produce surplus for the market; three to four hours a day in food processing and cooking; and two or more hours for such duties as water and firewood collection, washing, child care, and care of the sick. The United Nations' International Labor Organization (ILO) counts the Beti man as an "active laborer." But because none of the Beti woman's working day is spent "helping the head of the household in his occupation"—and because work done in the home that meets family needs directly is not counted as part of the economy—the ILO concludes that she is not an active laborer.[4]

Waring describes how the life-sustaining and self-renewing natural environment is also excluded from measures of economic productivity, except when it is dug up or chopped down and sold off to make money. The services that soil, water, and climate provide—for agriculture, waste disposal and neutralization, for recreation and aesthetic and spiritual inspiration—do not readily lend themselves to being counted through monetized measures. So when left alone, merely supporting and restoring our life and health, nature has no value according to conventional economic standards.

Furthermore, when air, land, or water are polluted in order to produce more products and provide more jobs, the conventional economic measures report that people's standard of living has risen. There's no way within the GDP to acknowledge that the pollution and destruction of the natural environment has also worsened people's health and overall quality of life.[5]

When Waring embarked on a campaign to persuade development agencies to include the value of women's unpaid work and the contributions of the natural environment in their measures of national productivity, she was told repeatedly that this could not be done because economists don't know how to measure the value of something unless someone pays money for it.[6]

Perhaps it would be more accurate to conclude that these institutions—which do the measuring, recommend the development policies, and hand out the money—didn't think it was important to acknowledge the contributions of women and nature. They could surely have developed an appropriate methodology if they believed it were necessary.

For example, they could have used the model developed by divorce lawyer Michael Minton, who had ample motivation for putting a monetary value on all the years of unpaid work that his female clients performed during their marriage. Minton combined several standard economic measures into a model through which he estimated that the average value of a homemaker's services came to about $40,000 per year (in 1983)—and he has won many settlements using this model.[7]

So as Marilyn Waring and other women's advocates and critical economists are pointing out, the exclusion of the economic contributions of women and nature from conventional economic measures has little to do with technical feasibility, and much to do with prejudice and power.

Growing environmental awareness and critical pressures have recently influenced the World Bank to incorporate some environmental criteria into its economic models. But observers say this is still mostly a token effort.[8] And, thanks to pressure from women activists, economists and development agencies are now paying more attention to women's role in economic development. Unfortunately, this often means that Third-World women are being integrated into a modernized economy that piles more work on them while failing to compensate them for their worsened quality of life.[9] Much still needs to be done to overcome the economic invisibility of women and nature.

THE DISAPPEARANCE OF CARING

While some family services, such as pregnancy, childbirth and breast feeding, can only be done by women, many other caring activities for one's family can be performed by either women or men. And in some modern nations men's participation in housework and child care is increasing. But since they are not paid for these activities either, men's caring activities for their families are also excluded from measures of the economy.

Unpaid domestic activities are not the only caring activities that are economically invisible. Millions of people in modern economies, both women and men, spend many hours on volunteer work in their communities, helping others. For example, a recent survey found that more than half the U.S. population 18 years of age and older participates in volunteer work! Yet the conventional measures of economic productivity ignore such unpaid community work.[10] So the conventional definition of the economy not only excludes women's unpaid activities for their families, but also ignores unpaid caring in general, whether for family or community, whether done by women or men.

THE CONSEQUENCES OF ECONOMIC INVISIBILITY

The economic invisibility of women, nature, and caring activities has serious harmful consequences. When women enter the paid economy, they earn on average three-fifths the average income that men earn, and the feminization of poverty is increasing.[11] Likewise, the natural environment is continually being damaged severely by careless economic development, pollution, and waste production, while people concerned about the health of the natural world have to fight intense struggles to assure that nature is protected.

Finally, some modern economies have now reached a crisis in caring for their own members. For many people, having children has become an unaffordable luxury. Finding the time to care for one's own children is difficult, and finding adequate paid child care from others is near impossible. Governments can no longer pay for the services necessary to assure community well-being. And the most vulnerable among us are simply being tossed out into the cold.

In other words, the modern economic paradigm devalues women, nature, and caring activities, and we are increasingly suffering the impact of this devaluation in our daily lives. In part, economic invisibility is the cause of this devaluation. In part, it is one more expression of this devaluation. At any rate, economic invisibility is a problem that can no longer be ignored.

NOTES

1. The GNP measures the production within a nation by businesses owned by that nation's residents. The GDP measures production by all the businesses located within a nation, whether these businesses are owned by residents or outsiders. Marilyn Waring says that during the past few years, political leaders around the world have switched to the GDP because so many businesses, especially in developing nations, are owned by multinational corporations rather than by local residents, and GNP figures alone give a limited—and unfavorable—picture of their nations' economic growth. See Marilyn Waring, *If Women Counted: A New Feminist Economics* (San Francisco: Harper & Row, 1988), 71.

2. The GDP is a complex measure, but in essence it measures the goods and services produced by a nation's businesses. For a more complete explanation of what the GNP/GDP includes and leaves out, see Herman E. Daly and John B. Cobb, Jr., *For The Common Good: Redirecting the Economy Toward Community, the Environment, and a Sustainable Future* (Boston: Beacon Press, 1989), chap. 3; or Waring, *If Women Counted,* especially chaps. 2 and 3.

3. Robert L. Heilbroner and Lester C. Thurow, *Economics Explained* (New York: Simon & Schuster, 1987), 77.

4. Waring, *If Women Counted,* 30.

5. Ibid., chap. 10.

6. Ibid., chap. 4.

7. Michael H. Minton with Jean Libman Block, *What Is A Wife Worth?* (New York: William Morrow & Co., 1983), 65.

8. Economic activist Hazel Henderson, a leading crusader for scrapping the GDP and replacing it with more meaningful social and environmental indicators, claims that the World Bank now pays lip-service to environmental and social issues, but its actual evaluation methods have not changed. See Hazel Henderson, *Paradigms in Progress: Life Beyond Economics* (Indianapolis: Knowledge Systems, 1991), chap. 6.

9. On problems of women's economic development, see Gita Sen and Caren Grown, *Development, Crises, and Alternative Visions: Third World Women's Perspectives* (New York: Monthly Review Press, 1987); or Kathryn Ward, ed., *Women Workers and Global Restructuring* (Ithaca, N.Y.: ILR Press, 1990).

10. Fifty-one percent of all U.S. residents age 18 and older do volunteer work, according to the Independent Sector, which studies voluntary and nonprofit activities. See "Giving and Volunteering Survey," the Independent Sector, 1828 L St. NW, Suite 1201, Washington, D.C. 20036, 1992. On exclusion of volunteer work from the GDP, see Waring, *If Women Counted,* 68–69.

11. On women's poor economic conditions, see Ruth Sidel, *Women and Children Last: The Plight of Poor Women in Affluent America* (New York: Viking Penguin, 1986); or Theresa Amott, *Caught in The Crisis: Women and the U.S. Economy Today* (New York: Monthly Review Press, 1993). On women's

economic conditions in the Third World, see Sen and Grown, *Development, Crises, and Alternative Visions.*

Chapter 2

RISING STRESS, DECLINING HEALTH: INVISIBLE COSTS OF THE WORKPLACE

The previous chapter focused on a major form of economic invisibility: how the modern economic paradigm denies the value of, or makes invisible, the economic contributions of socially devalued individuals, groups, and activities.

The modern paradigm also promotes the illusion that dominant, publically valued people or institutions are constantly producing wealth, when in actuality they are often destroying wealth, generating waste and garbage, and causing other harmful results. The modern economic paradigm makes invisible the destructive impacts of socially valued individuals, groups, and activities.

One of the most important examples of this second form of economic invisibility is the widespread destruction of the natural environment that has accompanied the continued expansion of affluent modern economies. The modern paradigm emphasizes the financial and material wealth that modern societies have created, while overlooking their destructive environmental impacts. But since the 1970s, the extent of environmental destruction, both local and global, has become increasingly visible. And many authors and activists have made visible the connections between environmental damage and the production-consumption activities of modern economies.[1]

This chapter explores another important example of economic invisibility. That is, how individual, social, and economic well-being are being destroyed by workplaces designed according to the conventional criteria for maximum efficiency, productivity, and business success.

STRESS IN THE MODERN WORKPLACE

One of the most troubling problems of modern economies today is the extent and severity of job-related stress.

23

In the United States, for example, back in 1985, approximately 20 percent of U.S. workers reported that their jobs were highly stressful. By 1991 this number had risen to include almost half of all U.S. workers. In one study, 70 percent of those interviewed reported that job stress was making them less productive and causing them frequent health problems.[2]

A recent study done by the United Nations International Labor Organization (ILO) concludes that job-related stress has become both a major economic problem for employers as well as a major health and economic problem for modern nations worldwide. In the workplace, job stress leads to such costly consequences as absenteeism and high employee turnover, lower productivity, on-the-job accidents, and rising health insurance and other medical expenses. The ILO estimates that in the United States alone job stress is costing employers approximately $200 billion a year![3]

The increasing seriousness of stress-related problems—for individual employees, for their workplaces, and for the larger economy—has led to numerous research and action programs by unions, employers, medical and other consultants, and government agencies around the world. Gradually, such efforts have revealed that job-related stress results from a traditional definition of economic success that is incompatible with human well-being. The most innovative and effective programs to reduce workplace stress have led to radically new workplace structures that challenge long-held assumptions about workplace organization, efficiency, and productivity. And they indicate that workplaces and work processes that are consciously designed to promote the health and respect the wholeness of workers will also be the most healthy and successful economic enterprises.[4]

CAUSES AND CONSEQUENCES OF JOB STRESS

We experience stress when we are presented with physical, social, or emotional demands that threaten our well-being. This can happen in any area of life—in personal relationships, at home, in recreational activities, or at work.

Physical stressors in the workplace can include such problems as excessively noisy work environments, poor lighting, excessively fast-paced machinery, or poorly designed equipment that requires injurious movements or postures. Organizational, emotional, or other psychosocial aspects of the workplace that can cause stress include work schedules, workload, relationships with supervisors and co-workers, the amount of autonomy or responsibility the job entails, or the constant fear of being laid off.[5]

Many studies have discovered that stress becomes harmful when people experience it on a continued basis, and when they are unable either to escape or eliminate it. Under such circumstances, people may eventually react with physical ailments or illness, with emotional or behavioral problems, or with any combination thereof. People who are under constant, inescapable stress—whether at work or elsewhere—may react with any one or more of the following: rashes, skin disorders, allergies, high blood pressure, stroke, heart disease, migraines, ulcers or other gastrointestinal disorders; arthritis; weakened immune system or chronic fatigue; insomnia or other sleep disorders; anxiety, depression, or other emotional problems; abuse of tobacco, alcohol, drugs, or other chemical substances; accidents; apathy or diminished self-esteem; or feelings of anger or physical violence directed against self or others.[6]

Thus, stress in the workplace can lead to more than just poor worker health, increased absenteeism, accidents, rising health-care costs, and lowered productivity. It can also lead to alcohol or drug use, on the job or in one's personal life. In extreme cases, it can provoke workplace sabotage or acts of violence against co-workers or supervisors. And its effects can extend beyond the workplace, vented against strangers in the world outside, or through emotional or physical abuse of family members in the so-called haven of the home. In such ways the stress so prevalent in today's workplaces harms not only the workplace and the larger economy, but also disrupts people's homelives and spreads through the community, diminishing well-being and quality of life both for affected employees and the many others their lives touch.

We should distinguish between unhealthy stress and the challenges and uncertainty that are a natural part of living. Even stresses at work can be a normal, positive aspect of the job. And for many people the responsibilities and demands of their jobs constitute a positive challenge, which when dealt with successfully lead to feelings of mastery and accomplishment, to prestige and financial reward.

But many people suffer excessive, harmful job stress because their paid work is demeaning and disempowering. The problem is not just that they face stress, demands, or challenges at work, but that their jobs have been designed to prevent them from having any control over the sources of stress imposed upon them.

EMOTIONS, JOB STRESS, AND HEALTH

Among the most disturbing and important new findings about job stress are the connections between workers' feelings of disempowerment at work and their likelihood of developing physical illness, especially heart disease.

Heart disease, which is relatively rare in many nonindustrial societies, is a prominent cause of illness and death in modern industrial civilization. Heart attacks are currently recognized as the leading cause of death for both men and women in the United States and were responsible for more than one out of every five U.S. deaths in 1990.[7]

In researching the causes of heart disease, physician Larry Dossey found that most heart attacks in the United States tend to strike at one particular time: 9 AM on Monday mornings. This is, of course, the standard starting time of many people's paid workweek. Is it possible that for some people, the prospect of returning to work is so upsetting that it induces heart attacks?

Dossey cites further evidence that suggests that negative feelings about one's paid work can be linked to physical illness, including heart disease. He found a 1972 Massachusetts study that concluded that the best factor for predicting if a person might get heart disease was not any of the usually cited physical links, such as smoking, high blood pressure, or high cholesterol, but the patient's feelings of dissatisfaction with his or her job. Furthermore, job dissatisfaction is often related to feelings of powerlessness over work. For example, Dossey found that workers who had no control over their workload were more likely to get heart attacks.[8]

The connections between feelings of powerlessness at work and physical illness have been studied intensively by U.S. industrial-systems engineer Robert Karasek. His complex and richly documented book, *Healthy Work: Stress, Productivity, and the Reconstruction of Working Life*, coauthored with Swedish occupational-health physician Töres Theorell, pulls together enormous amounts of evidence about work conditions that cause stress. He concludes that the problem is not exposure to stress per se, but jobs that place workers under constant stress while giving them little or no decision-making authority and little opportunity to utilize their skills. Not only are workers in such jobs more vulnerable to physical illness in general, but they are especially likely to suffer heart attacks.[9] In other words, people whose work activities are most restricted, disempowered, or tightly controlled by others are more likely to die of broken hearts.

JOB STRESS AND SOCIAL CLASS

Job stress and stress-induced ailments affect all modern workers: executives, professionals, white-, pink-, blue-collar, service, and unskilled workers.[10] However, while it's publicly acceptable to sympathize with highly paid managers who suffer from executive stress, many studies show that people at the bottom of the occupational hierarchy are actually most likely to suffer from illness and life-threatening afflictions caused by job stress. For example, several studies have shown that blue-collar and unskilled workers are at greater risk for stress-related illnesses and death than are white-collar workers and professionals.[11]

Since socially devalued groups, such as women, lower-income people, those with less formal education, members of disadvantaged racial or ethnic groups, and immigrants, tend to be funneled into these lower status jobs, this means that members of such groups are at higher risk for job-related illness and death.

Job stress is not just an unfortunate side effect of progress and modern life. Nor is it the unavoidable fate of those unskilled or unlucky enough to be trapped in bad jobs. As we shall now see, the modern workplace was consciously designed to dehumanize people in order to increase efficiency and productivity. And as long as workplaces adhere to the goals, values, and assumptions of the modern economic paradigm, this dehumanization will continue, resulting in constantly escalating job stress and workplaces that harm both their employees' health, and in the long term, the employers' own best interests.

INCREASING EFFICIENCY, DECREASING EMPOWERMENT: A BRIEF HISTORY OF THE MODERN WORKPLACE

For most of human history, people either produced everything they needed themselves or turned to highly skilled craftspeople for specific necessities or luxuries. While such production methods meant that almost everyone could learn and utilize a variety of skills and could experience the complete creative process from start to finish, these methods were also relatively slow, compared to modern production processes.

In Western Europe during the sixteenth and seventeenth centuries, a growing middle class demanded more material goods and a constantly rising standard of living. New kinds of businesses sought to meet the demand by employing increasing numbers of wage-workers in small centralized facilities called manufactories (literally, "places where things are made by hand"). Such facilities made production more efficient because they combined newly invented wind- and water-powered machinery with the division of labor—breaking up the production process into small, unskilled actions repeated over and over again by narrowly specialized workers. In Adam Smith's famous description of a late eighteenth-century pin factory,

> One man draws out the wire, another straights it, a third cuts it, a fourth points it, a fifth grinds it at the top for receiving the head. . . . I have seen a small manufactory of this kind where ten men only were employed and where some of them consequently performed two or three distinct operations. . . . Those ten persons . . . could make among them upwards of forty-eight thousand pins in a day. . . . But if they had all wrought separately and independently . . . they certainly could not each of them make twenty, perhaps not one pin in a day.[12]

The introduction of fossil-fuel powered mass-production machinery in the late 1700s precipitated the Industrial Revolution. Factories became larger, employed more workers, and turned out more goods more quickly and cheaply. The Industrial Revolution further accelerated the division of labor. More jobs were broken down into single, repetitive activities, and the speed and quantity of factory production increased.

Perhaps the crowning achievement in the search for constantly increasing productive efficiency was "scientific management," originated in the United States during the late nineteenth century.

The goal of scientific management was to restructure every job so that workers no longer had to think; they only had to learn one or a few simple movements and obey their supervisors. Scientific management had political as well as economic origins. Before its inception, even industries that used extreme job specialization were still dependent on skilled craftsmen in many operations. Being indispensable and difficult to replace, such skilled workers held considerable bargaining power, which they often used to their advantage during labor-management conflicts. A pressing goal of business management at the turn of the century was to eliminate the need for skilled workers.

Businesses achieved this goal by employing efficiency experts, who systematically broke every task involved in production into its smallest and least-intelligent components. These experts not only observed skilled workers but also interviewed them about their jobs, under the pretense of understanding their work in order to help them do it better. Instead, formerly skilled workers discovered that their jobs had evaporated, turned into mindless bits of repetitive physical operations. Such deskilled jobs were then reincorporated into the industrial system, making more workers replaceable and fewer individuals indispensable because of special knowledge or skills.[13]

Perhaps the most famous application of scientific management, also called "Taylorism," after one of its leading proponents, was at the Ford Motor Company. As the automobile-assembly process was broken up into the simplest tasks and integrated with the mechanically driven assembly line, the time required to assemble a complete Model T chassis fell from twelve and one half hours to a little over an hour and a half. As a result, from 1911 to 1914, Ford was able to double the number of cars produced, while actually reducing the workforce from 14,336 to 12,880 workers.[14] Other companies eagerly adopted this approach, which combined lower costs and higher profits with faster production and greater control over the workforce.

As we approach the end of the twentieth century, modern electronic technologies are an important new source of work degradation, worker disempowerment, and job stress. While such technologies have the potential to make work more interesting, challenging, and empowering (and some companies are using them in this way), the older assumptions about efficiency and hierarchical control in the workplace regularly lead to their abuse. In both office work and technical fields, electronic technologies are being used to make formerly skilled and diversified jobs more limited, isolated, and subservient, with escalating emotional and physical stress on millions of workers. They have also led to new occupational hazards, particularly cumulative trauma disorders (CTDs) of hands, wrists, and shoulders, caused by repetitive motions such as passing thousands of groceries over a checkout scanner, or typing at a computerized word processor for eight hours a day, five days a week. CTDs currently afflict some five million people in the United States—thus comprising almost half of all U.S occupational illnesses in 1988—and can lead to permanent disability. But all this is justified on the grounds of increasing productivity and profitability.[15]

CREATING GOOD JOBS AND BAD JOBS

The modern economic paradigm promotes a model of productive efficiency based on the degradation of work and the fragmentation of workers' lives. This has been accomplished by the conscious creation of two distinct categories of work: the good jobs, held by those who think and plan, and the bad jobs, held by those who mutely obey.

Although the popular ideology of modern economies says that anyone, based on their ability and willingness to work hard, can get a good job, the reality is that millions of people are forced to take demeaning, disempowering jobs because that's all that's available. Most paid work opportunities were designed to be bad jobs. So it should not be surprising that so many men and women today are experiencing job stress, dissatisfaction, feelings of disempowerment, anger, or low self-esteem around their jobs, and are suffering from physical and emotional ailments induced by the inherently disempowering nature of their paid work.

It should also be noted that the division of the workplace into good and bad jobs has regularly been used to reinforce the gender, racial, and other prejudices of the larger society. In modern economies up until very recently, the good jobs at the tops of workplace hierarchies were held exclusively by upper- and middle-class white males, while the secure, better-paying bad jobs were given to working-class and poor white males. But these patterns have changed significantly since the 1970s. Gradually, a few women and people of color have been allowed into the good jobs. Meanwhile, the many formerly secure, relatively well-paid bad jobs are increasingly being turned into insecure, part-time or temporary, lower-paid bad jobs, and are increasingly being given to women and people of color, who are replacing the working-class white men who formerly held these positions.[16]

DENYING WORKPLACE STRESS

To acknowledge the extent and devastating impact of job stress poses a challenge to the existing hierarchy of wealth and power. By focusing solely on conventional measures of economic success, such as rising profits or a growing GDP, business executives can continue to justify their own high salaries, while government officials can justify their economic policies and their right to remain in office for another term. To admit that workplaces are actively generating stress, ill health, and social unrest calls into question the ability of the managers and politicians who are currently shaping our workplace and national economic policies. However, those on top are not the only ones who have kept the existence and costs of job stress invisible. Over the years, union leaders and even average working people have also colluded in this denial.

The need to deny job stress is often related to gender identity. To be a "real man"—that is, to gain one's identity through participation in the paid workforce—means to grit one's teeth, get the job done, and never to complain or admit one's pain. Back in 1973, for example, when a controversial study, *Work in America*, first brought the problems of widespread job dissatisfaction and job stress to public attention, the report was attacked not only by the Nixon administration but also by prominent union leaders. According to *Newsweek* magazine,

> [United Auto Workers] president Leonard Woodcock concluded a meeting of his union's production workers . . . with a blast at "academics" whom he accused of

writing "elitist nonsense" that degraded factory workers. "Sure," Woodcock said, "work is dull and monotonous. But if it's useful, the people who do it are entitled to be honored and not degraded."[17]

Many people need to deny that their jobs are stressful for economic as well as emotional reasons. In this age of disappearing jobs, both women and men lucky enough to have paid work may feel they have no recourse except to put up with demeaning or stressful jobs—until they end up with stress disorders or have accidents and have to go on disability. In many workplaces today, where the constant pressure, speed-ups, and overwork are justified by the need to stay competitive, stressed-out workers may nevertheless feel they have no other option but to stay with the job. And sometimes, when workers are unable to leave degrading job situations, their only remaining source of pride is their toughness, their ability to endure. Even workers who participate in programs to alleviate job stress are often reluctant to admit that they experience stress, believing that it's their own fault or personal weakness if they can't cope.[18]

As the extent and costs of job-related stress have become ever more painfully apparent, a new form of denial has recently become popular: blaming the worker. Familiar responses to job stress today include programs in stress-management or relaxation techniques, or recommendations that sufferers should find less stressful, more rewarding jobs. But while such approaches have their place, to rely on them completely implies that job stress is purely a personal problem, which must be solved by each employee individually.

HEALTHY WORKPLACES, HEALTHY WORKERS: TOWARD A NEW PARADIGM

As the above history and many recent studies of the problem suggest, the social structure and organization of the workplace can be a primary cause of job stress resulting in widespread physical, emotional, and social ailments. Not only physical issues such as noise, lighting, pace, and equipment design, but also psychosocial factors, such as the requirements of a job, its scope, limitations, and position in the workplace hierarchy, all contribute to job stress. And such factors are not mere chance occurrences but the conscious result of prevailing economic values and assumptions.

But if the workplace can be designed intentionally to degrade work, disempower workers, and thereby produce job stress, it can also be redesigned to make jobs more fulfilling and empowering. Rather than merely training individual workers to accept and adapt better to stress, a more effective solution is prevention—actively involving workers in changing the workplace to reduce or eliminate the causes of stress.

This kind of participatory, preventive approach is being increasingly recommended by unions, medical practitioners, and many management consultants, and is gradually being adopted by more forward-thinking employers. It utilizes innovative programs that challenge, alter, or even eliminate the traditional workplace hierarchies and division of labor. For example, such programs involve workers in identifying their sources of job stress, then proposing and implementing solutions. In the most effective programs, workers are changing their own job descriptions, making their work more diverse and challenging, even working with management to open up access to company information and develop more participatory, less hierarchical decision-making processes throughout the organization.[19]

Because such approaches are so different from the prevailing paradigm, they are spreading slowly throughout modern economies, and they sometimes fail, due to fear, resistance, or lack of experience. But when they succeed, they can reduce workers' stress, improve physical and mental health, decrease absenteeism, and increase workplace performance and productivity, fulfilling both individual and organizational goals simultaneously.[20]

This kind of win-win approach, which tries to solve an economic problem by treating the people involved with respect, as whole human beings with their own needs and abilities, not merely as mindless actors serving larger economic goals, typifies the emerging postmodern economic paradigm.

NOTES

1. The publications of Worldwatch Institute, 1776 Massachusetts Ave. NW, Washington D.C. 20036–1904, document the connections between the materialistic excesses of modern economies and environmental degradation.

2. See "Employee Burnout: America's Newest Epidemic," a study sponsored by the Northwestern National Life Insurance Co., released May 6, 1991. Reported in "Third of Workers Surveyed Stress Point: I Want to Quit," *Boston Herald*, 7 May 1991.

3. Frank Swoboda, "Employers Recognizing What Stress Costs Them, U.N. Report Suggests," *Washington Post*, 28 March 1993, Sec. H.

4. On new approaches to reducing workplace stress, see Robert Karasek and Töres Theorell, *Healthy Work: Stress, Productivity, and the Reconstruction of Working Life* (New York: Basic Books, 1990); and "Preventing Stress at Work," *Conditions of Work Digest*, 11 (1992), available from ILO Publications Center, 49 Sheridan Ave., Albany, NY 12210, (518) 436–9686, x.123.

5. On causes of work stress, see "Preventing Stress at Work," 3–4; and "Third of Workers Surveyed Stress Point," *Boston Herald*, 7 May 1991.

6. On physical and emotional responses to stress, see "Preventing Stress at Work," 4 and 13; and *Work in America: Report of a Special Task Force to the Secretary of Health, Education, and Welfare* (Cambridge, Mass.: MIT Press, 1973), 79–89.

7. *1993 Heart And Stroke Fact Statistics*, American Heart Association, 7272 Greenville Ave., Dallas TX 75231–4596, 1992.

8. On correlations between job dissatisfaction and heart disease, see Larry Dossey, *Medicine and Meaning* (New York: Bantam, 1991), chap. 6; and *Work in America*, 79–81.

9. On correlations between lack of decision making at work and heart disease, see Karasek and Theorell, *Healthy Work*, chaps. 2–4.

10. For data that job stress affects all levels of worker see *Work in America*, 13–17; and "Preventing Stress at Work," 5–9.

11. For data showing that blue-collar and unskilled workers are at greater risk for job stress and related health problems, see "Preventing Stress at Work," 6; and Teresa Amott, *Caught in the Crisis: Women and the U.S. Economy Today*, (New York: Monthly Review Press, 1993), 100.

12. Adam Smith's description of the pin factory is cited in Robert L. Heilbroner, *The Worldly Philosophers: The Lives, Times, And Ideas Of The Great Economic Thinkers* (New York.: Simon and Schuster, 1953), 53.

13. On the development of scientific management, see David Noble, *America by Design: Science, Technology, and the Rise of Corporate Capitalism* (Oxford: Oxford University Press, 1977), chap. 10.

14. Robert Lacey, *Ford: The Man and the Machine* (New York: Ballantine Books, 1986), 113–117.

15. On electronic technologies deskilling office workers, see Bob Baker, "Assembly Line Stress in Offices," *Los Angeles Times*, 13 June 1991, sec. A. On the deskilling of technical workers, see Robert Howard, *Brave New Workplace* (New York: Viking Penguin, 1985). On cumulative trauma disorders (CTDs), see Andrea Gabor, "On-the-job Straining," *U.S. News & World Report*, 21 May 1990, 51–52.

16. On race, gender, and the changing composition of the U.S. workforce during the nineteenth and twentieth centuries, see Teresa L. Amott and Julie A. Matthaei, *Race, Gender, and Work: A Multicultural Economic History of Women in the United States* (Boston: South End Press, 1991).

17. The union response to the *Work in America* report is described in "The Job Blahs: Who Wants to Work?" *Newsweek*, 26 March 1974, 79–89.

18. On workers' reluctance to complain about job stress, see "Preventing Stress at Work," 39. An innovative project that helped workers move beyond self-blame to recognizing and changing sources of stress in the work environment is described in Dr. Michael Lerner, *Occupational Stress Groups and the Psychodynamics of the World of Work*, Institute for Labor and Mental Health, 3137 Telegraph Ave., Oakland, CA 94609, 1985.

19. New approaches to reducing workplace stress through creating a more participatory workplace are described in Karasek and Theorell, *Healthy Work*, chaps. 5–10; and "Preventing Stress at Work," 29–41.

20. Studies that show that reducing stress through participatory workplace reorganization leads to both increased profitability and productivity, and improved worker mental and physical health, are described in *Work in America*, 188–201. See also descriptions of new-paradigm workplaces in Karasek and Theorell, *Healthy Work*, chaps. 5–10; and "Preventing Stress at Work," 29–41.

Chapter 3

WOMEN'S ECONOMIC INVISIBILITY: IN THE HOME AND ON THE JOB

The phenomenon of women's economic invisibility not only reflects the devaluation of women, but also is related to other hierarchical systems in modern economies. When women cook or clean for their families or care for their children or older relatives, such activities are not recognized, nor counted as productive by official measures of the economy. When traditional women's domestic activities, such as cleaning, doing laundry, or caring for children are done for pay, which makes such activities economically visible, they are among the least well-paid and lowest-status jobs. And such jobs are frequently relegated to members of low-status groups, such as people with limited formal education or people of color. Thus, various types of hierarchical discrimination, whether based on gender, race, or class, are often intertwined.

Sexism, racism, classism, and other oppressive hierarchical systems appear throughout modern economies, affecting various groups and individuals in a multiplicity of ways. For example, although the top positions of our political and economic hierarchies are filled overwhelmingly by white males, many men, both white and of color, are economically and emotionally degraded by hierarchical workplace structures.

While each hierarchical form has unique characteristics, all hierarchical systems share certain dynamics. I focus on women's economic invisibility throughout this book not only because these processes run so deep and explain so much about the lives of women in particular, but also because exploring the dynamics of the patriarchy reveals so much about how all oppressive systems, including those that harm men, are maintained.

Modern economies have been shaped by a strong sex-role division: the economically productive male breadwinner, who works out in the world, is contrasted with the emotionally nurturing housewife and mother, whose domain is in the home. Although the reality has often been quite different, this idealized image of male and female roles, which developed with the Industrial Revolution, has remained one of the most important forces within the modern economic paradigm.

This chapter explores why this sex-role division of modern economies came into being. And it demonstrates the many ways that economic invisibility can be implemented, both to maintain an illusory and harmful ideal and to force people's real-life behavior to conform to this ideal.

WOMEN'S WORK BEFORE THE INDUSTRIAL REVOLUTION

For most of human history, family, home, and economic production have been inseparable, with all household members—women and men, children and elders—participating in gathering or growing the food they ate and producing the rest of the material goods they needed. In many preindustrial societies women have held considerable economic power. But even within the most patriarchal societies, where women are severely restricted and have little or no economic power, they have played an essential and recognized role in economic production.[1]

However, women's specific activities and degree of freedom have varied widely from place to place. For example, a U.S. woman who recently participated in an economic-development project for women in rural Pakistan describes their separate but ceaselessly productive lives:

> During the six days I was based in Chitral—the district capital and only town in this mountainous area a little larger than Connecticut—I never saw one Pakistani woman, even completely veiled, in public. The bazaar is Chitral's main street, both sides crammed with tiny stalls and shops selling everything from clothing to automatic weapons to hot tea, cooked rice, and *deal* (lentils). It is the center of life in Chitral. It belongs to the men.
>
> The women are at home and in the fields. They fetch water and firewood, cook, clean, care for the children, the men and their elders, make clothes, preserve and store food for the seven months of snow, card and spin sheep's wool, and weave colorful goat-hair carpets to cover their dirt floors. They tend the livestock, they plant, weed and harvest the crops from small terraced plots. They work from early sunrise until late in the evening, when they can no longer see by the dim light of their woodburning tin stoves centered in the middle of each mud hut. They have no heat, no electricity, no running water. Theirs is a frequently brutal life in a geographically brutal world of astounding beauty. And theirs is a life of courage.[2]

Western Europe throughout the Middle Ages and in the early modern, preindustrial period was also a patriarchal culture, although the specifics were somewhat different. Women were excluded from the male-dominated ruling institutions: government, higher education, the professions, the military, and the religious establishment. Often, women were not allowed to own land or property. But they still had a recognized, and public, role in economic production. Women worked in the fields next to men; they baked bread and brewed beer, spun thread, sewed clothes, performed a wide variety of other economically productive tasks, and often sold the surplus of their household production in the marketplace. Sometimes, businesses contracted out work to men and women who labored for pay in their own homes. Individual women occasionally worked as craftspeople or in other occupations commonly thought of as men's work. A few women even ran small businesses, and had some degree of economic power.[3] Women usually worked in or near their homes, since this was where most preindustrial economic production took place. But all that changed dramatically with the Industrial Revolution.

INDUSTRIALIZATION AND THE ECONOMIC DISAPPEARANCE OF WOMEN

In Western Europe, the development of fossil-fuel powered mass-production technologies spurred the movement of production from the home to the factory. Since factories could produce goods far more quickly and cheaply than either skilled craftspeople or home producers, home production gradually declined as people began to buy commercially mass-produced necessities and luxuries. In Europe and North America during the nineteenth century, the home slowly lost most of its economic identity, except as a place of consumption. But at the same time, it was given a new role.

Historians have described how during the nineteenth century, as industrialization spread, the rigid sex-role division of male breadwinner/female housewife emerged. The new, fast-paced, money-driven business world, characterized by laissez-faire economics, selfishness, and unrestrained competition, was a harsh, amoral realm in which men now had to earn their daily bread. In contrast with the male domain was the "women's sphere." The home was frequently described in literature of the time as a "haven in a heartless world," a source of peace and concord, love and devotion, where men returned to refresh themselves after a hard day's work. Historian Alice Kessler-Harris refers to this new role for women as "the cult of domesticity." She notes that as the new market economy obliterated such standards as compassion, charity, and caring for others, someone had to maintain moral and ethical values. This responsibility was assigned to women, especially in their role as mothers, in the sanctity of the home.[4]

I would also like to suggest another reason for assigning women to the home. The new commercial and industrial sectors were turning into the major centers of wealth and power in industrializing nations, bringing new fortunes, influence, and prestige to factory owners, entrepreneurs, and other businessmen. In order to maintain men's domination within society, women had to be excluded from this newly emerging source of wealth, power, and prestige. After all, men already controlled all the other institutions—government, religion, education, the professions, and the military. Now that the formal business sector was becoming such an important source of wealth and power, it too had to become an exclusively male domain.

MAKING WOMEN IN MODERN ECONOMIES ECONOMICALLY INVISIBLE

The patriarchal prejudices of modern Western nations meant that women could not be allowed access to the new sources of wealth and power in the emerging industrial economy. Yet modern societies still needed women's skills and labor for numerous tasks, both in the paid workforce and at home. The patriarchal solution was to keep women working, but to make them and their work economically invisible.

Many feminist scholars point out that it is insufficient to speak about the experiences of women in generalities, as if women constituted a uniform, undifferentiated group. Even in patriarchal societies, different kinds of women are treated differently, depending on their age, role in the family, social class, or race. Thus, modern economies have used a variety of strategies to make different kinds of women economically invisible.

A groundbreaking study of women's diverse experiences in the modern economy is *Race, Gender, and Work: A Multicultural Economic History of Women in the United States*, by feminist economists and activists Teresa Amott and Julie Matthaei. They follow the distinct economic histories of Native-American, Chicana, European-American, African-American, Asian-American, and Puerto Rican women in the United States over the last five centuries, emphasizing how the privileges, opportunities, or restrictions placed on each group of women affected their particular history, and also interacted to affect all the other groups, both in and out of the paid workforce. Their book is essential reading for anyone interested in better understanding the interaction of race, class, and gender in modern economies.[5]

Rather than repeating Amott and Matthaei's approach, this chapter will instead describe some of the methods through which women in modern economies have been disempowered and kept economically invisible, pointing out at a fairly broad level of categorization the different kinds of women against whom these strategies have been applied.

Keeping Women Out of the Visible Economy

Upper- and middle-class men were the most active enforcers of the new ideal that a woman's place is in the home—at least, when it applied to their women. Not only could such economically successful men afford to keep their wives, sisters, or daughters out of the paid workforce, they could also hire lower-class women as domestic servants to do most of the work necessary to make their homes into peaceful, pleasant havens. Having a wife who stayed at home and did not work became a symbol of a man's economic success.

In order to maintain the patriarchal hierarchy, it was essential to keep women out of the most powerful positions and lucrative money-making opportunities available to middle- and upper-class men. This was accomplished through a combination of informal pressures and formal, even legal prohibitions aimed at excluding women from higher education and the most prestigious occupations.

For example, according to the new ideology of nineteenth-century industrial society, respectable women, while morally superior, were also physically weak and emotionally delicate, too delicate to deal with the harsh realities of the workaday world. This assumption justified the exclusion of middle- and upper-class women from paid work, while it stigmatized as "unwomanly" women who sought to enter prestigious male fields such as law, politics, or medicine.

A typical case was women's exclusion from the medical profession. In the United States during the nineteenth century, as the practice of medicine became more formalized and graduation from medical school became required, medical schools and professional societies, established by men, erected numerous barriers to keep women out. Women's attendance was either prohibited outright, or male teachers and students openly harassed and discriminated against the few women who were let in. Women's exclusion was justified by the desire to keep women pure, the belief that no woman of true delicacy would want to attend medical lectures with male students, where such physically explicit activities as surgery and dissection of corpses were regularly presented. When a few medical schools for women were opened, some professional societies attempted to penalize male doctors who taught at them, and women who graduated from these schools were listed separately in medical directories, implying that they were less than full-fledged physicians.[6] Nineteenth-century women who attempted to enter higher education or law faced similar battles.

Gradually it became acceptable for respectable women to participate in the paid workforce—especially in clean, docile, ladylike jobs. For example, in the United States following World War I, office work and retail sales turned into women's occupations, filled almost exclusively by white, single women.[7] But while such women's participation in the paid workforce became acceptable—and therefore visible—the official ideology still maintained that these women were not serious workers, but rather were just helping out the real breadwinner, or passing the time until they found a husband and left the paid workforce. Furthermore, many workplaces that welcomed single women as employees had strict prohibitions against employing married women.[8]

Although most formal and legal prohibitions against women's entry into the paid workforce have now been eliminated, more subtle forms of discrimination still exclude women from many areas of the visible economy. Girls and women are discouraged from acquiring education in science, technology, or other fields that could provide them with entry into the most prestigious and highest-paid occupations. And in the business world, once female executives begin to approach the higher levels of management, they regularly bump up against the corporate "glass ceiling," which keeps most white women (as well as women and men of other racial or ethnic groups) from making it to the very top.[9]

Devaluing Women in the Visible Economy

While respectable women have been excluded in a variety of ways from the visible economy over the last two hundred years, women of less prestigious backgrounds have regularly sought paying work. And they have readily been hired by employers who needed their skills and labor. In the United States, poor and lower-class women, immigrants, and women of color have always been active wage-earners in the modern industrial economy, where they have held the poorest paid, least prestigious, and often extremely unpleasant and physically arduous jobs as, for example, household servants, laundresses, agricultural and factory workers. But because of their position in the social hierarchy, such women are already invisible. And their paid work merely reinforces the image of lower-class women as undelicate, unwomanly women who don't deserve the protections and respect reserved for their higher-class sisters.

Perhaps the most important strategy through which employers have utilized women wage-workers while maintaining the patriarchal hierarchy has been through the creation of separate occupational spheres for women and men. This pattern characterizes industrial nations around the world.[10]

At the upper levels of the occupational hierarchy, women have been shunted into specialized female professions, such as nursing, librarianship, social work, and teaching younger children, where they are usually supervised by or serve as assistants to men. At the middle and lower levels, for example in offices and factories, women have been massed into work that is more physically restricted, routine, and unskilled than the jobs done by men in the same workplaces. Throughout modern nations, the special occupational categories that have been systematically reserved for women are considered inferior to, and therefore receive less financial compensation than, the much broader range of paid work opportunities open to men.[11]

The creation of distinct occupational sectors for women has not only maintained the patriarchy directly, it has also reinforced the belief that women are less skilled than men, or are only capable of performing work which is an extension of their "natural" nurturing tendencies. Such assumptions and occupational structures, combined with the belief that women are not serious workers or breadwinners, further justify keeping women out of more skilled, prestigious, and highly paid positions.

Devaluing Women's Work in the Home

But women workers are not only penalized in their roles as workers. In modern economies, women—regardless of whether or not they do paid work—still have primary responsibility for care of children, home, and family. This means that most women with paying jobs end up working two shifts: one on the job, then another in the home.

The double shift has always caused hardship for women from economically and socially disadvantaged groups, who have often had to earn a living in addition to their domestic duties. But it was not perceived as a broad social problem until large numbers of middle-class women began entering the paid workforce, a phenomenon that started in the 1970s and still continues.

More women than ever in the paid workforce today have young children, including preschoolers and even infants. For example, in the United States in 1990, women constituted 45 percent of the paid workforce. These wage-earning women included two-thirds of all married women with children, and two-thirds of all single mothers.[12] As a result, growing numbers of women today are suffering increased physical and emotional stress as they desperately try to juggle both paid work and family responsibilities.

In *The Second Shift*, U.S. sociologist Arlie Hochschild describes in painful detail the stress on both women and family relationships in two-earner families with young children. In such families, plagued by incessant time and emotional pressures, women scramble to fulfill household and child-care duties after coming home from their paid work. Often they fight with their men over their need for more help and support in the home, over what is a fair share of the housework, and who should do it. Usually they lose their battles, learn to hold their tongues, and just do as much as they can themselves. The most common result is a rushed pace, resentful children, and lack of sleep, all problems which fall disproportionately on women. Hochschild estimates that in such families, women put in an extra month of work more per year than their male partners in order to meet family responsibilities.[13]

Furthermore, conventional perceptions have denied the economic value of women's unpaid activities in the home, focusing instead on the emotional and relational aspects of women's domestic activities. Women are idealized as hugging babies, drying away tears, baking cookies, making Halloween costumes, and driving the kids to after-school activities. And then they are expected to provide a warm comforting home, a supportive listening ear, and sexually gratifying receptivity to their husbands who come home to recuperate after a hard day's work out in the real world. In this way, social attitudes and cultural expectations sustain the myth that women's activities in the home are primarily emotional, not economically productive.

Official government policy also reinforces the illusion that women's work for their families is not real work. As the British feminist Ann Oakley points out:

> Not only is the housewife not paid for her work, but in almost all industrialized countries the housewife as houseworker has no right to the financial benefits—sickness benefit, unemployment benefit, and so on—which accrue to other workers through state insurance systems. Any benefits for which she qualifies come to her indirectly, through marriage, and because, in marriage, she acknowledges her condition of economic dependence [on her breadwinner husband]. As a worker, she does not exist.[14]

One study of women's work identifies six tasks which women throughout the world are expected to perform: bearing children, feeding people, clothing people, tending the weak and sick, bringing up and educating young children, and being in charge of the household.[15]

All of these tasks are essential to the maintenance of human life and are the central responsibilities that women are expected to perform for their families today. But in modern economies, such activities are only recognized as having economic value when working parents—that is, those who can afford it—begin to pay others to provide such services for their families. Today one can purchase everything from prepared meals to child care, from nursing services to housecleaning, and can even hire people to do one's shopping. And many households find it necessary to pay for such services in order to keep the family healthy and maintain some semblance of family life. Considering the cost of such services, there can no longer be any doubt about the economic importance of women's traditional, unpaid activities in their own homes.

Defining Women as Consumers, Men as Producers

While the modern economic paradigm devalues women's contributions as workers and producers, women are enthusiastically assigned the role of consumer.

Women's new identity as consumers arose in Europe and the United States during the late nineteenth century. Respectable wives and mothers, when not performing their domestic duties, could spend their leisure hours in those new innovations—department stores—which encouraged their elegant customers to become addicted to the latest fashionable luxuries.[16] By the twentieth century, continued increases in societal affluence enabled women of all income levels and classes to become stereotyped as consumers.

The image of men as producers and women as consumers fills popular U.S. culture. It is reflected in such phrases as "Men earn, women spend"; T-shirts for women that proclaim "Shop till you drop," or "When the going gets tough, the tough go shopping"; or country music laments about the unfortunate man caught robbing a bank, a crime to which he was driven by his love for a luxury-craving woman. Of course men also consume, sometimes compulsively. They buy auto accessories, electronic gadgets, computers, software, and power tools. But such purchases are labelled important, unlike the frivolous personal luxuries that women buy.

The image of men as producers and women as consumers reinforces the belief that men do the important work of the world, while women are dependent on men's work not only for money but also for the goods and services women consume. While men may gripe about women's spending and consuming, it plays an important role in affirming male self-esteem. Especially in the United States, the male earner's rise up the economic ladder is expected to be accompanied by his family's regular move up the consumption scale, to a bigger house, a better neighborhood, better schools for the children, and more elaborate entertaining and recreational activities. By spending money on the right clothes, food, and household furnishings for her home and children, the wife conveys to the outside world her husband's economic and social success.

Even the assumptions of mainstream economists reflect this imagery. According to conventional economic theory, the modern economy functions because of the interactions of two distinct sectors: firms (businesses) and households. Firms produce, and households consume. Notice the gender imagery encoded in this model: Businesses—that is, the male economic domain—produce. Households—that is, the female economic domain—consume. In conventional economic theory, households are never defined as producers.[17]

Through all the strategies described above—keeping women out of the paid workforce, devaluing women in the paid workforce, denying the economic value of women's work in the home, and identifying women primarily as consumers—the modern economic paradigm has maintained men's economic superiority.

THE ECONOMIC INVISIBILITY OF THIRD WORLD WOMEN

Although this book emphasizes changes taking place in modern economies, we need to look briefly at the situation of Third-World women, because their lives are increasingly intertwined with the changes in modern nations,

Over the last five hundred years, Westerners have busily exploited Asia, Africa, and the Americas, at first for resources such as precious metals, slaves, and fertile lands for growing plantation crops. During the nineteenth and twentieth centuries, as industrialization radically transformed Western Europe and North America, the cultures and economies of their Third-World colonies also had to be changed drastically to meet new Western needs. Over the past two hundred years, modern industrial nations have actively been turning the people of Third-World societies into low-paid wage-workers employed by, and ever-expanding markets for goods mass-produced by, Western-owned businesses.[18]

Central to this transformation has been the imposition of modern Western gender roles onto Third-World societies. Anthropologist Peggy Reeves Sanday, in her comprehensive study *Female Power and Male Dominance*, shows that women's status and economic power in nonindustrial Third-World societies has varied widely. In some nonindustrial societies women have owned land, bought and sold goods, made money, and participated openly in economic and political decision making. In other societies, women have been subjected to extreme patriarchal domination, including overwork and physical brutality, with little liberty or power of their own.[19]

Yet regardless of women's status, their work has always been central to the survival of nonindustrial societies. Even today, women in Third-World nations are primarily responsible for gathering, growing, or otherwise securing their households' food supplies and for such essential services as child-rearing, health care, fuel and water collection, and sanitation.[20]

As the modern economic paradigm was imposed onto Third-World societies, men's and women's roles were redefined according to the Western ideal of male breadwinner vs. female housewife. This does not mean that Third-World women have stopped working — just that their economic contributions have become invisible.

In many instances, the imposition of Western economic and cultural patterns has actively weakened Third-World women's economic power and increased their workload. Where women owned land or held political power, their lands and power were often transferred by Western colonizers to local men. Third-World economic development programs have emphasized the creation of paying jobs for men, while ignoring the needs and considerable unpaid economic contributions of women. The ongoing conversion of the most productive Third-World lands from self-sufficient farming to the growing of cash crops for export has made it harder for women to grow food for their families.[21]

In addition, over the last few decades, Third-World women have increasingly been hired to work in clothing, electronics, and other multinational-owned factories, many of which have relocated from the West to the Third World. Like women wage-earners in modern nations, Third-World women are also treated as secondary workers and are shoved into the least skilled, poorest-paying jobs. As a result, Third-World women now play a crucial economic role as the lowest rank in the global assembly line.[22] And, of course, even when they have paying jobs, Third-World women are still responsible for child care and other domestic duties, which means that they often work an exhausting double day.

The years 1975 to 1985 were named the United Nations Decade for the Advancement of Women. At the end of this decade, the DAWN Collective, an international network of women activists and researchers concluded that

> rather than improving, the socioeconomic status of Third World women has worsened considerably throughout the Decade. With few exceptions, women's relative access to economic resources, income, and employment has worsened, their burdens have increased, and their relative and even absolute health, nutritional, and educational status has declined.[23]

Many Third-World and feminist activists also point out that because the economic contributions of Third-World women are so important to the larger well-being of their societies, women's economic decline is a key unrecognized cause of the overall worsening of many Third World economies.

We must add one final form of economic invisibility. Many Third-World women have migrated to more affluent modern nations in search of paid work. Often undocumented, they frequently find jobs in sweatshops or as underpaid health or child care workers. They are regularly subjected to dangerous working conditions and are often paid at or below minimum wage. But because such women are afraid to lose even these jobs, they have no recourse but to endure. To the outside world, they must remain invisible.

ECONOMIC INVISIBILITY AND THE MAINTENANCE OF HIERARCHIES

Modern economies are characterized by many hierarchical structures and constraints that sharply limit people's opportunities. As we saw in chapter 2, corporate industrial workplaces are consciously hierarchical, with a few good jobs at the top and large numbers of purposely designed bad jobs at the bottom. As we've seen in chapter 3, during two centuries of industrialization, employers have regularly hired men for skilled, well-paying jobs, while shunting women off to less skilled, lower-paying work. Patriarchal beliefs that women are inferior, and that their real place is in the home, are invoked to justify gender discrimination, while such discriminatory employment practices further reinforce women's overall social and economic inferiority.

But ironically, the patriarchal assumption that women are less skilled or less serious workers can also be used against men. One instance of this occurred in the United States during the Great Depression. As millions of men were thrown out of work and jobs became scarce, more women tried to enter the workforce to help support their families. Because they could be hired for less money than men, white women during the 1930s actually had higher employment rates than white men. Of course a backlash occurred, as women were accused of stealing men's jobs. One response was a series of mostly unsuccessful efforts to pass state and federal laws that would have prohibited employers from hiring married women.[24]

And many analysts note that since the 1970s women are increasingly being hired at lower wages in deskilled job slots, often for part-time or temporary work, to replace higher-paid, more skilled, formerly fulltime male workers.[25] Not only are male workers being replaced by less well-paid women in modern nations, but their jobs are also being transferred to even lower-paid Third-World women.

We've seen how women's economic invisibility has kept them out of the paid workforce or restricted them to inferior paid positions. But women's economic invisibility hurts more than just women. It hurts their families, hurts men, and can be detrimental to an entire economy.

Gender distinctions are not the only source of oppression in modern nations; modern societies are shaped by many separate but interacting hierarchical systems. People are also classified, divided, privileged, or constrained on the basis of race, class, nationality, age, sexual preference, and other criteria. Sexism, racism, classism, and other systems of domination and discrimination interact and intertwine, opening up opportunities and enhancing wealth, power, and self-esteem for some people, cutting off opportunities and limiting wealth, power, and feelings of self-worth for others.[26]

But as the example of women's economic invisibility has demonstrated, hierarchical systems disempower individuals and divide communities on the basis of artificially created differences and illusory criteria of superiority and inferiority. As a result, the destructive influences of such systems can extend far beyond the harm done to the group characterized as inferior. A central challenge of the emerging economic paradigm is to acknowledge all forms of economic invisibility and to move beyond the unjust, destructive systems they maintain.

NOTES

1. The range of women's economic activities in preindustrial societies is described in Peggy Reeves Sanday, *Female Power and Male Dominance: On the Origins of Sexual Inequality* (New York: Cambridge University Press, 1981), chaps. 4 and 6.

2. Sandra Willett, "How was the spinning wheel working?," *Boston Sunday Globe*, 11 November 1990, sec. B.

3. On women's economic roles in pre-industrial Europe, see Ann Oakley, *Woman's Work: The Housewife, Past and Present* (New York: Vintage, 1974), chap. 2.

4. See Alice Kessler-Harris, *Out to Work: A History of Wage-Earning Women in the United States* (New York: Oxford University Press, 1982), 49–50. On how industrialization changed women's economic roles, see also Oakley, *Woman's Work*, chap. 3.

5. See Teresa L. Amott and Julie A. Matthaei, *Race, Gender, and Work: A Multicultural Economic History Of Women in the United States* (Boston: South End Press, 1991).

6. Mary Roth Walsh, *Doctors Wanted: No Women Need Apply (Sexual Barriers in the Medical Profession, 1835–1975)* (New Haven, Conn.: Yale University Press, 1977).

7. Amott and Matthaei, *Race, Gender, and Work*, 127.

8. On the exclusion of married women from the workforce in the U.S., see Amott and Matthaei, *Race, Gender, and Work*, 300–301. In Canada, see Bruce O'Hara, *Working Harder Isn't Working* (Vancouver: New Star Books, 1993), chap. 10.

9. On the glass ceiling, see Sarah Hardesty and Nehama Jacobs, *Success and Betrayal: The Crisis of Women in Corporate America* (New York.: Simon & Schuster, 1986).

10. On the occupational segregation of women in the U.S., see Amott and Matthaei, *Race, Gender, and Work*. In Great Britain, see Harriet Bradley, *Men's Work, Women's Work : A Sociological History of the Sexual Division of Labour in Employment* (Minneapolis, Minn.: University of Minnesota Press, 1989). In Japan, see Larry S. Carney and Charlotte G. O'Kelly, "Women's Work and Women's Place in the Japanese Economic Miracle," in Kathryn Ward, ed.,*Women Workers and Global Restructuring* (Ithaca, N.Y.: ILR Press, 1990), 113–145.

11. Diane Lewis, "Two Studies Show Women Still Trail Men in Earnings,"*Boston Globe*, 18 March 1993, 46.

12. Data on working women with young children comes from "Alternative Work Patterns," *Facts on U.S. Working Women*, U.S. Dept. of Labor, Women's Bureau, Fact Sheet No. 86-3, August 1986. Data on U.S. women's participation in the paid workforce in 1990 comes from a fact sheet, "Are Mommies Dropping Out of the Labor Force? No!" published by the Institute for Women's Policy Research, 1400 20 St. NW, Suite 104, Washington, D.C. 20003 (no date), 3.

13. On stresses in two-earner families with young children, see Arlie Hochschild, *The Second Shift* (New York: Avon Books, 1989). Hochschild's comparisons of men's and women's total work-time, both paid and unpaid, is on pp. 3–4. Sociologist Cynthia Negrey cites numerous U.S. studies of two-parent families which show that, regardless of how many paid hours each parent works, the women still perform approximately 70 per cent of the housework. See Negrey, *Gender, Time, and Reduced Work* (Albany: State University of New York Press, 1993), 23–28.

14. Oakley, *Woman's Work*, 3.

15 . Universal characteristics of women's domestic work are described in Virginia Novarra, *Women's Work, Men's Work* (London: Marion Boyars, 1980).

16. On nineteenth-century department stores and women's lives, see Elaine S. Abelson, *When Ladies Go A-Thieving: Middle-Class Shoplifters in the Victorian Department Store* (New York: Oxford University Press, 1989).

17. Marilyn Waring explores why, in conventional economic theory, households are never defined as producers; see *If Women Counted: A New Feminist Economics* (San Francisco: Harper & Row, 1988), chap. 3.

18. On Western nations' economic domination of the Third World, see Gita Sen and Caren Grown, *Development, Crises, and Alternative Visions: Third World Women's Perspectives* (New York: Monthly Review Press, 1987), 28–34; also Arjun Makhijani, *From Global Capitalism to Economic Justice* (New York: Apex Press, 1992), chaps. 2, 4, and 6.

19. On the range of women's economic and political power in preindustrial societies, see Sanday, *Female Power and Male Dominance*, chaps 1, 4, and 6.

20. Third World women today have primary responsibilities for essential economic production; see Sen and Grown, *Development, Crises, and Alternative Visions*, 23–24; Waring, *If Women Counted*, chaps. 1, 3, and 8; and Vandana Shiva, *Staying Alive: Women, Ecology And Development* (Atlantic Highlands, N.J.: Zed Books, 1989).

21. On how Western influence in Third-World nations has worsened women's social, economic, and political status, see Sanday, *Female Power and Male Dominance*, chap 7; and Sen and Grown, *Development, Crises, and Alternative Visions*, chap. 2.

22. On Third World women at the bottom of the global assembly line, see Kathryn Ward, ed., *Women Workers and Global Restructuring* (Ithaca, N.Y.: ILR Press, 1990).

23. Sen and Grown, *Development, Crises, and Alternative Visions*, 16.

24. On women's employment advantage during the 1930s Depression, see Kessler Harris, *Out to Work*, chap. 9; or Amott and Matthaei, *Race, Gender, and Work*, 128.

25. A discussion of how, since the 1970s, lower-paid, parttime, and temporary women employees have been replacing higher-paid men appears in Teresa Amott, *Caught in The Crisis: Women and the U.S. Economy Today* (New York: Monthly Review Press, 1993), 58–65.

26. There is an ongoing debate over whether or not one hierarchical system, such as gender or class oppression, is the basis of all other forms of domination. I agree with feminist economist Nancy Folbre, who—in one of the best discussions of the issue—says that structures of domination are distinct, but regularly interact, and are often mutually reinforcing, but sometimes conflicting with each other. See Nancy Folbre, *Who Pays for the Kids?: Gender and the Structures of Constraint* (London and New York: Routledge, 1994), chap. 2.

Chapter 4

VISIBLE AND INVISIBLE CONTRIBUTIONS: DISCOVERING THE WHOLE ECONOMY

As the previous chapters have outlined, the modern economic paradigm makes many essential wealth-producing and life-sustaining activities invisible. But as the problems related to economic invisibility become more apparent, an increasing number of professional economists and others concerned about social, economic, and environmental justice are developing more comprehensive and accurate models of what the whole economy includes. This chapter draws on their work to examine the breadth of the invisible economy in modern nations and the relationship between the visible and invisible areas of the whole economy.

I define the visible economy as the production and distribution of goods and services by individuals and institutions whose activities are officially assumed to increase national wealth and are therefore counted in the GDP.

The invisible economy consists of all the wealth-producing, wealth-distributing, and life-sustaining activities, institutions, and relationships that are officially considered nonproductive and are therefore not included in the GDP.

Together, these visible and invisible sectors constitute the whole economy.[1]

(Note that I use the terms "the visible economy" and "the visible sectors of the economy" interchangeably; likewise, "the invisible economy" and "the invisible sectors of the economy.")

SEEING THE WHOLE ECONOMY: HAZEL HENDERSON'S LAYER CAKE

One of the most memorable images of the whole economy was offered in 1982 by the pioneering economic critic and activist Hazel Henderson, in her mind-expanding layer cake diagram (see Figure 4.1.).[2]

At the top—the icing, as Henderson so pointedly calls it—is the private or market sector, which includes the production and sales activities of businesses, as well as the paid work, savings, purchases of goods and services, and investments of individuals, businesses, and other organizations. This layer consists exclusively of *monetized* activities—that is, transactions and relationships that involve the use of money. Since the activities of this layer are regularly included in the GDP, it is the essence of the visible economy.

Next is the public or government layer. According to conventional definitions, government is distinct from but interacts with the economy, and some of its activities increase the GDP. When federal, state, or local governments pay individuals or businesses to provide services on the public's behalf—for example, to teach kids in public schools, put out fires, build weapons, or wage wars—this is counted as wealth production in the GDP. But when governments give money directly to people in order to help them and their families survive—for example, as Social Security, unemployment, or disability benefits, or aid to mothers with dependent children—these are called "transfer payments." According to one introductory economics book, because transfer payments are "the public equivalent of private charity," they are not counted as wealth production in the GDP.[3]

Henderson places the public sector just below the private business sector to emphasize that government provides an underlying set of services—public safety, firefighting, education, and roads, for example—which make possible both business and general well-being.

Figure 4.1:   Total productive system of an industrial economy— Hazel Henderson's three-layer cake with icing.

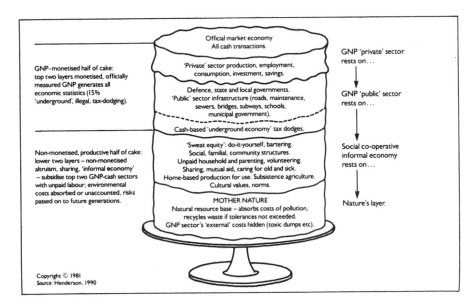

Official market economy
All cash transactions.

GNP 'private' sector rests on...

GNP-monetised half of cake: top two layers monetised, officially measured GNP generates all economic statistics (15% 'underground', illegal, tax-dodging).

'Private' sector production, employment, consumption, investment, savings.

Defence, state and local governments. 'Public' sector infrastructure (roads, maintenance, sewers, bridges, subways, schools, municipal government).

GNP 'public' sector rests on...

Cash-based 'underground economy' tax dodges.

Non-monetised, productive half of cake: lower two layers – non-monetised altruism, sharing, 'informal economy' – subsidise top two GNP-cash sectors with unpaid labour; environmental costs absorbed or unaccounted, risks passed on to future generations.

'Sweat equity': do-it-yourself, bartering. Social, familial, community structures. Unpaid household and parenting, volunteering. Sharing, mutual aid, caring for old and sick. Home-based production for use. Subsistence agriculture. Cultural values, norms.

Social co-operative informal economy rests on...

MOTHER NATURE
Natural resource base – absorbs costs of pollution, recycles waste if tolerances not exceeded. GNP sector's 'external' costs hidden (toxic dumps etc).

Nature's layer.

Copyright © 1981
Source: Henderson, 1990

The economic role of government is highly controversial. In some industrialized nations, especially in Japan, government is openly active in the visible economy through planning and coordination of business activities. In other modern societies, most notably the United States, there is a long-standing belief that any economic activities by government are inherently unproductive. Since, according to this free-enterprise tradition, business is the most efficient source of economic production and the free market is the ideal vehicle for optimum distribution, the most desirable role for government is to get out of the way and let business and the market operate according to their own best interests.

Critics of government waste and involvement in the economy are quick to cite excessive government bureaucracies and regulations of dubious value. They fail to mention the enormous government contracts, tax breaks, and other domestic policies that provide the largest corporations with numerous economic and legal advantages, not to mention the trade agreements, international policies, and periodic military ventures in which modern nations engage, in order to advance the interests of their largest business corporations.[4] Nor do they point out that many government regulations harass individuals and small businesses, while ignoring the much more serious social, economic, and environmental harm done by the wealthiest and most powerful businesses.

The debate over appropriate government involvement in the economy has gone on for many years, at all levels of economic and political life, and is still taking place heatedly today. I am not trying to resolve it here. I only mention it to remind my readers that economic activities performed by government are often categorized as nonproductive or wasteful. But while some government activities are clearly wasteful, even destructive, so are many activities initiated by businesses. And some government-sponsored services are actually more socially and economically beneficial than comparable business activities.[5]

The bottom layer of Henderson's cake—the natural environment—is gaining increasing recognition today as public and private groups around the globe realize that a healthy economy is inseparable from a healthy environment and explore the possibilities for sustainable economic development (see Bibliography and Resources). But because it is not yet considered part of the economy by conventional standards, the environment is in essence economically invisible.

THE INFORMAL ECONOMY

The economic sector that has received the least public and professional attention to date is what Henderson calls the "sweat equity" or "social cooperative" layer. This includes all those unpaid personal and neighborly activities that play such a large but officially unrecognized role in sustaining our lives. Professional economists are aware that this layer exists, and they even have a name for it: the informal economy. However, they do not pay much attention to it or include it in the GDP because it is assumed to have little importance in modern economies.[6] To rectify this omission, this chapter emphasizes the essential but largely overlooked role of this unpaid sector in our lives.

Incidentally, the informal economy is of considerable interest to economists who study and advise on development in the Third World. However, in this context the term has a somewhat different meaning than in relation to industrialized nations. In underdeveloped countries, the informal economy often refers to the intricate networks of production and exchange that have spontaneously developed in urban slums and squatters' quarters. Characterized by numerous one-person businesses—street vendors, food sellers, barbers, among others—this informal economy, to some extent monetized, is considered by many development specialists an entrepreneurial base that can be built into more formal business activities.

Increasingly, the term is also being used (incorrectly, I believe) to refer to paid work that businesses in the Third World subcontract to unreported enterprises or homeworkers in order to avoid paying minimum wages, withholding taxes, and providing other standard benefits. Women in particular are trapped in such exploitative ventures.[7]

The Informal Economy Is Not the Underground Economy

Like many of the writers cited below, I believe we must make a clear distinction between the informal economy and the so-called underground economy. The underground economy is essentially illegal. It includes both legitimate money-making activities, which are not reported in order to avoid taxation, and overtly criminal activities such as selling illegal drugs. In modern nations, enormous amounts of money pass through the underground economy.

By contrast, the activities of the informal economy are completely open and legal—they are just not considered part of the economy. Ironically, some informal activities, such as barter networks, may actually be subject to taxation (see chapter 16), even though the activities involved do not utilize money.

Extent of the Informal Economy in Modern Societies

A powerful and comprehensive study of the informal economy in the United States, *Home, Inc.: The Hidden Wealth and Power of the American Household*, was published by financial writer Scott Burns in 1975. Although Burns uses the term "the household economy," he is actually disscussing all economic activities that take place outside of profit-oriented market institutions and relationships. He defines this enormous but invisible household economy as

> the sum of all the goods and services produced within all the households in the United States. This includes, among other things, the value of shelter, home-cooked meals, all the weekend-built patios and barbecues in suburban America, painting and wallpapering, home sewing, laundry, child care, home repairs, volunteer services to community and to friends, the produce of the home garden, and the transportation services of the private automobile.[8]

Although we are taught that the household is a consuming institution, Burns declares that it is beyond doubt a productive economic institution as well, employing both labor and capital and producing goods and services that have a tangible economic value. But since the household economy pays neither cash wages nor issues dividends, and since its economic product is both produced and consumed within the family, it is invisible to official perceptions of the economy.[9] Burns recognizes that gender bias also contributes to this invisibility:

> The invisible household economy might also be called the matriarchal economy, because it is dominated by women. They perform most of the labor, make most of the household decisions, and are employed as managers for the labor and assets of the household. More than a few observers have noted that the household economy is invisible precisely *because* it is controlled by women and that present accounting conventions have the effect of demeaning the work and value of women.[10]

Although a few other U.S. writers have examined specific small segments of this nation's invisible economy,[11] to my knowledge Burns' book is the only comprehensive study of the nonmonetized economy in the United States. Not surprisingly, observers in other nations take their societies' informal economic activities much more seriously.

In Canada, the Vanier Institute of the Family has sponsored several studies of the informal economy in advanced industrial societies such as Canada, England, and the United States. In *From the Roots Up: Economic Development as if Community Mattered*, one of the most comprehensive analyses to date, authors David P. Ross and Peter J. Usher define the informal economy as consisting of those institutions and relationships that are small-scale and are guided by both social (nonmonetary) as well as economic goals. According to their definition, big business and government comprise the formal economy, while the informal economy includes small businesses, collective and cooperative enterprises, community organizations and enterprises, voluntary activities performed for community organizations, barter and skills exchanges, mutual aid, and household activities.[12]

Usher and Ross estimate that for nations such as England, Canada, and the United States, the size of the informal economy is at least half again the size of the visible economy.[13] Since they include small businesses in the informal economy, this certainly exaggerates the informal sector's contribution to the whole economy. Other studies, which do not include small businesses in the informal sector, still suggest that a staggeringly large amount of unpaid economic production and distribution is taking place in our advanced industrial societies. Scott Burns notes three separate studies that concluded that the household economy (as they defined it) was about one-third again the size of the monetized economy. Burns estimates that if all the work done within the household by both men and women were monetized, its total value would equal the entire amount paid out in wages and salaries by every corporation in the United States And he cites a 1965 study that put the value of all goods and services produced in the U.S. household economy at about $300 billion.[14]

Another estimate of the informal economy comes from the Finnish feminist economist Hilkka Pietila, who developed a model of the economy designed to identify and acknowledge the unpaid and therefore officially unrecognized economic contributions of women. She conceives of a modern economy as having three separate sectors:

— the "fettered economy," the realm of large-scale production for export, which is tied to the world market;

— the "protected sector," including commercial production for the domestic market, and public services such as food production, construction of houses and infrastructure, schools, health, transportation, and communication, which in most countries are provided or heavily regulated by the government; and

— the "free economy," the work and production that people do voluntarily for the well-being of their families, or for pleasure, without requesting or receiving pay.

Pietila estimates that in Finland in 1980, the free, informal, sector involved 54 percent of people's time, and provided 35 percent of the productive value of the total economy.[15] Her work reaffirms the enormous importance of informal, unpaid activities in modern nations.

Considering the extent and universality of the informal economy, it seems almost incomprehensible that it is entirely omitted from GDP measures of society's wealth production. This omission reflects the biases of the modern economic paradigm: activities that are small-scale, done to help others without involving money or the goal of maximizing profit, and primarily the province of women simply cannot be relevant to the important business of the economy.

THE UNIQUE ROLE OF THE INFORMAL ECONOMY

Denying the crucial productive role of the household and other nonmonetized sectors of the economy keeps the informal economy at a serious disadvantage. And this is unfortunate, because the informal economy provides unique contributions to modern societies. Many of the studies on the informal economy describe how it is kept in a subordinate status and the special contributions it provides despite its limitations.

The Informal Economy Is Deprived of Material Resources and Social Support

Because it's not recognized as a legitimate economic realm that provides essential economic services, the informal economy is deprived of access to society's resources. It is forced to subsist on the resources already available to its individual creators and their surrounding communities.

In a materially rich community, the informal economy can also be materially rich. Members of affluent communities can devote many resources to the care of their children, elders, and other dependents, to aesthetically pleasing household production, fulfilling volunteer work, and rewarding neighborly interaction and exchange. But in a materially poor community, the informal economy, while even more important to people's survival and well-being, can be severely limited. Children, elders, and other dependents may be deprived of needed resources, and the caretakers suffer under enormous strain as they try to care for dependents. People in poor communities often show impressive ingenuity in making the best of what they have, but their courageous and loving efforts are hampered by lack of material resources.

The Informal Economy Is Often More Efficient and Responsible Than the Visible Economy

Most informal economic activities are small-scale, using local resources to meet people's needs. As a result, participants are keenly aware of the impact of their activities on their community and the immediate natural environment. This can make participants in informal economic activities use resources more carefully; they are also more likely to be socially and environmentally responsible. By contrast, large economic organizations whose decision-makers are far removed from the effects of their decisions are more likely to ignore any harmful impact and to allow pursuit of monetary goals to obscure their effects on the real world.

Informal Economic Activities Can Be More Personally Fulfilling and Empowering Than Formal Economic Activities

The informal economy is self-directed, shaped by the participants themselves to meet their own needs. In contrast with paid work activities, which are often driven by the need to cut costs, speed up the pace, and constantly increase efficiency, informal economic activities can be much more interesting, diversified, congenial, and playful. Their pace can be much slower, and the results much more personally, emotionally, and aesthetically satisfying. And they can offer full opportunity for people to socialize, express their whole selves, and enhance their skills and learning.

The Informal Economy Provides Caring

In the modern economic paradigm, monetary value and the ability to pay determine the worth of all things. Unfortunately, people with the greatest needs are also most likely to lack money to pay for what they need. Babies and children can't earn money. Many older people are ill or frail and can't earn money. Sick or injured people often can't earn money—they may be too weak, immobilized, or unconscious. Mentally and physically disadvantaged people are less able, or unable to earn money. Poor people, by definition, lack money. But all these groups of people still have to eat and be sheltered. They need the services we all need and may require additional care or even exceptional help and support, temporarily or permanently.

Because the modern economic paradigm equates the economy with monetized activities, it turns dependent people, who by definition can't pay for what they need, into aberrations. Since such people don't fit within the criteria of the economy, they are redefined as "noneconomic" problems, to be dealt with by unpopular, underfunded government programs, nonprofit or religious-based charities, community volunteers, and fellow family members, especially women. Since in many cases these caregivers are not paid for what they do, they too are devalued, considered unproductive.

While from the perspective of the modern economic paradigm caring for dependent people has no value, it is nevertheless a natural fact of human existence that every one of us is sometimes unable to be productive and must depend upon others to meet our needs during various phases of life. Since the visible economy, driven by the goal of money-making, is inherently unable to deal with the fact of human dependency, caregiving must therefore fall to the informal economic sector, which is guided by different rules and values. This does not mean that the informal economy is inferior, but rather that the monetized market economy is inherently unable to serve essential human needs.

DISPLACING THE DYSFUNCTIONS OF THE VISIBLE ECONOMY ONTO THE INVISIBLE ECONOMY

In essence, the visible economy is the realm of monetized activities—of businesses, the buying and selling of goods and services, of paid work and other money-making endeavors. The invisible economy consists of nonmonetized activities—household production of goods and services for one's family, neighborly exchanges of goods and services, and unpaid volunteer work for the community. The life-giving, wealth-producing, self-renewing activities of the natural environment are also part of the invisible economy.

This extensive invisible economy suffers not only because it is deprived of material resources and denied recognition as a legitimate, productive sector of the economy. In addition, the problems and damage caused by the visible economy are regularly displaced onto the home, family, and community; onto other supposedly nonproductive institutions such as government and charitable organizations; and onto the natural environment. This puts an even greater strain on all these sectors. But because they are considered nonproductive or are economically invisible, nobody notices.[16] A major example of this displacement regularly occurs regarding the environmental destruction caused by modern economies. This damage can be found everywhere: in the mounting litter and spreading landfills; the polluted rivers, lakes, and forests; the depleted topsoils; and poisonous pesticide and herbicide residues and runoffs.

Nature is not the only victim. Wastes and toxins also end up where people live, harming human health and making communities unlivable. But modern economies make the garbage and poisons they produce invisible. Symbolically, the costs of producing and cleaning up the wastes are counted as wealth-production in the GDP. Physically poisonous wastes are moved from the mainstream into out-of-the-way places, or to the Third World. And socially, they are dumped into communities of poor people and people of color, who are less valued and therefore invisible—a process called environmental racism. These practices are being opposed by the growing movement for environmental justice.[17]

When people are poisoned in this way, the care of the victims usually falls on their own family members, especially on women. And organizing to oppose further dumping, or cleaning up after the fact, is usually carried out by unpaid volunteers from the affected communities. So this healing work is also excluded from measures of the economy, both because it is unpaid and because it is done by people who are already economically invisible.

This displacement of destruction is legally permitted by the concept of "externalities." According to conventional economics, any harm caused by a business that doesn't directly affect that business or the people who buy its products is technically defined as an "externality," and is not traditionally held against that business by law or accounting systems. So a business is responsible for the costs if a piece of its productive equipment wears out, or its customers get sick from its products. But if a business generates poisons in the process of manufacturing and gets rid of them by pouring them into the river or dumping them onto unused land in a distant community, the end results of such activities are no longer relevant to that business, according to the concept of externalities.[18]

Because the concept of externalities is enshrined in conventional economic models, public policy, and the legal system, businesses can engage in all kinds of wasteful, even overtly destructive, activities but do not have to take responsibility for their mistakes. Meanwhile, their profits and sales increase, and the visible economy, measured by the GDP, continues to grow. The nonbusiness, nonmonetized, invisible sectors of the economy are left to clean up the messes, pick up the pieces, absorb the blows, become the victims, care for the victims, and try to heal the wounds being caused by the destructive activities of the visible economy.

REVALUING THE INVISIBLE ECONOMY

As Figure 4.2 summarizes, the visible and invisible economies have distinctly different goals and values and operate according to different rules. At the same time, despite its inferior position and many burdens, the invisible economy constantly creates and sustains life.

A key challenge of the new economic paradigm is to create a more balanced relationship between the visible and invisible sectors of the economy. There are at least two ways this must happen. First, the extensive and essential contributions of the invisible economy must be fully acknowledged. Since it is deprived of resources and social recognition, the nonmonetized, invisible economy can look like an economy of last resort, from which people should be seeking to escape. However, despite the real problems noted here, we've also seen that the voluntary, self-directed economic activities of the informal economy can offer us models for more humane, empowering, and environmentally supportive economic activities. Thus, a crucial issue for the emerging economic paradigm is how the positive social

FIGURE 4.2: COMPARISON OF THE VISIBLE AND INVISIBLE SECTORS OF THE ECONOMY

The Visible / *Monetized Economy*	*The Invisible /* *Non-Monetized Economy*
Centered around businesses and money-making.	Centered around household, neighborhood, community.*
Perceived as the real economy.	Perceived as secondary (if at all).
Monopolizes resources, public attention, and power.	Deprived of resources and power.
Shaped by efficiency and the bottom line: The producers are working for others.	Shaped by the needs of the producers: The producers are working for themselves.
Serves those who can pay.	Serves everyone, including dependent people (those who can't pay).
Its costs and mistakes are displaced onto the invisible economy.	Bears the brunt of the visible economy's dysfunctions, and cleans up its messes.
Traditionally men's work: the masculine realm.	Traditionally women's work: the feminine realm.

* Note: The invisible economy also includes the natural environment. Many of the characteristics listed here also apply to nature and its relation to the visible economy.

values and self-directed structure of the informal economy can be transferred to all our economic activities. Or conversely, how more skills and resources can be brought into our freely self-directed activities, to enhance both our freedom and economic empowerment.

Second, both the positive contributions and harmful effects of the visible sectors of the economy must be evaluated more realistically. By denying the economic contributions of the invisible sectors, the modern economic paradigm maintains the illusion that the formal business sector is the primary source of wealth generation and well-being in modern societies, and therefore deserves special support and privileges. In fact, the visible (business) economy is directly dependent upon, and could not grow and prosper without, the devalued or unrecognized wealth-creating, healing, and life-sustaining activities of the invisible economy of households, families, communities, and nature.

I call this overvaluing of business and the visible economy "economism." I will return to the dynamics of economism in chapter 9.

WHY ECONOMIC INVISIBILITY?

Economic invisibility maintains the hierarchical values and existing distribution of wealth and power in modern economies. By promoting the illusion that the business sector is the primary source of wealth production and distribution, the phenomenon of economic invisibility justifies why the largest business corporations have become so extraordinarily wealthy and powerful, and why the people who own, run, and receive the most money from these businesses deserve their privileges, prestige, and hefty rewards. Meanwhile, by maintaining the prevailing gender, racial, class, and institutional hierarchies, economic invisibility also helps to justify the inferior wealth, power, and status of the inferior categories—women, poorer men, people of color, local institutions, small businesses, and community organizations—and justifies the continued pollution and exploitation of communities and the natural environment.

Economic invisibility also prevents people from considering the possibility of alternatives. To some extent, inequitable social and economic systems are maintained by force and violence. But a destructive system must also keep its hold over people's hearts and minds by creating the illusion that it provides the best possible answers, that all the alternatives are worse, or by denying that any other alternatives exist.

As we have seen, the invisible areas of the economy, such as our unpaid caring activities and the contributions of nature, follow very different models, and operate according to very different principles, than the visible economy. Since the alternative models offered by these sectors present a direct challenge to the dominance of the modern economic paradigm, they must therefore be kept invisible.

Societies throughout history have used various forms of invisibility to maintain the existing system and repress perceptions that threaten the official view of reality. The established system may be described as divinely ordained, scientifically proven, or human nature, while people who question the standard explanations and categories are labeled weird, crazy, heretical, immoral, or not team players. People who are suffering may be taught that they deserve it because they are innately inferior, while the official view of reality teaches others not to notice that injustices are taking place. A society may not have words to describe unacceptable perceptions, experiences, or emotions, which makes it not only difficult to talk about but even to think about them.

But invisibility is created in order to cover a society's dysfunctions. When the destructive consequences of such systems become too serious and widespread, as is happening today, then the invisible starts to become visible, and people begin to create new paradigms and new systems.

NOTES

1. For a conventional explanation of what is and is not counted in the GDP, and why, see Robert L. Heilbroner and Lester C. Thurow, *Economics Explained*, updated edition (New York: Simon & Schuster, 1987), 52–56 and chaps. 5–8. For a critical analysis of the GDP, and a powerful and comprehensive exposure of the forces behind economic invisibility, see Marilyn Waring, *If Women Counted; A New Feminist Economics* (San Francisco: Harper & Row, 1988).

2. The layer cake diagram is from Hazel Henderson, *Paradigms in Progress: Life Beyond Economics* (Indianapolis: Knowledge Systems, 1991), 30.

3. On which government expenditures are considered wealth-producing and included in the GDP, and which are considered nonproductive expenses, see Heilbroner and Thurow, *Economics Explained*, 49–51, 63–67, and 73–74. Heilbroner and Thurow equate transfer payments with charity on p. 74. See also Waring, *If Women Counted*, 65–68 and 72, for a critical interpretation.

4. Examples of foreign and military policy that support business objectives are described in Arjun Makhijani, *From Global Capitalism to Economic Justice* (New York: Apex Press, 1992), 18–31; and Walden Bello et al., *Dark Victory: The United States, Structural Adjustment, and Global Poverty* (Oakland, Calif.: Institute for Food and Development Policy, 1994), chaps. 4–8.

5. Examples of efficient and effective federal, state, and municipal-sponsored enterprises in capitalist nations are described in Gar Alperovitz and Jeff Faux, *Rebuilding America: A Blueprint for the New Economy* (New York: Pantheon Books, 1984), 244–248; and Christopher Gunn and Hazel Dayton Gunn, *Reclaiming Capital: Democratic Initiatives and Community Development* (Ithaca, N.Y.: Cornell University Press, 1991), chap. 6.

6. Marilyn Waring cites official UN guidelines that state that unpaid household production is "of little or no importance" to national wealth production. See *If Women Counted*, chap. 3, especially p. 78.

7. The informal economy in Third-World nations is described in Kathryn Ward, ed., *Women Workers and Global Restructuring* (Ithaca, N.Y.: ILR Press, 1990), 2–3, and chaps. 2–4.

8. Scott Burns, *Home, Inc.: The Hidden Wealth and Power of the American Household* (Garden City, N.Y.: Doubleday & Co., 1975), 5.

9. Ibid, 4–5.

10. Ibid., 7.

11. Studies of parts of the informal economy in the U.S. include Mirra Komarovsky, *Blue-Collar Marriage* (New York: Random House, 1967) and Carol Stack, *All Our Kin: Strategies for Survival in a Black Community* (New York: Harper & Row, 1974).

12. David P. Ross and Peter J. Usher, *From the Roots Up: Economic Development as if Community Mattered* (Croton-on-Hudson, N.Y.: Bootstrap Press, 1986), chap. 4. Other studies of the informal economy in modern nations include William M. Nicholls and William A. Dyson, *The Informal Economy: Where People Are the Bottom Line* (Ottawa, Canada: Vanier Institute of the Family, 1983), which covers theory and specific examples from Canada; and Graeme Shankland, *Wanted Work: A Guide to the Informal Economy* (New York: Bootstrap Press, 1989), which covers theory and facts from England. All these books are available from Apex Press, 777 United Nations Plaza, Suite 3C, New York, NY 10017, (212) 953-6920 or (914) 271-2039. See also Alfredo L. de Romaña, "The Autonomous Economy: An Emerging Alternative to Industrial Society," *Interculture*, 22 (Summer 1989) and 22 (Fall 1989), which includes theory and examples from both Canada and the Third World. *Interculture* is published by the Intercultural Institute of Montreal, 4917 St. Urbain St., Montreal, Quebec H2T 2W1, Canada, (514) 288-7229.

13. Ross and Usher, *From the Roots Up*, 98.

14. Burns, *Home, Inc.*, 6.

15. Hilkka Pietila's work is described in Waring, *If Women Counted*, 300–301.

16. I would like to thank radical economist and activist Randy Albelda for first bringing the concept of displacement to my attention.

17. The environmental justice movement is described in Richard Hofrichter, ed., *Toxic Struggles: The Theory and Practice of Environmental Justice* (Philadelphia: New Society Publishers, 1993).

18. Conventional economists are well aware of the existence and problematical nature of externalities. But they do not find the concept so anomalous as to require changing their underlying theoretical assumptions about what constitutes the economy. Instead, they recommend dealing with externalities through external mechanisms, such as government taxes on pollution. See, for example, Heilbroner and Thurow, *Economics Explained*, 170–173. New-paradigm economists, on the other hand, cite the problem of externalities as a major reason for why economic assumptions must be changed radically. See Herman E. Daly and John B. Cobb, Jr., *For the Common Good: Redirecting The Economy toward Community, the Environment, and a Sustainable Future* (Boston: Beacon Press, 1989): "When vital issues (e.g. the capacity of the earth to support life) have to be classed as externalities, it is time to restructure basic concepts [of economics so as to] . . . embrace what was previously external," p. 37.

Recent environmental legislation attempts to make corporations financially responsible for cleaning up some kinds of pollution and tries to prevent the emission of some toxics. Ideally, businesses should be required to take social and environmental externalities into account in their planning. For suggestions on how this can be done, see Paul Hawken, *The Ecology of Commerce: A Declaration of Sustainability* (New York: HarperCollins, 1993).

PART II

The Problem of Economic Addiction

Chapter 5

THE BIRTH OF THE ADDICTIVE ECONOMY

ADDICTION AND THE MODERN ECONOMY

One of the most troubling problems in modern societies today is the prevalence of addictions. People are becoming addicted not only to chemical substances such as alcohol, tobacco, or other legal or illegal drugs, but also to activities, such as eating, dieting, exercise, or romance. Even healthy activities can turn into destructive obsessions. As people become engrossed in their addictions, both the addict and the people around him or her suffer.

This epidemic of addictions is related to the fragmentation of modern life. Fragmentation is a key component of modernism, central to the intellectual visions of seventeenth-century philosopher-scientists such as Francis Bacon, René Descartes, and other fathers of modern science. Their paradigm declared that the mind was separate from, and superior to, the body, and humans were separate from, and superior to, nature—and that both the body and nature were merely collections of lifeless, physical pieces that interacted mechanically.[1]

Their conception of the world provided a philosophical foundation for the subsequent fragmentation of experience. In the following centuries, industrialization and the spreading market economy tore apart the traditional connections of everyday life. Skilled work was broken down into narrowly specialized operations. Home and family were separated from production, men's work from women's work, industrial workers from knowledge and skills, thinking from doing, production from consumption, and women and children from the larger world.

Meanwhile, in imitation of the industrial model, modern life has also become fragmented spatially, as different kinds of activities—family life, education, production, distribution, and consumption—are carried out in separate physical locations. And our lives have been fragmented temporally, divided into distinct segments—dependency, schooling, work, retirement—with each segment concentrated in a different period of life.

These processes of fragmentation have increasingly destroyed people's feelings of wholeness and connectedness, replacing them with feelings of pain, loss, meaninglessness, powerlessness, and spiritual emptiness. Deprived of everyday sources of integrity and emotional and spiritual health, many people in modern societies have sought to restore their feelings of well-being and power—or at least to wipe out feelings of pain, loss, and powerlessness— by turning to addictive substances and activities.

Some of the most common addictions today are related to economic activities: work, money, and shopping. So it's surprising that most experts in the addiction-recovery field view addiction as entirely an individual problem, which must be dealt with primarily on an individual basis (or, occasionally, at the family level). Even 12-step groups, a popular form of addiction-recovery, focus on changing the individual. But our larger societal goals, values, and institutional structures are constantly encouraging addictive behaviors of all kinds. In order to recover from the modern addiction epidemic, addiction must be addressed at the social and institutional, as well as at the personal, levels.

One of the few writers on addiction and recovery who has drawn connections between the spread of addictions and the prevailing culture and values of modern economies is Anne Wilson Schaef, in such books as *When Society Becomes an Addict* and *The Addictive Organization*. Perhaps Schaef's most important insight on this issue is her assertion that not only individuals but also organizations, such as businesses, can behave like addicts. Addictive organizations engage in addictive activities that harm both the addictive organization as a whole, along with the many individuals whose lives the organization affects. But the people at the top of addictive organizations deny that any destructive activities or addictions are taking place. Instead, the individuals or groups in power continue to escalate the addictive behaviors and policies, thereby increasing their destructive impact, not only inside the organization, but also for society in general.[2]

In this and the following four chapters, I will apply Schaef's insights about addictions to the modern economy. I will discuss why the economy became dependent on addictions, and explore how this addictive system has altered business and government institutions and our daily lives. Finally, I will examine the connections between economic addictions and economic invisibility, and will discuss why the modern economic paradigm, which is characterized by economic invisibility and which promotes economic addictions, is now vulnerable to change.

THE MEANING OF ECONOMIC ADDICTION

Let's start with a few key definitions:

— *Economic addiction* is the inability to say No to, or to set limits on, the activities of the visible economy.

— *An addictive economy* is that economic system that is maintained by, and therefore promotes, addictions.

— *Addictive businesses* are businesses that cannot put limits on their production, sales, or money-making activities, addict their employees to work, and addict the general public to buying and consuming their products. The addiction-promoting activities of addictive businesses are justified by the sacred incantation "More is better."

Note that what is being defined here as addictive economic behavior is defined by the modern economic paradigm as the proper functioning of healthy, growing businesses in a healthy, growing economy.

Addictions are not unique to modern societies. The Bible contains references to addictions to money and material possessions that were condemned thousands of years ago. And opium addiction has been a problem for several centuries in China. What's new is a society in which the economic system depends on addictions for its continued functioning. The addictive economy was made possible by the Industrial Revolution, as new mass-production technologies brought forth floods of material goods with minimal human labor. But the addiction-based economy did not fully come into its own until the 1920s, in the United States, as the imbalances inherent in the modern industrial economy finally led to what I call the Unavoidable Dilemma.

IMBALANCES IN THE MODERN ECONOMY

The new industrial economy generated constant imbalances: imbalances between the quantities of goods produced and the numbers of people able to buy them, leading to overproduction; between the numbers of people needing paid employment and the numbers of available jobs, leading to excessive unemployment; and between the quantities of goods offered for sale and the amount of money in circulation, leading to inflation. At the same time, the existence of class, gender, racial and other hierarchies promoted the concentration of wealth and power among a small proportion of the population, while preventing more equitable distribution of resources.

Such imbalances periodically produced a devastating new phenomenon unique to modern industrial society: the business cycle. In all modern economies, periods of prosperity have regularly been followed by depressions—when banks and businesses fail, thousands of people lose their jobs and savings, and poverty, homelessness, and hunger reappear on a large scale.[3]

For example, in the United States there have been thirty-five discernible business cycles of prosperity followed by depression. The most severe, which occurred in 1807, 1837, 1873, 1882, 1893, 1920, 1929, and 1937, were marked by widespread panic, unemployment, poverty, hardship, and worse for thousands, sometimes millions of people.[4] The great depression of 1837–1839 brought unemployment to one-third of New York City's working population, and to thousands of factory workers in New England. As people panicked and withdrew their savings from banks, impoverishment spread dramatically, and it was widely feared that the jobs that had disappeared would not reappear.[5]

The stock market crash of 1873 triggered a new round of bankruptcies and failures, with six thousand businesses in the United States closing in 1874, and as many as nine hundred a month folding during 1878. During the next twenty years, recurring recessions brought wage cuts, extended layoffs, irregular employment, and worsening conditions, even starvation, for many industrial workers.[6] The financial panic of 1893–1894 deepened into the most severe industrial depression yet. Businesses collapsed, banks failed, and eventually a staggering three million people became unemployed. For the first time in U.S. history, organized groups of the jobless appealed to the government for direct relief.[7] Regardless of their severity, however, most depressions ended within a few years. With recovery, the visible economy continued to expand, new jobs were created, and ever cheaper and more diverse kinds of mass-produced goods became available.

In the United States during the early twentieth century, industrial abundance generated increasing optimism that for the first time in the history of the world, material poverty might actually be eliminated. Utopian novelists of that period regularly wrote about a not-too-distant future when each person would be required to work only four hours a day to meet their material needs. After work, everyone could enjoy the fruits of social and technological progress, and it was anticipated that most people would, in their newly acquired free time, voluntarily improve themselves and upgrade society through involvement in education, the arts, and civic participation.[8]

Instead, the 1920s began with yet another severe depression. Although it was brief (1920–1922), many businesses collapsed and large numbers of people lost their jobs. Since programs such as unemployment insurance and Social Security had not yet been created, to lose one's business or job in those days could have devastating consequences. The depression of the early 1920s was not only unexpected but also ominous, especially for the U.S. business community. Many businessmen of the time concluded that this depression had occurred because the modern economy had not only achieved the long-awaited goal of producing sustained abundance, but that businesses were now producing *more* than people needed or wanted to buy.[9]

In other words, the success of the modern economy might now be its undoing. It seemed that the economy had finally come up against its underlying nemesis: the Unavoidable Dilemma.

THE UNAVOIDABLE DILEMMA

A common problem for modern businesses is market saturation: reaching all one's potential customers. Once this has happened, sales may level off as customers periodically make repeat sales; or, if the product in question is a one-time-only purchase, sales will actively decline. And unless companies which have reached this point are somehow able to increase their sales once again, they may eventually have to lay off employees, or even go out of business, causing many other individual, social, and economic calamities.

The problem of market saturation is only made worse by businesses' drive for constantly increasing sales and profits. As companies find faster, cheaper ways to produce more products and get them to market, they simply bring closer the inevitable day when they reach all their potential customers.

Many businesses have tried to avoid reaching market saturation by making products that break down quickly and need to be replaced more often, or by regularly introducing "new, improved" models. But such strategies are constrained by limits on raw materials and landfills. They also lead to eventual consumer outrage and demands for better-made, longer-lasting products. Ironically, selling high-quality products that don't wear out is no guarantee of business longevity. There are many examples of good, honest companies that had to go out of business because their excellent products rarely broke down and didn't need to be replaced.[10]

You would think that once people have enough, utopia would have been achieved. Instead, in the modern economic paradigm, once people's needs are met and they stop buying, the result is economic disaster. This is the ultimate Unavoidable Dilemma of the modern economy. Once a business—or an economy—has achieved saturation, it has three alternatives: 1) to let sales decline and businesses fail, which can lead to more widespread economic disasters; 2) to further increase sales, by inducing people who already have enough to keep buying and consuming even more; 3) to redefine the concept of business and economic success, and restructure economic goals, values, and institutions, so everyone can benefit from a society in which people have enough.

In the 1920s, the first alternative was unthinkable, the third far too radical. Instead, the United States chose to create the world's first addictive economy.

BIRTH OF THE ADDICTIVE ECONOMY

After the depression of 1920–1922 had ended, the U.S. business community actively set about transforming the basis of the economy. By any means possible—through new attitudes, new economic approaches, and favorable government policies—they would ensure constantly increasing sales.

It may be overstating it to say that the dramatic economic and cultural transformations of the 1920s took place solely because business wanted them. But there is no question that the business community played a dominant role in shaping that decade's economic trends, cultural developments, and public policies. Even the *Wall Street Journal* asserted, "Never before, here or anywhere else, has a government been so completely fused with business."[11] Business was publicly acknowledged as the dominant institution of the decade. And you have only to read the statements of numerous business and advertising executives during the 1920s to appreciate their awareness that they were literally giving birth to a new society, one in which people would constantly buy more.[12]

The rapidly growing advertising industry was central in promoting this new way of life. Scientifically placed advertisements touted the latest products from every street corner. From 1918 to 1929, the amount spent on magazine ads alone more than tripled, reaching $196 million in 1929, with millions more spent on newspaper, billboard, and streetcar advertising. And ads no longer merely announced the availability or described the merits of the products. The new ads increasingly alluded to the customer's inadequacies and threatened dire consequences, including loss of job, friends, or love life, for failing to buy the advertised toothbrush, skin cream, mouthwash, manicure aids, or labor-saving appliances.[13]

During this decade, businesses also introduced the concept of buying on the installment plan. Prior to the 1920s, society praised discipline, hard work, and obedience in the workplace, and modesty and frugality in the home. Going into debt was considered morally shameful. But during the 1920s, wonderful new products now filled the stores: cigarette lighters, wrist watches, all kinds of electric appliances, and, most wonderful of all, the automobile. This new abundance demanded a new kind of person—the never-satisfied consumer—to keep the economy going. As one historian put it, "Unless [the average person] could be persuaded to buy and buy lavishly, the whole stream of six-cylinder cars, super heterodynes, cigarettes, rouge compacts, and electric ice boxes would be dammed up at its outlets."[14]

So advertisements and articles in the mass media now proclaimed that saving and frugality were actually harmful, while spending, consuming, and going into debt on the installment plan were socially and economically beneficial. And the campaign succeeded. From 1922 to 1929, the sales of radios jumped from $60 million to $852 million per year. And while in 1900 the U.S. auto industry produced a mere 4,000 cars, by 1929 production reached 4,800,000, and 26 million cars and trucks were on the road. Not coincidentally, three out of every four radios, and three out of every five automobiles, were purchased on the installment plan.[15]

During the 1920s, to buy and enjoy the latest products and services offered by business came to mean that one was smart, modern, and in tune with the latest trends. Increasingly, people began to base their identity and self-esteem on what they bought. The worship of business and its miraculous accomplishments became the new U.S. religion. The expanding mass prosperity was described as the achievement of heaven on Earth. The most successful businessmen, such as Henry Ford, were referred to as society's new spiritual leaders. President Calvin Coolidge described the factory as a temple, with the worker the devotee who worshiped there. And the good news of the public's ever-increasing propensity to consume was referred to as "the new economic gospel of consumption."[16]

The Coolidge administration, concerned that this incredible economic progress not be halted, also established a presidential committee to study current economic trends. The committee's report, published in 1929, concluded triumphantly that the nation need not worry:

> [Our] survey has proved conclusively what has long been held theoretically to be true, that wants are almost insatiable; that one want satisfied makes way for another. The conclusion is that economically we have a boundless field before us; that there

are new wants which will make way endlessly for newer wants, as fast as they are satisfied. . . . By advertising and other promotional devices, by scientific fact finding, by carefully predeveloped consumption, a measurable pull on production has been created which releases capital otherwise tied up in immobile goods and furthers the organic balance of economic forces . . . it would seem that we can go on with increasing activity. . . . Our situation is fortunate, our momentum is remarkable.[17]

But the president's committee was misled by its own optimism. In 1929 the stock market crashed, setting off the most severe and longest-lasting depression the United States had ever experienced.

THE FAILURE OF THE ADDICTIVE ECONOMY

Historians now recognize that the 1920s marked a major turning point in the nature of the modern economy. Prior to that time, the industrial economy was driven by the goal of constantly increasing production. The official ideology said that poverty existed because society was not yet able to produce enough material wealth to meet everyone's needs. If only people worked hard enough and production could be made more efficient, then the business system could eventually bring about prosperity for all. To support this goal, nineteenth-century society promoted the work ethic, thrift, and frugality. Respectable people saved their money, bought carefully, lived modestly, and paid cash for their purchases. It was considered almost immoral to go into debt. Savings were reinvested in more efficient production facilities, and the business economy grew.

But when it appeared that businesses were finally able to produce enough—and more than enough—to meet people's needs, then the character of individuals and the society had to be changed. A new system had to be created, driven by the constantly expanding consumption of goods and services, in order to absorb businesses' constantly increasing output. This change marked the birth of the addictive economy.

While this addictive economic strategy appeared to solve the problem of excess production during the 1920s, it was in reality a superficial, short-term solution. In essence, U.S. business and government leaders chose to expand consumption for those who already had enough, while failing to resolve the underlying inequities and imbalances of the economy. Unemployment still plagued many areas of the nation. Even many steady wage-earners received barely enough to pay for basic necessities. Women were either excluded from the paid workforce outright or were concentrated in inferior jobs, at inferior pay. And many people of color—African-Americans, Native Americans, and other groups—still suffered extreme poverty.[18]

By the 1930s, this strategy of expanding consumption had reached its limits, and the economy again collapsed, stagnating in the Great Depression for the next ten years. It was not until World War II, when the endless needs of the battlefield and then postwar reconstruction created new demands, that the economy began moving again.

During the 1950s and 1960s, the consumption-based lifestyle that began in the United States during the 1920s became a standard for imitation around the world, stimulating a new wave of global prosperity. However, starting in the 1970s the oil crisis, the environmental crisis, global competition, and other unanticipated developments have disrupted economies worldwide.

Yet modern nations are not yet ready to give up the addictive illusion that they can consume their way to prosperity. In the 1990s, increasingly troubled modern economies are still trying to restore their economic health by expanding consumption—among their own populations and among customers in other nations, especially in the Third World. And they are still choosing to ignore, and failing to resolve, the local and global imbalances and inequities that characterize the world today. As a result, their addictive economic strategies are exacerbating the imbalances, leading to ever more disastrous social, economic, and environmental consequences.

NOTES

1. On the essential connections between fragmentation and modernism, see Fritjof Capra, *The Turning Point: Science, Society, and the Rising Culture* (New York: Bantam, 1983), 53–62.

2. On addiction as an organizational and societal problem, see Anne Wilson Schaef, *When Society Becomes an Addict* (San Francisco: HarperSanFrancisco, 1987); and Anne Wilson Schaef and Diane Fassel, *The Addictive Organization* (San Francisco: Harper & Row, 1988), especially chaps. 2 and 3.

3. The *Encyclopedia Americana* states, "Business cycles are distinctly characteristic of private enterprise industrial [i.e. modern capitalist] economies." *Encyclopedia Americana*, vol. 5 (Danbury, Conn.: Grolier, 1993), 45.

4. Ibid., 46.

5. Alice Kessler-Harris, *Out to Work: A History of Wage-Earning Women in the United States* (New York: Oxford University Press, 1982) 45.

6. Alan Trachtenberg, *The Incorporation Of America* (New York: Hill and Wang, 1982), 39.

7. Alice Wexler, *Emma Goldman: An Intimate Life* (New York: Pantheon Books, 1984), 74.

8. On utopian optimism in the early twentieth-century United States, see Benjamin Kline Hunnicutt, *Work Without End: Abandoning Shorter Hours for the Right to Work* (Philadelphia: Temple University Press, 1988), 29–34. My analysis in this chapter is indebted to Professor Hunnicutt's richly documented and insightful study of attitudes toward, and the interaction of, production, consumption, and paid work in the United States during the first half of the twentieth century.

9. Businessmen in the early 1920s believed that the economy was finally producing more than people needed or wanted to buy, says Hunnicutt, *Work Without End*, 37–39.

10. A classic example of quality being "bad for business": The grandfather of a friend of mine owned a successful company in the Midwest that manufactured heavy-duty, all-steel vises for woodwork and metalwork. Since the vise was so well made and affordably priced, it was purchased widely by do-it-yourselfers and professional carpenters and machinists. The company thrived during the 1930s and 1940s (especially during World War II), finally reaching market saturation in the 1950s. Because this simply designed, hefty piece of equipment never broke down or wore out, customers rarely needed to replace it. (My friend reports that one of these vises, purchased back in the 1930s, is still in use in our local neighborhood hardware store.)

11. From the *Wall Street Journal*, quoted in William E. Leuchtenberg, *The Perils of Prosperity: 1914–1932* (Chicago: University of Chicago Press, 1958), 103.

12. Descriptions of how business had the dominant role in shaping U.S. economic and public policy during the 1920s, and how businessmen consciously created a new, consumption-driven culture are given

in Hunnicutt, *Work Without End*, chap. 2; Leuchtenberg, *The Perils of Prosperity*, chaps. 5, 10, and 13; and Stuart Ewen, *Captains of Consciousness: Advertising and the Social Roots of the Consumer Culture* (New York: McGraw-Hill, 1976).

13. The growth of the U.S. advertising industry is described in Ewen, *Captains Of Consciousness*, 31–39. How ads encouraged insecurity and self-doubt is described in 37–48, 94–100, and 177–184.

14. Hunnicutt, *Work Without End*, 45.

15. On how business introduced installment buying and encouraged consumers to go into debt, see Leuchtenberg, *The Perils Of Prosperity*, 198–203.

16. On business as the new U.S. religion during the 1920s, see Leuchtenberg, *The Perils of Prosperity*, 186–189. The new economic gospel of consumption is mentioned in Hunnicutt, *Work Without End*, 42.

17. Committee on Recent Economic Changes, *Recent Economic Changes in the United States* (New York: McGraw-Hill, 1929), xv.

18. On low wages, poverty, and unemployment during the 1920s, see Leuchtenberg, *The Perils of Prosperity*, 193–194 and 245–248; also Ewen, *Captains Of Consciousness*, 58–59. On racial and gender inequities during the 1920s, see Teresa L. Amott and Julie A. Matthaei, *Race, Gender, and Work: A Multicultural Economic History of Women in the United States* (Boston: South End Press, 1991), 48–49, 75–77, 126–127, 164–170, and 223–225.

Chapter 6

WHY WE CAN'T JUST SAY NO, AND OTHER CONSEQUENCES OF THE ADDICTIVE ECONOMY

THE DECLINE OF TRADITIONAL VALUES

Many people today are concerned about the loss of traditional values such as hard work and self-discipline, a weakening of moral standards, and a rise in selfishness and the desire for instant gratification. The current social breakdown and economic decline of modern nations is often attributed to these trends, which are frequently blamed on such popular scapegoats as liberals, hippies, permissive parents, secular humanists, foreigners, or the underclass.

In fact, the loss of traditional values and much of today's social, economic, and moral crisis can be traced directly to the addictive economy, the new kind of economic system that the U.S. business community initiated during the 1920s. Until that time, modern industrial societies were centered on the work ethic. People were encouraged to live soberly, work hard, delay gratification, and save for the future. But by the 1920s, the U.S. industrial economy had become so productive that a new, addictive economic system had to be created, sustained by constantly increasing consumption. This required the full-scale transformation of people's personal beliefs and behaviors, along with deep changes in society's commonly held moral and cultural values.

In almost every respect, the new consumer personality required by the addictive economy is the exact oposite of the traditional, work-oriented personality. In essence, the capitalist business system had to destroy society's traditional values in order to keep the economy going (see Fig. 6.1.).

Gradually these new values have spread around the world. But not everyone has adopted the new consumer values. Some people have integrated the two personality types; they follow the work ethic in the workplace, the consumer ethic at home. Other individuals and communities have stubbornly resisted the allure of the consumer personality, and even today in some areas of modern nations, the old-fashioned values of the work ethic and frugality are still prevalent.

But for many people, the addictive consumer personality gradually expanded into all areas of life, driving out old-fashioned, traditional values such as self-control, perseverance, and dedication to doing a good job, not only in leisure time activities, but even in the workplace. Eventually the new values led to the

FIGURE 6.1 COMPARISON OF THE WORK ETHIC AND THE CONSUMER PERSONALITY

The Work Ethic	*The Consumer Personality*
Early industrial period (1800s-1920). (Desired behavior, especially in the workplace.)	*The addictive economy (1920 to the present). (Desired behavior in one's free time, especially when shopping.)*
Work hard.	Don't work at all. Your purpose in life is to enjoy yourself and be entertained.
Learn a skill. This takes time, self-discipline, effort, and patience.	Don't bother to learn anything. It's so easy to buy ready-made products and services. Patience is old-fashioned. Buy on impulse. Gratify your whims of the moment.
Avoid waste. Be careful with your tools and materials.	Be careless and waste things. You can always buy more.
Be frugal. Limit your needs and desires. If you want less, you won't be bothering the boss for constant salary increases.	Think of yourself first. Let your desires be unlimited. Buy, possess, consume as much as you can. Go into debt.
Be restrained and obedient. Obey your supervisor and be loyal to your employer.	Let yourself go. Eliminate the old. Go with what's new. Treat yourself—you deserve it.
Practice self-control. Save for the future.	If it feels good, do it.

materialistic excesses of the late twentieth century: the me-generation, the yuppies, and the get-rich-at-any-cost morality of the Reagan years.

Officially, the work ethic is still highly valued by modern economies. Imagine the outrage that would occur if our leaders dared to admit publicly that our economic and other established institutions actively encourage greed, addictions, and self-serving behavior. The official assumption is that people "naturally" want to earn, spend, own, and consume in ever-increasing quantities, and they'll work hard in order to do so, as long as economic conditions make it possible. Accordingly, since business leaders have created the institutions that provide the jobs and produce the goods that foster constantly increasing consumption, they and other official shapers of the modern economy are justified in earning society's highest rewards.

I don't mean to imply that all our problems would be solved if we returned to the puritanical self-sacrifice of the work ethic personality. That too was an artificially created personality type, designed to fit the needs of the factory system and rigidly hierarchical businesses. Now the postmodern paradigm must promote an economic system that does not depend on work addiction, consumption addiction, money addiction, or any other kind of addictions in order to be successful.

NO LIMITS: THE BASIS OF THE ADDICTIVE ECONOMY

Just open any conventional economics textbook and you will find the cheerful assertion that because human wants and needs are limitless, the economy can keep growing infinitely. The addictive economy is justified by the belief that more is better, that an economy constrained by limits will suffer reduced sales, layoffs, and eventually will slide into recession or depression.

This rejection of limits is an extreme example of how the modern economic paradigm is out of touch with the realities of daily life. Of course people have limits. There are limits to how much food we can stuff into our bodies, how many possessions we can crowd into our closets, attics, basements, and garages, limits to how quickly we can rush around a shopping mall or dial the home shopping network in pursuit of new goodies. There are limits to how many repair people or consultants we can keep busy, to how many recreational activities we can cram into our leisure moments. And when we tire of what we already have and try to throw it away so we can make room for more, we discover that there are limits to how much land we can turn into garbage dumps.

Furthermore, in the real world, limits are a natural and healthy part of life. Our limits define who we are and enable us to say no to excessive intrusions or demands. And our limits let us know when we have enough. If you're hungry, you eat until you have eaten enough. If you're cold, you turn up the heat or pile on more clothes until you're warm enough. In the real world, by honoring our limits, we can recognize when we are happy and satisfied, protect ourselves when necessary, and maintain our balance and health.

But in the addictive economy, to reach one's limits and have enough is calamitous. In order to keep the addictive economy going we must always be ready to say yes to each new fad and fashion, to another new car, to the latest electronic gadgets. Proponents of the U.S. "War on Drugs" tell us that we should "Just Say No." It should not be surprising that this approach has made little difference in stopping drug use. In the rest of our lives all the messages around us are telling us that we can't say no. The continued prosperity of the addictive economy depends on our never saying no, on our continuing to work, to produce, to sell, to buy, and to consume as if we have no limits.

FURTHER CONSEQUENCES OF THE ADDICTIVE ECONOMY

In a healthy economy, people are encouraged to recognize and honor their limits. In addictive systems, as people are taught to ignore their limits, individuals' lives and the goals, values, and activities of businesses, governments, and other institutions become increasingly distorted in order to serve the limitless needs of the addictive modern economy.

Product Buying Replaces Problem Solving

Addictive economies inhibit the search for real solutions to personal or social problems because they discourage people from having faith in their own skills and inner resources and from trusting and relying on each other. In an addictive economy we are supposed to look outward to big corporations and experts and the products and services they sell to solve our problems, ease our longings, and take away our pains. In the addictive economy, the response to any personal or societal trouble is the question: "What new products or services can businesses develop to sell to people affected by this problem?"

But while the product-selling approach may increase sales, it rarely solves problems. For example, enormously popular medications such as tranquilizers and painkillers temporarily mask our natural response to stress—they do not eliminate the causes of stress in our lives. So the pain keeps coming back, and people buy more painkillers. From the perspective of addictive businesses, to find real solutions would be self-defeating. A product that actually eliminated a problem would not generate repeat sales.

What Sells Becomes the Criterion of Morality

In an addictive economy, the need to generate constantly increasing sales erodes ethical standards. The new standard of morality is the quantity of sales generated. A high rate of sales becomes proof of a product's social value, proof of the producer's and seller's moral contribution to society. It doesn't matter that customers may be squandering their own or their family's money, buying unnecessary or overtly harmful items, such as alcohol or tobacco. It doesn't matter that salespeople may be pandering to customers' short-term impulses, vanity, insecurity, or inability to set limits, that advertisers employ psychologically manipulative, belittling, or sexually exploitative advertising, or that our privacy is invaded by computer-dialed phone calls, scientifically targeted junk mail, and other high-tech commercial intrusions.

Anything goes in order to make another sale, and that's perfectly acceptable, because more sales generate more jobs and higher profits, and keep the economy going. In the addictive economy, the criterion for making moral judgments is not "How does this act affect the integrity of the people involved?" but "Is it good for the economy? Will it increase sales?"

The Pace of Life Is Speeded Up and Leisure Disappears

Addictive businesses increase work hours and speed up the pace of paid work in order to get more out of their employees. In their remaining free time, people rush to fulfill all their responsibilities, becoming ever more dependent on fast foods and numerous other convenience products and services. But there's still not enough time for family, friends, or self, and little or no time for neighborhood, community, or civic involvement. So many essential activities remain undone, and the quality of our lives worsens.[1] In the modern economic paradigm, the ceaselessly productive machine is the ideal against which we are expected to measure ourselves. And because our mechanical and electronic technologies are able to produce seemingly instant results, the achievement of instant results has become a positive value in modern life.

In the natural world, change and transformation are always taking place, but they happen slowly. Since human beings are also part of nature, slow but dynamic processes of change, growth, healing, creation, and transformation are constantly taking place inside our own minds, bodies, and souls. By convincing us that instant is better, the modern paradigm teaches us to scorn both our inner selves and the leisurely rhythms of nature. Instead, we are encouraged to use up vast amounts of unnecessary resources and energy in order to make the machines and products that seem to so magically bring about those instant results. The addictive economy separates us from our innate powers and makes us more dependent upon the system's pace and products.

We Have to Buy Things That Were Formerly Free or That Were Never Before Considered Necessary

In addictive economies, any new disaster is a guaranteed source of new needs and expanding sales. It may seem somewhat perverse to refer to environmental and health disasters as business opportunities, but the destruction of the natural environment has created markets for many new products. As pollution increases, clean air and water, which we have always taken for granted, become scarce. And new products, such as air and water filters and bottled water, become health necessities. Businesses that reduce their polluting activities, and that provide products and services to help restore the environment and protect people's health certainly deserve commendation, and more companies should follow their lead. However, to a significant extent, the cost of living in modern nations is escalating because we have to pay for repairing the considerable damage to human, social, economic, and environmental health caused by addictive economic activities.

Acquisitiveness Is Celebrated, the Rich Become More Wasteful, and the Poor Become Poorer

In an addictive economy, where the purpose of life is to acquire ever more money and possessions, there's no reason to be moderate or frugal, or to share what you have with other people. Those who already have the most are encouraged to get more. Those with the least are labeled failures and fall further behind. And the people in the middle try to appear successful by imitating the irresponsibility of those on top. (I'm not immune. I'm ashamed to admit that when I first started writing this book, I owned forty cotton turtleneck sweaters. I have since given some away. But that's not as bad as my teenage neighbor, who told me she owns seventy sets of high-fashion underwear.)

While the gap between rich and poor in modern nations is now increasing, it is even wider between modern nations and the Third World. For example, the United States, with about 5 percent of the world's population, annually consumes about 30 percent of the world's resources. The amount of energy used by one U.S. resident each year is equivalent to the energy used annually by 6 Mexicans, 14 Chinese, 38 Indians, 168 Bangladeshi, or 531 Ethiopians. Although in part these figures convey the real poverty of the Third World, they also represent the increasingly unnecessary excesses and waste that characterize life in addictive modern economies, especially in the United States. Because of this enormous waste and excess consumption, one person in the United States causes 100 times more damage to the global environment than does a person in a poor country.[2]

People Are Reduced to Markets

As market researchers discover new groups with money to spend, addictive businesses develop advertising campaigns aimed at convincing each group—whether it be employed women, black professionals, senior citizens, teens, or preteens—that they cannot live without the latest products designed especially for them. Buying the right products becomes the easy, instant substitute for the time-consuming tasks of affirming one's identity and building real connections with other people.

Marketing campaigns aimed at our youngest children are especially insidious, because they undermine parents' abilities to set limits and teach children to say no. Meanwhile, politicians scold parents for being too permissive. Then they complain about the lack of consumer confidence and encourage everyone to go out and buy more in order to save the economy.

Other Countries Are Turned into Markets and National Policies Become Distorted

After businesses have run out of customers in their own country, one option is to turn people in other parts of the world into consumers. Historically, industrial nations have systematically made Third-World societies into markets by destroying their indigenous economies and cultures and using political, even military, power to force their products into less developed nations.[3] The struggle for foreign markets is still taking place today, in the form of trade wars and destructive trade agreements such as the General Agreement on Tariffs and Trade (GATT). Although these policies are implemented by national governments, they are propelled by the needs of addictive multinational corporations, which seek to increase their sales, accumulate more wealth, and consolidate their power.[4]

Occasionally, the battle for control of foreign markets leads to open warfare among nations. Because war and the preparation for war consume tremendous quantities of goods and services, addictive economies regularly promote military expenditures and policies while opposing more peaceful solutions to international conflicts.

THE ADDICTIVE ECONOMY AND THE DECLINING QUALITY OF LIFE

An addictive economy is a system in which people who already have enough—and more than enough—are constantly increasing their consumption. The growing production, sales, and steadily rising GDP of addictive economies supposedly indicate that their inhabitants are increasingly better off.

But as we have seen, when people reach their limits, then sales and consumption can only be expanded by increasing stress and ill health, disempowering individuals, eroding families and communities, destroying moral and ethical values, distorting public policy, degrading the environment, and in many other ways diminishing the quality of life. In addictive economies, consumption keeps rising largely because people are buying more goods and services that enable them to cope with—or to temporarily escape from—the mounting personal, social, economic, and environmental problems that have been caused by an addictive way of life.

So in an addictive economy, a rising GDP is actually an indication that stress and disease, waste and garbage, economic and social inequities, and environmental destruction are steadily getting worse. And as the quality of life declines, people are driven to even more addictions, which further worsen their well-being.

WHO SETS THE LIMITS?

Since around 1970, many people have begun to question the possibility or desirability of an economy based on constantly increasing consumption. This is often framed as an environmental problem, and frequently generates heated controversies over whether the natural world or human well-being is more important.

In the course of such debates, environmentalists and even nature can easily be cast as uncaring villains, standing in the way of people's right to economic betterment. For example, environmentalists are often stereotyped as back-to-nature cranks, or as tyrannical idealists who want to force the rest of us to sacrifice the comforts of modern life in order to save a few trees or fish. And nature is often depicted as an uncaring, untamable realm that must be forced, by modern science and technology, to hand its wealth over to human beings.

This controversy is made more complicated because expressions of concern over the environment are sometimes misused by already affluent individuals or nations to prevent people who still live in poverty from improving their lives. For example, it's often claimed that the masses of the poor, whether in modern or Third-World nations, will put excessive pressure on and cause irreparable damage to the environment. The materialistic excesses of the affluent critics are conveniently overlooked.[5]

The problem of environmental limits is real and cannot be denied. Obviously there are limits to fossil fuels such as oil and gas, to naturally occurring minerals and other resources, and to the amount of wastes that nature can successfully neutralize. And the more we produce and consume, the more resources we use up, the more waste we create, the more severe the disruption we cause to the natural environment. Nevertheless, perceiving the question of limits as essentially an environmental problem is both misleading and counterproductive for building a more humane and fulfilling economy.

The most important limits to economic expansion are not "out there," in the environment, but inside us—in the inherent patterns, cycles, and natural rhythms of our own bodies. Addictions can make it seem as if we have no limits, as if we can work and buy, produce and consume endlessly. But eventually the addictive beliefs, values, and behaviors that sustain unnecessary production and consumption also harm our individual, social, even our economic well-being. The addictive economy is bad for *us*. That's why one of the most important challenges of the postmodern economic paradigm is to create an economy characterized by balance —a system in which no one is forced either to suffer poverty or driven to overconsume, but everyone is able to have enough.

NOTES

1. On the time crunch, see Barbara Brandt, "Less is More: A Call for Shorter Work Hours," *Utne Reader*, July/August 1991, 81–87. See also *Utne Reader*, January/February 1994, 52–71, for a feature section on people who feel too busy.

2. On the effects of consumption by industrialized and Third-World societies, see *All Consuming Passion* (Seattle: New Road Map Foundation, 1993), 10. Available from Quality Tape Services, P.O. Box 15352, Seattle, WA 98115, for $1.00 (includes postage).

3. On U.S. government policy to assure foreign markets, see Arjun Makhijani, *From Global Capitalism To Economic Justice* (New York: Apex Press, 1992), 24–31.

4. On trade policies that favor the industrialized nations, see Walden Bello with Shea Cunningham and Bill Rau, *Dark Victory: The United States, Structural Adjustment and Global Poverty* (Oakland Calif.: Institute for Food and Development Policy, 1994), chap. 8.

5. On industrialized nations with affluent lifestyles which criticize the consumption of the world's poor, see Makhijani, *From Global Capitalism to Economic Justice*, chap. 14.

Chapter 7

MONEY AS AN ADDICTIVE SUBSTANCE

For most of human history, people grew or made what they needed or obtained it through giving or by trading with others. It was not until industrialization and mass production, as people came to depend upon commercially produced goods and services to meet their needs and upon paid employment for income, that money addiction as a widespread phenomenon became possible. Money addiction is more than just greed, the obsessive desire for money. Money addiction also includes:

— confusing money with real wealth;

— believing that self-worth can be obtained by having and flaunting money;

— and assuming that money, its accumulation and movements, provide information about the state of the real world.

As people in modern economies become ever more money-addicted and focus on the accumulation and movements of money, society grows increasingly out of touch with the realities of individual, social, and environmental well-being. On paper, ever larger amounts of money move around in modern economies. Meanwhile, our real quality of life declines. Money addiction prevents individuals from taking necessary actions and prevents institutions and the larger society from choosing policies that can improve well-being. This chapter discusses why money is an addictive substance, how money addiction leads to the destruction of real wealth, and how people today are recovering from money addiction.

Money Provides a Simple Linear Scale by Which Life Can Be Measured

Since money is expressed in terms of numerical quantities, it easily lends itself to a simplistic, hierarchical view of life. Less money is worse, more is better. People who have less money are inferior, stupid, lazy; people who have more money are qualified, intelligent, hard-working, superior. As the world becomes more complex, the simple hierarchical nature of money provides an ever more tempting basis to help make sense of reality and guide our personal and societal choices.

Money Enables Feelings of Power to Be Condensed into Small, Tangible Symbols

Money is convenient. We can carry it around in small physical representations: coins, bills, checks, plastic credit cards. Or we can indicate it by a few scratches on a piece of paper or some figures on a computer printout. In any case, it doesn't require much space to write down "$10" or "$10,000,000." But what power is contained in such small packages! We can exchange them for homes, cars, servants, trips around the world, or anything else imaginable. As a result, it is easy for people to become intellectually or emotionally attached to these symbols.

This power is demonstrated in that classic plot of the mystery novel—which sometimes occurs outside of fiction—murder for the insurance money. There may be no reason to want Mr. Doe dead as long as he's just plain old Mr. Doe. But as soon as he takes out a $1,000,000 insurance policy on his own life, then his beneficiary, John Doe, Jr., starts thinking of all the things he could do with that $1,000,000. Once a monetary value has been placed on someone's life, it is now possible to imagine all the other things for which that money might be used. And if someone is cold-hearted or desperate enough (as apparently some people are), it may become acceptable to them to decide that those new possessions and activities are worth more than having Father Doe remain alive. The infinite range of goods and services for which money can now be exchanged multiplies its addictive power.

The Experience of Spending Money Provides a Magical High

People have always been intrigued by the power to instantly create what they wished for: the story of Aladdin and his magic lamp, featuring a powerful genie who materialized whatever his master requested; the European folktales about the supernatural being who granted three wishes; and the image of the magic wand that can make any desire appear with a single wave are all expressions of this longing. And money, in its universal presence today, has made these fairy tales a reality. Money is the magical wish-granting fairy, the genie in the jar, the magic wand that instantly fulfills our deepest desire.

Consider: You walk into a shopping mall with money (or its even more addictive plastic version, a credit card) in your pocket. Imagine anything at all—a portable radio, a car, a coat, a VCR, some candy, a computer—and in a moment it's yours. All you have to do is wave your magic money and the desired object instantly materializes and comes into your possession. Stores, shopping malls, TV home-shopping networks, and all the other purveyors of goods are well aware of the addictive experience of spending and do everything they can to enhance the experience. They put the glamour and fun of buying up front, while they conveniently ignore the pain of paying or bury the unpleasant details in the fine print.

Modern Societies Glorify People Who Have and Flaunt Money

Modern addictive economies, dependent upon people's constantly increasing consumption, glorify the making and spending of money. Although the affluent consumer lifestyle was born in and most typifies the United States, the popular media now promote such values in every corner of the globe, captivating millions of people seeking to become modern. Notes Alan Durning in *How Much Is Enough?*:

> One fourth of Poles deem "Dynasty," which portrays the life-style of the richest Americans, their favorite television program, and villagers in the heart of Africa follow "Dallas," the television series that portrays American oil tycoons. In Taiwan, a billboard demands "Why Aren't You a Millionaire Yet?" A *Business Week* correspondent beams: "The American Dream is alive and well . . . in Mexico."[1]

Addictions to money and excessive material possessions run counter to the wisdom of many traditional societies and the teachings of all major religions.[2] Yet it's difficult for people to adhere to a more modest lifestyle and less materialistic values when social pressures constantly encourage economic addictions.

Money Addiction Distorts Our Values

Because of its power and pervasive nature, money has increasingly become a filter through which individuals perceive and make judgments about their own lives and the basis on which institutions make decisions and set goals and policies. But the more money we have and the more we base our decisions and actions on money, the more disconnected we become from the real world, and the destruction of nonmonetary values and real wealth increases.[3]

Money addiction alters the criteria for judging actions, both public and private. From the money-addicted perspective, the criterion for making decisions is no longer "Is this right or wrong?" but "Will this make money?" For example, if someone chopped down a bunch of trees and left them in splinters, we would describe this as "senseless vandalism." But in a money-addicted economy, if those trees were cut down and sold, and the seller made money from their sale, that person would be described as enterprising and resourceful. Nevertheless, the same trees would be gone, the animal and plant life they supported would suffer, as would the regional and ultimately the global ecosystem.

Likewise, companies that increase profits by laying off thousands of employees or by moving to other locations where wages are lower and worker protections minimal are praised for making wise business decisions, even though such actions harm the well-being of many individuals, even of entire communities. Ironically, when environmentalists oppose new economic development on the grounds that it will destroy endangered species or unique ecosystems, they are labeled uncaring elitists who are more concerned about owls than about human well-being. But money addiction means that the natural environment, along with human lives and whole communities, can be blithely destroyed if someone stands to make money from the destruction.

Money addiction means that people measure their worth by how much money they have; the lives of people with less money are less valued; and people without money-making opportunities learn to devalue themselves.

Money addiction also means that poor people are always vulnerable to being uprooted when the land on which they live can be used for new luxury highrises, condos, a hotel, or some other commercial or industrial developments that will turn a profit for someone else. Since the people already living on that land are generating so little money compared with the proposed new development, it only makes sense—according to the logic of money addiction—to remove the current residents from their homes, ostensibly for the sake of the larger good. Such disruption of communities has happened repeatedly in both modern and Third-World nations, and is still taking place today.[4]

Money Addiction Leads to Loss of Information

Since money is a linear system of measurement, it provides only two possible criteria for making judgments: more is better, and less is worse. Furthermore, the assumption that only activities that produce money are worthwhile—and that more money means more value—ignores the value or existence of economic activities that don't produce and may not even use money. As modern economies rely on solely monetary criteria for making judgments and policy decisions, they increasingly eliminate information about the complexity and quality of life.

The GDP epitomizes the way in which the reliance on monetized measures of economic activity eliminates essential information about people's well-being. As many new-paradigm economists have pointed out, a key shortcoming of the GDP is that it doesn't distinguish between "good" or "bad." The GDP simply counts up the monetary value of all the products and services produced and sold by businesses. According to conventional assumptions, a rise in GDP means that people are producing and consuming more wealth, which must mean that their quality of life is improving. But a rising GDP does not tell us whether people are buying and consuming more organically grown fruits and vegetables, or are increasing their intake of alcohol and tobacco, whether more people are taking music lessons and planting gardens, or are getting sick and paying enormous hospital bills. We are told, simply, that a rising GDP is desirable, and that all our economic and political policies should be geared to keeping it rising.

Also, GDP figures alone tell us nothing about jobs. A rising GDP does not tell us how many new jobs are being created, whether these jobs are high-quality and well-paying or oppressive and poorly paid, or which groups are getting the good or bad jobs. In fact, in the United States today we are actually seeing an increase in business output and profits without comparable increases in job creation. This is because businesses both large and small have now discovered that they can spend less and increase productivity and profits by employing new electronic technologies rather than human workers.[5]

The GDP does not tell us about the distribution of the goods and services it counts. A rising GDP may mean, for example, that the rich now have even more, while the poor may be growing poorer. Neither does the GDP tell us about the workplace stress being generated, or about the toxic waste that addictive businesses produce in order to achieve their increased bottom lines. Nor does it tell us about the harm done to the cultures or political stability of Third-World nations in order to increase the income and material wealth of modern nations, nor about the environmental damage throughout the world caused by the pursuit of money-making.

Finally, because the GDP does not include nonmonetized activities, it eliminates many human and environmental sources of well-being from its measurements, which means that conclusions about societal well-being based on GDP measures are essentially worthless.[6] As new-paradigm economist and activist Hazel Henderson wryly notes, "The social costs of a polluted environment, disrupted communities, disrupted family life and eroded primary relationships may be the only part of the GDP that is growing. We have no idea whether we are going forward or backward."[7]

Even more ironically, if we improve our lives by cutting down on waste and thereby reducing expenditures, or if we give up some consumer activities and replace them with self-reliant creative activities in our homes or communities and feel that we have improved our quality of life, the GDP merely registers this as a decline in wealth creation. Since the GDP equates improved well-being with increased spending of money, then any time we are able to spend less, conventional economists conclude that people's lives and the economy are worsening.

Money Addiction Leads to the Destruction of Real Wealth

Money addiction means that people confuse money and monetized measures with real wealth. They make decisions and choose actions on the basis of appearances, not reality. As a result, money-addicted individuals, organizations, and governing institutions regularly destroy real wealth—in the form of human health, the natural environment, or community well-being—especially over the long term, in order to make money in the short term. For example, individuals may choose uncongenial jobs, which deny their real interests, for the sake of making more money.

Businesses often make money by destroying real wealth. Disposable products are a prime example. When King Gillette invented disposable razor blades, hardly anyone was concerned about all the metals his product would use up, or all the waste that would be generated. Back in the early twentieth century, few people thought about the environmental impact of the mass production-mass consumption economy. Instead, Gillette was celebrated as an economic genius because he had discovered a way to replace a long-lasting item—the straight-edged razor — with a more convenient product that would generate constant repeat sales.[8]

And things have only gotten worse. Even as public concern grows over the environmental impact of business activities, disposable products have proliferated. We can now buy disposable ball-point pens and markers, disposable printing cartridges, disposable convenience-food containers, disposable cameras, and of course, entirely disposable razors. The waste of raw materials and generation of garbage has multiplied enormously. But by the logic of money addiction, businesses have no choice. If disposable products make money, then they represent good business decisions.

Another example: Businesses today often close local branches ("profit centers") that aren't making "enough" profit. Instead, they may invest their money in speculative ventures. Never mind that the eliminated facility may have been producing a good product, satisfying its customers, and providing employees with a decent living. The logic of money addiction means that businesses should eliminate their actual productive activity, even though it is serving a variety of real needs, if they can generate a higher rate of profits by employing their assets in speculative financial activities.[9]

Perhaps most ominous, as the Indian environmentalist and feminist activist Vandana Shiva warns, the drive to make money often leads to such severe environmental destruction that formerly self-renewing natural resources, such as complex forests, are being made nonrenewable.[10] Such destruction has been sanctioned worldwide, not only by businesses but by government policy. For every tree chopped down and every forest destroyed, the constantly increasing amounts of money on the computer printouts, and the rising curves on the economic growth charts convey the illusion that our wealth and well-being has increased. What has actually increased is short-term money-making, obscuring the continuing destruction of real wealth.

RECOVERING FROM MONEY ADDICTION

Since money addiction occurs at all levels—societal, institutional, and individual—recovery from money addiction must also be implemented at each of these levels. At the societal level, Hazel Henderson reports that some nations and international agencies are now using new economic indicators in addition to, or instead of the GDP, in order to gain a more accurate picture of real social, economic, and environmental well-being. Examples include the United Nations' Human Development Index, Physical Quality of Life Index, and Basic Human Needs Indicator, and Japan's Net National Welfare (NNW). Many new indicators include such measures as status of women and minority populations, infant mortality rates, literacy, human rights and democratic participation, and resource depletion and pollution.[11]

At the institutional level, businesses need to challenge their assumption that a rising bottom line is the best, or only, indicator of economic health and success. In his recent book *The Ecology Of Commerce*, socially responsible business pioneer Paul Hawken describes new accounting systems and other methods through which businesses can recover from their money addiction.[12] However, since modern economies are built on the assumption that more money is better, there is only so much that individual businesses can do on their own to recover from money addiction. When most financial and investment criteria and government policies are based on the assumption that more money is better, it becomes clear that we also need to change the larger values, government policies, and legal structures that promote institutional money addiction and prop up addicted businesses.

Addiction-recovery therapist Donna Boundy writes that because the larger culture, especially in the United States, perceives of money addiction as good and "natural," it is difficult for individuals to recognize and recover from their dysfunctional attitudes and behaviors around money. Her book *When Money Is the Drug* identifies such destructive patterns as compulsive spending and compulsive indebtedness, and points out that many people are addicted to money because it appears to be the source of deeper things they really want, such as love, security, or power. She helps the reader identify sources of love, power, and other values inside themselves, and suggests how to use money appropriately to express one's real values.[13]

Another compassionate yet powerful approach to recovery from money addiction for individuals has been developed by the New Road Map Foundation, a nonprofit organization based in Seattle. Their publications, such as their best-selling book *Your Money or Your Life*, encourage people to discover what is personally important to them. Authors Joe Dominguez and Vicki Robin provide detailed programs through which individuals can break addictions to unfulfilling work and debilitating consumption, change their relationship to money so it does not control them, and do the work and live the life that truly fulfills their values.[14]

REVALUING MONEY

Since money is a numerical representation of reality, it's easy to imagine constantly increasing profits, make projections about the compound interest that will increasingly swell your bank account, or draw economic growth curves that rise to infinity. It's easy, on paper, to imagine neverending growth and declare this an achievable and desirable goal. But such images are only abstractions, and unhealthy ones. When we try to shape our lives to fit the image of a constantly rising curve, we lose touch with our inherent sources of health and well-being: our own cycles and limits. In order to produce more money, we and our machines must continually work harder and faster. We must keep consuming more in order to absorb the mounting production and keep people in paid employment. Both businesses and nations must constantly borrow more money in order to finance new economic growth. And we have to use up more and more of the natural environment, more quickly, in order to pay back our debts.[15]

In the modern economic paradigm, money is assumed to be a neutral medium of exchange and a reliable measure of value. Mainstream economists teach that people will spend more money for what they value more, and that any choice which generates more money must therefore be more socially beneficial. According to these assumptions, a few ounces of caviar costing several hundred dollars are of far more value than a free plate of food that might save the life of a starving person. Unfortunately, this faulty equation of price with value shapes the policy decisions of businesses and nations.

As this chapter shows, money is neither a neutral substance nor a consistently reliable measure of value. People can become intellectually and emotionally addicted to money, confusing it with real wealth, or valuing it even more than the real wealth it represents.

In response to money addiction, growing numbers of people in modern economies have been choosing to work less and earn less, in order to have more time for relationships and activities that are of even more value to them than the money they are giving up.[16] In essence, such "downshifters" are demonstrating that while money has its uses, it is neither an ultimate source nor an impartial measure of value. These people have discovered that other things—such as more free time, improved health, more community involvement, and a slower pace of life—are of more value than money. This is a key to recovery from money addiction.

NOTES

1. Alan Durning, *How Much Is Enough? The Consumer Society And The Future Of The Earth* (New York: W.W. Norton & Co., 1992) 22.

2. Ibid., 142–145.

3. The substitution of economic for moral criteria is called "economic imperialism" by Mark A. Lutz and Kenneth Lux, *Humanistic Economics: The New Challenge* (New York: Bootstrap Press, 1988), chapter 9.

4. The systematic destruction of low-income communities in modern nations in order to benefit wealthier individuals and institutions is documented in *Building The American City*, Report of the National Commission on Urban Problems (Washington, D.C.: U.S. Government Printing Office, 1969); destruction of communities in the Third World is described in Vandana Shiva, *Staying Alive: Women, Ecology And Development* (Atlantic Highlands, N.J.: Zed Books, 1989).

5. "Jobs, jobs, jobs," *Business Week*, 22 February 1993, 29–30.

6. Extended critiques of the GNP/GDP are presented in Marilyn Waring, *If Women Counted: A New Feminist Economics* (San Francisco: Harper & Row, 1988); Herman E. Daly and John B. Cobb, Jr., *For The Common Good: Redirecting The Economy Toward Community, The Environment, And A Sustainable Future* (Boston: Beacon Press, 1989), chap. 3 and 401–455; Hazel Henderson, *Paradigms In Progress: Life Beyond Economics* (Indianapolis: Knowledge Systems, 1991), chaps. 4 and 6; and Victor Anderson, *Alternative Economic Indicators* (London and New York: Routledge, 1991).

7. Henderson is quoted in James Robertson and Andre Carrothers, "The New Economics: Accounting for a Healthy Planet," *Greenpeace*, January/February 1989, 11–14.

8. The story of Gillette razor blades is described in Susan Strasser, *Satisfaction Guaranteed: The Making Of The American Mass Market* (New York.: Pantheon Books, 1989), 97–102.

9. How U.S. corporations are substituting financial speculation for real wealth production is described in Robert B. Reich, *The Work Of Nations* (New York: Random House, 1992), 74–75.

10. On renewable resources made nonrenewable, see Shiva, *Staying Alive*.

11. On new economic indicators, see publications cited in note 6, above.

12. On new, nonaddictive goals for businesses, see Paul Hawken, *The Ecology Of Commerce: A Declaration Of Sustainability* (New York: HarperCollins, 1993).

13. Donna Boundy, *When Money Is the Drug: The Compulsion for Credit, Cash, and Chronic Debt* (San Francisco,: Harper San Francisco, 1993).

14. On combating personal money addiction, contact New Road Map Foundation, P.O. Box 15981, Seattle, WA 98115; or see Joe Dominguez and Vicki Robin, *Your Money or Your Life: Transforming Your Relationship with Money and Achieving Financial Independence* (New York: Penguin, 1992).

15. On monetary and economic growth vs. the cycles and limits of the real world see Donella H. Meadows, Dennis L. Meadows, and Jorgen Randers, *Beyond The Limits: Confronting Global Collapse, Envisioning A Sustainable Future* (Post Mills, Vt: Chelsea Green, 1992).

16. On U.S. workers who are choosing to work and earn less, see Carol Hymowitz,"Trading fat paychecks for free time," *Wall Street Journal*, 5 August 1991, sec B; also Amy Saltzman, *Downshifting: Reinventing Success On A Slower Track* (New York: HarperCollins, 1991).

Chapter 8

THE TROUBLE WITH JOB ADDICTION

In the modern economic paradigm, productive work is equated with having a paying job. But while the opportunity to perform truly productive work is necessary for both individuals' self-esteem and society's economic success, the paid work available in modern economies is often inadequately compensated, personally unsatisfying, even demeaning, and may produce goods or services of limited social value. The resentment that many people increasingly feel in regard to their jobs is reflected in popular references to "the daily grind," the widespread jubilation at reaching the end of the work week ("Thank God it's Friday"), and depression at having to return to work ("Monday morning blues").

Nevertheless, a paying job is essential not only for bringing in income, but in modern economies is considered a defining characteristic of responsible adulthood. Furthermore, because of the power of the visible economy in modern nations, our leaders may give elaborate verbal praise to other aspects of life, such as the family, community or civic participation, and spiritual values but in reality such areas are often shortchanged by both business and government policies, while the demands of earning a living have increasingly taken precedence in people's lives. This overemphasis on the role of paid work, compared with both unpaid work and non-work activities, could be called job addiction.

Job addiction is different from work addiction, another common ailment of modern society. Work addiction refers to the quality of one's activities. Work addicts, or workaholics, must be constantly busy, and can turn anything, including a hobby or a vacation into relentless hard work. But work addiction most often expresses itself on the job. Workaholics constantly find more tasks to accomplish, more reasons to stay overtime, and often demand that co-workers make similar sacrifices. They can become obsessed with their jobs, at the expense of personal life, health, family and other social relationships. Unfortunately, many employers encourage work addiction among their employees in the misguided notion that work addicts are more productive. Gradually, it is becoming understood that workaholics are harmful not only to themselves but also to the morale and effective functioning of their workplaces.[1]

By comparison, job addiction is characterized by the belief that to have a fulltime paying job is a central obligation of one's adult life. But many people who accept this assumption because they need to earn income do not enslave themselves to their jobs. They may try to conduct their paid work activities at a leisurely, sociable pace, and value their lives outside of work. In fact, many workers who are committed to their jobs often struggle to balance the demands of their paid work with other obligations, particularly to their families.

While job addiction affects individuals, it is perhaps most destructive at the institutional and societal levels. It finds expression in employers who believe that the job is more important than any other interest or obligation of their employees. Job addiction also leads to business and government policies that make good employment opportunities available to socially valued people, while limiting employment opportunities for socially devalued people. It leads to government misuse of statistics to disguise the full extent of unemployment. And it encourages public officials to offer cheerful platitudes about creating more jobs-jobs-jobs, rather than acknowledging the forces that continue to eliminate jobs.

Job addiction developed with the Industrial Revolution, when finding a job and being able to earn enough to support one's family became the new basis of male identity. The sex-role division of industrialism said that women's place was in the home, caring for household and family, while men went out to work and earned money. Although women were also employed in the new industrial workforce, they were considered "secondary" workers, helping out the primary—male—breadwinner. The assumption that men are the wage-earners is demonstrated by the fact that throughout the nineteenth and most of the twentieth centuries, the U.S. labor movement continually fought for the right of white, male wage-earners to be paid a "family wage"—earnings high enough to support a wife and children.[2]

Because paid work not only provides jobholders with essential income, but also serves important psychological functions, any discussion of how work is changing or the changing availability of jobs becomes highly emotionally charged. It is especially difficult to talk calmly about the possibility that modern societies are now failing to create as many jobs as people need. But rather than considering that the elimination of jobs that is now taking place can lead to shorter work hours and a more balanced life for everyone, many leaders in modern nations are still insisting that we can and will create more jobs—meaning that we will create more work, even if it is not needed. This inability to deal with the changing nature of employment is a prime example of job addiction.

For individuals, job addiction appears in the belief that one's worth and value come from having a fulltime, paid job. It is also expressed in the feelings of depression and low self-esteem common to unemployed people. Job addiction is especially relevant to male identity and self-esteem, although as more women enter the paid workforce, they too are being judged, or judging themselves, by the criteria of job addiction. For businesses and other employing organizations, job addiction is expressed in the belief that employees' paid work is their most important obligation.

It doesn't matter what other responsibilities employees may have outside of work—if they can't make the hours and do the work, they're out of a job. From the societal perspective, job addiction is expressed in the beliefs that only paid work—especially regular, fulltime work—is real work, that there will always be enough jobs for those who really want them, and that people who do not have jobs are lazy, unproductive parasites on society. By recognizing how job addiction shapes both individual actions and business and public policy, we can better understand what is happening to jobs today, and will be better able to participate in the creation of more fulfilling work opportunities and a more balanced life for all members of society.

THE ELIMINATION OF JOBS IN MODERN ECONOMIES

Modern economies have created millions of jobs. They have done so by replacing self-directed household and community production for one's own use with wage labor for others, and by constantly inventing new products and services that people are hired to produce and sell.

But at the same time, factors inherent in modern economies are continually changing the kinds of jobs that are available, as well as eliminating many of the jobs that the system creates. In recent years, these job-eliminating forces have become ever more important, wiping out manufacturing jobs and creating the postindustrial economy. Some of the most influential job-eliminating factors include new technologies and forms of workplace organization, which increase productive efficiency and allow layoffs; market saturation, which reduces sales and jobs in the saturated fields; plant relocations (capital flight) to regions that have lower wages, weaker unions, and fewer environmental regulations; and competition from products made by lower-paid, Third-World workers.

Because of such factors, modern economies over the past few decades have been experiencing severe and steadily increasing unemployment. From the early 1960s to the late 1980s, average unemployment rates in industrialized nations jumped from 3 percent to 7.5 percent, according to official statistics.[3] The International Labor Organization says that Western Europe now has the most persistent, long-term unemployment rates since the Great Depression of the 1930s.[4]

Observers in the United States and Canada say that the criteria by which these nations measure unemployment are misleading, designed to show a rosier picture of employment than the facts would reveal. A critical study of unemployment in the United States says that 17.9 million people are actually unemployed or inadequately employed, for a true jobless rate of 14.3 percent. A critical Canadian estimate says that in reality, at least 20 percent of the Canadian workforce is unemployed or underemployed.[5]

Since the 1970s, as the factors cited above have grown in impact, modern nations have been making the unpleasant discovery that increases in production and profitability do not necessarily guarantee increases in new employment opportunities. Or as today's cover story on my daily newspaper says: "Welcome to the 1990s, where record profits and an expanding economy no longer guarantee you will have a job tomorrow." The article explains that in order to lower their costs and keep up with international competition, companies are eliminating human employees and replacing them with electronic equipment.[6]

INEQUITABLE ACCESS TO JOB OPPORTUNITIES

One of the myths related to job addiction is the assertion that in modern economies there are always enough jobs for all who want them. In fact, there have probably never been enough jobs for everyone needing employment—certainly not enough *good* jobs. Until very recently, modern economies have coped with inadequate employment opportunities by defining only certain groups—primarily white males in young adulthood and middle age—as serious workers, preserving the most secure, highest-paying jobs for them, and preventing other groups from entering or participating fully in the paid workforce.

For example, child-labor laws, while essential for protecting young people from exploitative labor practices, have at the same time kept children and teens out of the paid workforce. Women's protective legislation, passed in the United States during the early years of the twentieth century, restricted the hours and kinds of paid work for which women could be hired. And Social Security programs enabled employers to enforce compulsory retirement for workers over the age of sixty-five. While the purpose of all these laws was to protect the targeted groups from dangerous working conditions and exploitation, another effect of such laws has been to reserve society's limited job opportunities for prime-age males, and to strengthen the illusion that only men are, or should be, the breadwinners.[7]

Outright gender, racial, and ethnic discrimination have also been used to keep others besides the most acceptable workers from taking the best available jobs. In the nineteenth-century United States, less-favored white groups such as Irish, Eastern European, and Southern European immigrants faced rigid employment barriers. And everything from hiring restrictions to organized violence have long excluded Mexicans, Asians, African-Americans, and other people of color from secure, higher-paying blue- and white-collar jobs, forcing them into casual wage labor, seasonal agriculture, and other arduous and economically insecure work.[8]

Ironically, as white, prime-age men have been channeled for almost two centuries into the most desirable jobs they have become dependent upon their jobs, not just economically, but also emotionally, as a primary source of identity and self-esteem. As a result, rather than supporting better job opportunities for all, many all-white, all-male unions have focused on preserving the existing job opportunities for their limited constituency, while systematically excluding women and people of color from their ranks.[9]

As the workforce today becomes more diverse, and as job opportunities fail to keep up with the numbers of people needing paid work, conflicts over which groups will get the best jobs, or any jobs at all, are increasing. These battles are exacerbated because many employers are systematically laying off formerly high-paid, fulltime white men and replacing them with poorly paid, often parttime workers, usually women and people of color.[10] The lack of good jobs can not be resolved by separate groups fighting over the limited turf, but instead by redefining the problem so that more good job opportunities can be created, and so they can be distributed more equitably.

THE PHENOMENON OF MAKE-WORK

One response to the elimination of jobs in modern economies is the creation of make-work. It's fashionable to consider government-created jobs as wasteful make-work, but in fact make-work is created everywhere: in government, the nonprofit sector, and especially in business. I define make-work as the creation of jobs that do not serve real social needs (other than providing the jobholders with paid employment) and that may have destructive consequences.

Familiar make-work opportunities include jobs for bureaucrats, paper shufflers, and many middle managers. It is especially difficult for well-paid people at the tops of business hierarchies, who spend most of their time writing reports or memos and attending meetings, to acknowledge that their jobs might be make-work, designed to justify their incomes and social position, rather than work that actually accomplishes anything.

Many social-welfare programs, whether sponsored by the government or private agencies, contain aspects of make-work. Most of the money allocated for such programs goes to social workers, administrators, bureaucrats, and other middle-class professionals, while little of it actually gets to the hungry, homeless, jobless, and others who most need it. In many cases, our taxes and charitable donations could be used more effectively if instead of being spent on experts, it were given directly to poor people.[11] However, this would throw many middle-class professionals out of work, creating a new group of unemployed.

Many construction projects are make-work. Because they can be justified on the grounds that they put union members back to work, improve the infrastructure, and stimulate new business development, they have a universal appeal that transcends right-left politics. Unnecessary new highways, shopping malls, and industrial parks eat up a little more of the natural environment, but nature is always expendable when jobs are at stake.

Whenever economic conditions worsen and poverty and unemployment increase, crime and imprisonment rise. The United States now has a larger percent of its population in prison than in any other country in the world. At the same time, job opportunities in the security and surveillance fields are increasing. Prison inmates are disproportionately men of color, with nearly 25 percent of African-American men between the ages of twenty to twenty-nine in jail or on probation. It is no coincidence that African-Americans and Hispanics are also experiencing disproportionately higher-than-average rates of unemployment, underemployment, and poverty.[12] These two trends—the increase of both criminals and the crime-prevention professions—epitomize the inadequacy of the U.S. response to the elimination of good job opportunities.

JOB ADDICTION AND OVERWORK

In the late 1980s and early 1990s, modern nations became aware of the "time crunch"—hurried, harried employees who have no time for personal life or family responsibilities, working parents who rarely see each other or their children, and a "sandwich generation" of women who have to care for both children and older relatives after a full day of paid work. When Harvard economist Juliet Schor's book *The Overworked American: The Unexpected Decline of Leisure* came out in 1991, she became a national media figure because she had articulated the desperation of so many people.[13]

Schor made the startling claim that in the United States, paid work hours, which have consistently declined throughout two centuries of industrialization, have begun to rise since the 1970s.[14] Other observers of the time crunch around the world note its connection to the increasing entry of married women into the paid workforce since the 1970s, a phenomenon taking place throughout modern nations.

But while women are most severely affected because of their double responsibilities, they are not the only victims of the time crunch. In many working-class and middle-class families, where until recently a single—male—breadwinner had been able to provide adequate income for his stay-at-home wife and children, two wage-earners are increasingly needed to maintain a decent standard of living. In other words, not just individuals but *families* are now required to give more of their time to paid work, to the detriment of home life and family responsibilities.[15]

In Western Europe, where unions are fairly strong and government social policy regularly takes workers' needs into account, individual work hours have continued to fall, without loss in pay, so that many fulltime workers now average around thirty-five hours a week. In addition, workers in most Western European nations have ample benefits, such as paid family leave, medical leave, and government-mandated paid vacations of as much as four to six weeks a year.[16] While such policies have not eliminated overwork, especially for women, they represent somewhat more balanced attitudes regarding paid work. By contrast, in the United States and Canada, where unions are weaker and job addiction is more deeply ingrained, the forty-hour a week, fulltime job, for forty-nine or fifty weeks a year, almost seems like a law of nature. And most people who work fulltime must actually devote considerably more than forty hours a week to their jobs. To paid hours, add job-related tasks such as preparation of clothing and lunches, commuting, and time spent on recovering from work.

To make matters worse, many employees in the United States and Canada are putting in even more than forty hours a week on their jobs. It's cheaper for employers to pay existing workers overtime rather than hire additional employees, each of whom would require costly benefit packages. In the United States, manufacturing employees are now working the most overtime since the government started keeping records in the 1950s.[17]

Unionized workers must be paid extra for overtime work. However, professional employees in the United States, a group not covered by federal work-time legislation, are often obligated to work more than fulltime in order to demonstrate their commitment to their careers, while not even being paid for their overtime. Employers who insist that one's paid work is one's primary obligation, along with employees who are unable to say no to paid-work demands, are both increasing the imbalances caused by job addiction.

OVERWORK AND UNEMPLOYMENT: EXACERBATING THE IMBALANCES

Job addiction is characterized by the belief that only a fulltime job is real work, that a responsible adult devotes a substantial portion of daily life to paid work. Parttime work is not enough—it connotes laziness or lack of commitment. This belief is rationalized by the assumption that we need to spend long hours at work in order to produce the abundance of goods and services enjoyed by modern affluent societies.

But this assumption is false. For one thing, technological advances have constantly increased the productivity of human labor, making it possible to produce more with less work. Juliet Schor notes that since 1948, the productivity of the U.S. worker has doubled. This means that we could all now be working four hours a day, or six months a year, and still enjoy the same high standard of living as people in the middle of the twentieth century.[18]

Ironically, while many people today need more work and more money-earning opportunities, many fulltime workers—both women and men—would gladly give up a few hours or a day's work each week, even if it meant reduced pay, in order to have more time for themselves and their families. Working parents with young children are most willing to make this trade-off. However, workers desiring shorter hours are often at the mercy of inflexible, job-addicted employers who refuse to create reduced or more flexible work schedules. And many employees are afraid to ask for reduced work-time because they feel lucky to have any job at all and fear that if they complain about their jobs, they may lose them.[19]

Shorter work hours would not only help release individuals from the burdens of overwork but would also help relieve unemployment by enabling job opportunities to be distributed more equitably, a process sometimes called "sharing the work."[20] The U.S. AFL-CIO estimates, for example, that if workers today were no longer required to perform the overtime added on since 1982, 3 million new jobs would instead be created.[21]

Ironically, parttime work has also increased dramatically in modern economies during the past twenty years, but not in response to employees' need for shorter work-time. Employers have increasingly laid off well-paid fulltime workers and replaced them with parttime or temporary workers who recieve no benefits and often get paid considerably less for doing exactly the same work as fulltime employees. In the United States, approximately 25 to 30 percent of the paid workforce now holds parttime or temporary jobs. These low-quality, poorly paid jobs are taken primarily by women and people of color, replacing the predominantly while male workers who are being laid off as their formerly secure, high paying jobs disappear.[22]

CHALLENGES TO JOB ADDICTION

Recently, various groups in modern nations, including women activists and labor unions, have begun to challenge job addiction. In the United States in 1990, the Boston-area Shorter Work-Time Group issued a policy paper titled "Less Time for our Jobs, More Time for Ourselves." This group, of which I am a member, claimed that the time crunch is not merely an individual or family problem but a societal problem, caused both by economic necessity and by values and policies that elevate paid work over the rest of life. We noted that because people today are forced to spend so much time earning a living, our personal, family, and social lives, our neighborhoods, and the quality of our communities and public life have all been seriously diminished. We recommended that both men and women should be able to spend less time at work—without loss in pay—so they could have more time for sharing domestic responsibilities, rebuilding community life, hanging out and socializing, and simply attending to personal needs and self-enhancement. Our article was reprinted in a national magazine and continues to receive enthusiastic responses from people of all backgrounds.[23]

In Italy in 1990, a national women's organization called The Cherry Orchard proposed a law entitled "Women Changing the Times: A Law to Make the Time for Work, the Schedules of the Community, and the Rhythm of Life More Human." Their proposal begins: "Everyone needs time to study, to work, and to care for others and for themselves." They emphasize that the typical modern life cycle of school-work-retirement is designed to fit men's lives and completely overlooks the ongoing need to provide caring, a responsibility that has traditionally been shoved onto women in the invisible economy. They propose a more integrated approach, so that students can combine work with studies; both men and women can take time off to care for their families during their prime working years; and older people can do paid work in their later years, in exchange for time off when they are younger. Over 300,000 people signed their petition, which has since been delivered to the Italian parliament for further action.[24]

The Canadian Autoworkers union has taken some of the most advanced positions in favor of reduced work-time of any union in that nation. Their pamphlet *More Time: For Ourselves, Our Children, Our Community* provides a comprehensive statement of their positon.[25]

In the United States, the New Directions Movement (NDM), a national reform caucus within the United Autoworkers, has been especially active in fighting for reduced work-time. In September 1994 an NDM-led local won a precedent-setting victory in Flint, Michigan, where General Motors' policy of layoffs, speedups, and forced overtime had created 57-hour work weeks, was depriving employees of time for family life, and causing excessive injuries. Following a brief strike, the union got General Motors to hire 779 more workers (many of them recently laid off) to share the workload and help reduce current work hours.[26]

While many business leaders, professional economists, and public-policy makers focus solely on the needs of the visible economy, these women and men who are aware of the needs of the unpaid, invisible sectors of the economy are able to provide an alternative perspective to the job addiction of the modern economic paradigm.

NOTES

1. On work addiction as an individual problem, see Bryan E. Robinson, *Work Addiction* (Deerfield Beach, Fla.: Health Communications, 1989), or Diane Fassel, Ph.D., *Working Ourselves to Death and the Rewards of Recovery* (New York: Harper & Row, 1990). As an organizational dysfunction, see Anne Wilson Schaef and Diane Fassel, *The Addictive Organization* (San Francisco: Harper & Row, 1988). See also Walter Kiechel III, "The Workaholic Generation," *Fortune*, 10 April 1989, 50–62.

2. On labor's fight for the family wage for male workers, see Theresa L. Amott and Julie A. Matthaei, *Race, Gender, and Work: A Multicultural Economic History of Women in the United States* (Boston: South End Press, 1991), 26 and 102–105.

3. On declining employment in modern nations, see Michael Renner, *Jobs in a Sustainable Economy*, Worldwatch #104 (Washington, D.C.: Worldwatch Institute, 1991), 6–12.

4. The ILO's assessment of the unemployment situation in Europe is cited in "Record Unemployment Worldwide," *Society for the Reduction of Human Labor Newsletter*, 4 (Winter 1993–94), 1, available from the Society for the Reduction of Human Labor, c/o B. K. Hunnicutt, 1610 E. College St., Iowa City, IA 52245.

5. On the inaccuracy of official unemployment statistics in the United States, see David Dembo and Ward Morehouse, *The Underbelly of the U.S. Economy: Joblessness and the Pauperization of Work in America* (New York: Apex Press, 1993), chap. 1. In Canada, see Bruce O'Hara, *Working Harder Isn't Working* (Vancouver: New Star, 1993), chap. 4.

6. Charles Stein, "Economic Recovery is Producing Pain for Many Workers," Boston Globe, 10 March 1994, 1. See also "Jobs, Jobs, Jobs," *Business Week*, 22 February 1993, which reports that while profits and productivity in U.S. businesses continue to rise, job creation lags behind as employers substitute technology for human workers, overwork fulltime employees, or take on more low-paid part-timers, creating a two-tiered workforce.

7. On the exclusion of women, children and seniors from the paid workforce, see O'Hara, *Working Harder Isn't Working*, chap. 10. On women's protective legislation, see Alice Kessler-Harris, *Out to Work: A History of Wage-Earning Women in the United States* (New York: Oxford University Press, 1992), chap. 7.

8. On the exclusion of various racial and ethnic groups from the paid workforce, see Amott and Matthaei, *Race, Gender, and Work*, chaps. 4, 6, 7, and 8; and O'Hara, *Working Harder Isn't Working*, chap. 10.

9. On U.S. labor unions' discrimination against women, see Kessler-Harris, *Out to Work*, chap. 6; against people of color, see Amott and Matthaei, 25, 154–157, 197, and 240–241.

10. Commentators of all political stripes have noted the decline of high-quality, secure, well-paying jobs since the 1970s. See, for example, conservative Kevin Phillips, *The Politics of Rich and Poor: Wealth and the American Electorate* (New York: HarperCollins, 1991), 14–23; liberal Robert B. Reich, *The Wealth of Nations* (New York: Random House, 1992), 202–207; and labor-left writer Philip Mattera,

Prosperity Lost: How a Decade of Greed has Eroded Our Standard of Living and Endangered Our Children's Future (Reading, Mass.: Addison-Wesley, 1990), esp. chaps. 4 and 5. On the replacement of male by lower-paid female workers, see Teresa Amott, *Caught in the Crisis: Women and the U.S. Economy Today* (New York: Monthly Review Press, 1993), chap. 3.

11. For a scathing critique of both government anti-poverty and welfare programs, and private charities, see Theresa Funiciello, *Tyranny of Kindness: Dismantling The Welfare System to End Poverty in America* (New York: Atlantic Monthly Press, 1993).

12. On rising poverty and unemployment among African-Americans, see Dembo and Morehouse, *The Underbelly of the U.S. Economy*, 23–24. On imprisonment in the United States, see Amott, *Caught in the Crisis*, 100. On increases in crime and imprisonment with rising unemployment, see also Michael D. Yates, *Longer Hours, Fewer Jobs: Employment and Unemployment in the United States* (New York: Monthly Review Press, 1994), 66–68.

13. Juliet B. Schor, *The Overworked American: The Unexpected Decline of Leisure* (New York: Basic Books, 1991). Since publication of her book, Schor has been regularly interviewed on national TV programs and cited in national print media on the problem of overwork.

14. On rising work hours in the United States see Schor, *The Overworked American*, chap. 2. See also Peter T. Kilborn, "Tales from the Digital Treadmill," *New York Sunday Times*, 30 June 1991, sec.4.

15. On declining U.S. wages, see note 10 above. Strains on family life from overwork are documented by the five-year National Study of the Changing Workforce, described in Julia Lawlor, "Workers Want to Get a Life," *USA Today*, 3 September 1993, sec. B.

16. Pro-worker policies and shorter work-time in Western Europe are described in Suzanne Gordon, "Prisoners of Work," *Boston Globe Magazine*, 29 August 1989, 16–60; Schor, *The Overworked American*, 81–82; and Jeremy Brecher and Tim Costello, "The Great Time Squeeze," *Z Magazine*, October 1990, 102–107.

17. On employers' preference for making workers work overtime: in Canada, see O'Hara, *Working Harder Isn't Working*, 100–101; in the United States, Schor, *The Overworked American*, 66–68. See also Mike Feinsilber, "U.S. Says Overtime in Factories Soaring," *Boston Globe*, 18 March 1993, 46.

18. For more information on increased productivity in the United States since 1948, see Schor, *The Overworked American*, 2.

19. See "California Poll Finds a Wish for More Family Life at Careers' Expense," *Boston Globe*, 13 August 1990, 6; Lawlor, "Workers Want to Get a Life"; and Carol Hymowitz, "Trading Fat Paychecks for More Free Time," *Wall Street Journal*, 5 August 1991, sec. B

20. In the United States during the Great Depression of the 1930s, the labor movement and many politicians supported a 30-hour work week in order to reduce massive unemployment by sharing the available jobs more widely. Their proposal was defeated by the business community's support for a 40-hour week. See Benjamin K. Hunnicutt, *Work Without End: Abandoning Shorter Hours for the Right to Work* (Philadelphia: Temple University Press, 1988), chaps. 5 and 6.

21. Feinsilber, "U.S. Says Overtime in Factories Soaring," 46.

22. On the size and make-up of the parttime (contingent) workforce, see Carol Kleiman, "As Jobs Shift to Contingency Work, More Women Are Left Outside," Washington Post 18 April 1993, H 3. See also New Ways to Work, ed., *New Policies for Part-Time and Contingent Workers* (San Francisco: New Ways to Work, 1992) available from NWTW, 785 Market St., Suite 950, San Francisco, CA 94103, (415) 995-9860.

23. Barbara Brandt, "Less is More: A Call for Shorter Work Hours," *Utne Reader*, July-August 1991, 81–87.

24. The Cherry Orchard campaign to make work-time in Italy more compatible with other human needs is described in Margaret M. Quinn and Eva Buiatti, "Women, Time, Stress and Work: A Proposal from Italy", in *New Solutions: A Journal of Environmental and Occupational Health Policy*, 1,(Winter 1991) 48–56. (Available from *New Solutions*, P.O. Box 2812, Denver, CO 80201, (303) 987-2229.)

25. Contact Canadian Autoworkers, 205 Placer Court, Willowdale, Ontario M2H 3H9, Canada, (416) 497-4110.

26. See Gabriella Stern and Neal Templin, "GM, in a Switch, Agrees to Hire New Workers," *Wall Street Journal*, 3 October 1994, Sec. A. See also "Lasting One Day Longer Works—Flint GM Strike

Means Jobs," *Voice of New Directions*, Vol. 6, No. 3, October 1994, available from New Directions Movement of the UAW, P.O. Box 6876, St. Louis, MO 63144, (314) 531-2900.

Chapter 9

THE ECONOMY AND THE REST OF LIFE: TOWARD A NEW PARADIGM

Modern societies are characterized by numerous hierarchical systems, such as the elevation of men over women, of white people over people of color, employers' control over their employees, the political and economic domination by modern nations over the Third World, and the belief that human beings are separate from and superior to nature.

In addition to all these familiar systems, our explorations of economic invisibility and economic addiction suggest the existence of yet another hierarchical system—one not widely recognized—which is central to modern economies. This is based on the belief that the economy is separate from, and superior to, the rest of life. I call this structure ''economism."

THE MEANING OF ECONOMISM

Just as sexism is discrimination on the basis of gender, and racism is discrimination on the basis of race, economism is a system of discrimination based on whether or not an individual, institution, or activity is part of the economy. Crucial to this hierarchy is the fact that economism defines "the economy" as the visible economy—the realm of businesses, the buying and selling of goods and services, of paid work and money-making.

Economism is based on the following assumptions:

— Society can be divided into two separate spheres: the economy, and the rest of life.

— The economy consists of the activities of businesses—producing and selling goods and services, employing people, and making money.

— The economy—that is, the business sector—is the primary source of society's wealth and well-being.

— The rest of life—which includes people in their homes, families, and communities, volunteer activities and charitable organizations, the government, education, arts and culture, religion and spirituality—is defined as "not-the-economy."

— The rest of life is dependent upon the economy—that is, dependent upon the activities of the business sector—for wealth and well-being.

CONSEQUENCES OF ECONOMISM

Economism is a multi-layered hierarchical system. It both incorporates, and builds upon, the other hierarchical structures of modern nations.

For example, hierarchical systems such as sexism, classism, and racism are manifested in the visible economy through the prevalence of white men at the top of corporate hierarchies and in control of the richest and most powerful businesses and financial institutions, and the predominance of women and people of color in the lower-status, poorer-paying jobs. In the rest of life, sexism is expressed as discrimination against women in education and politics, or as violence against women on the streets and in their homes. In the rest of life, racism is expressed as discrimination against people of color in education, politics, and many other areas, and as overt violence on the streets, while classism is expressed through educational or public policies that discriminate against poor or lower class people.

At the same time that sexism, classism, racism, and other hierarchical systems shape people's lives in both the visible economy and the rest of life, the distinctive hierarchy of economism shapes the relations *between* the visible economy and the rest of life. Economism equates the goals and well-being of businesses with the well-being of society as a whole. Or as a familiar phrase puts it, "What's good for General Motors is good for America." And this assumption has important consequences both for the status of businesses in modern nations and for the well-being of the rest of society.

By equating the economy with the business sector exclusively, economism justifies why, in modern nations, business goals and needs take precedence over the supposedly noneconomic goals and values of the rest of life. Since, according to economism, the rest of life is dependent upon the business sector for its wealth and well-being, the institutions and activities of the rest of life have an obligation to support and nurture the business sector. As a result, the needs and values of the business sector come to dominate the rest of society, our resources, and the realms of moral and political legitimacy.

Thus, in modern economies, the purpose of home and family is to enthusiastically consume the products of business, raise good future workers and consumers, and help people recharge so they can go back to work the next day. The purpose of our schools is to teach our children the skills they will need at work, so that our businesses can remain competitive in the new global economy and so that we can invent new products and technologies that our businesses can sell. The purpose of religion is to teach us to be honest, obedient, and respectful of authority, so we will be good workers. The purpose of government is to promote policies that will help business (often at the expense of nonbusiness realms). The purpose of the creative arts is to help sell products. The purpose of nonprofit and charitable organizations is to pick up the pieces by caring for those aberrant individuals who through some deficiency or emergency are not able to earn their living. The purpose of Third-World nations is to provide cheap labor, raw materials, and new markets for the businesses of modern nations. And the purpose of the natural environment is to provide resources that can be turned into more products to be sold by addictive businesses.

The structure of economism is depicted graphically in Figure 9.1. However, it should be emphasized that economism describes the relationship between the rest of life and the hierarchical, addictive businesses of the old paradigm. As we shall see in the second half of this book, new-paradigm economic institutions, such as socially responsible businesses, are moving toward nonaddictive goals and are developing a more balanced relationship with the rest of life.

THE ECONOMY AND THE REST OF LIFE

What economism identifies as the economy is in reality only a small part of the whole economy. In every modern society there is also a vast invisible economy, which includes women's work in bearing and raising their children, the unpaid work that both women and men do in their homes for their families, the countless neighborly interactions and volunteer activities that people do with and for each other in their communities, and the constantly productive and self-regenerating processes of the natural environment.

Economism promotes an imbalance between the visible economy and the rest of life. It makes invisible the harm generated by the visible economy, such as workplace stress with its resulting pressures on individuals, families, and communities, or business pollution of the human and natural environment. It ignores all the work constantly being done in the invisible economy to pick up the pieces, clean up the messes, heal the wounds, and in countless other ways bear the costs of the visible economy. And it denies the economic value of all the productive work done regularly in the invisible economy to meet people's daily needs.

Economism perpetuates the illusion that only individuals who have paying jobs are making a productive contribution to society. It ignores the fact that women and other people who are discriminated against because of race, ethnicity, class, age, or other reasons are systematically denied full participation in the visible—paid—economy. It decrees that people who do not perform paid work—housewives, children, unemployed people, and retired people—have no value.

These injustices and imbalances are made even worse because the visible economy has increasingly become an addictive system, driven by the addictive business goals of constantly increasing sales and profits. The need to keep selling more must be supported by addictive individual behaviors, and addiction-promoting public policies. People's health, and the health of the natural environment are being destroyed in order to increase the bottom lines of addictive businesses, while economic indicators such as the GDP, which are based on money addiction, make this destruction invisible. And people's time and energy is monopolized by their employers, while work addiction and job addiction justify the resulting destruction

FIGURE 9.1: THE STRUCTURE OF ECONOMISM

Economism:
The belief that the economy is separate from, and superior to, the rest of life.

The Economy *(the superior category)*	*The Rest of Life* *(the inferior category)*
Economism equates the economy with the visible economy—the realm of businesses and monetized production and exchange. The visible economy is identified as the source of wealth production in society.	Economism defines the rest of life as "not-the-economy." In reality, the rest of life includes the essential activities of the invisible economy—non-monetized production and exchange in home, family, and community; volunteer activities; and the natural environment.
Hierarchical systems—e.g., sexism, classism, racism—shape the visible economy.	Hierarchical systems—e.g., sexism, classism, racism—also operate in the rest of life.

A hierarchical relationship also operates across the two categories, expressed in such beliefs as:

— People with paying jobs are superior to people without paying jobs.

— The needs of businesses take precedence over the needs of communities in which businesses are located.

— The needs of businesses take precedence over the needs of the natural environment.

— The needs of businesses to keep selling more products and services take precedence over people's needs to stay healthy and free from addictions.

of personal, family, and community life. Thus economism both denies and increases the destructive results of economic addictions.

THE VULNERABILITY OF THE MODERN ECONOMIC PARADIGM

Through economism and many other hierarchical beliefs and structures, the modern economic paradigm shapes the lives of individuals, the well-being of households and communities, the functioning of institutions, the direction of national economies, and the fate of the natural environment. Its hierarchical structures and addictive processes are maintained through officially accepted teachings, beliefs, and value systems, through institutionalized traditions and relationships, through coercion and control, and when necessary, through force and violence. Nevertheless, despite its power over people's lives and over entire economies, the modern economic paradigm is vulnerable to change.

The Vulnerability of Hierarchical Systems

Any system that divides humanity into artificial categories, that classifies some kinds of people as superior, others as inferior and justifies domination by the so-called superiors over the inferiors is inherently unstable and vulnerable. One reason is because both groups must give up their wholeness in order to fit the hierarchical stereotypes.

In *Toward A New Psychology of Women*, the pioneering feminist psychiatrist Jean Baker Miller describes the dynamics of this process as it applies to the patriarchy. She notes that in patriarchal systems, certain kinds of feelings and activities are relegated to the inferior group—women—including:

— providing for the bodily needs and comforts of others;

— making pleasant or clean those parts or experiences of the body perceived as unpleasant, uncontrollable, or dirty;

— providing sexual services and being sexually "available";

— caring for infants and children; and

— dealing with feelings of vulnerability, weakness, helplessness, dependency, and the emotional connections between people.

Miller notes that all these activities have three things in common: 1) they are classified as inferior; 2) they remind us of our own vulnerability, helplessness, dependency, and need for others; and 3) they are essential to the human psyche and to human survival.[1]

The feminist therapist and addiction-recovery pioneer Anne Wilson Schaef further illuminates the dynamics taking place here. In her book *Women's Reality: An Emerging Female System In A White Male Society*, Schaef notes that hierarchical systems such as patriarchy are maintained by creating the illusion that the superiors are always in control, that they never experience fear or weakness. In order to sustain such obvious falsehoods, universal human experiences such as weakness and dependence must therefore be eliminated from the province of the superior group and made the exclusive province of the inferior.[2]

Schaef's insights complement those of Miller. As Miller points out, because of their association with weakness and vulnerability, universal human experiences of dependency and caring are removed from the culture's definition of what is "masculine." Redefined as "women's" concerns and relegated to the private realms of home, family, and intimate personal issues, these universal human experiences become invisible. In essence, Miller concludes, women (along with members of other supposedly inferior social and racial groups) have been turned into "carriers" for society of these frightening but absolutely essential aspects of the total human experience.[3]

Miller and Schaef were writing about the patriarchy, but we can expand these insights to the larger modern economic paradigm. In modern economies, the activities that represent human physical and emotional vulnerability are relegated to all the groups and sectors classified as inferior. In the visible sectors of the economy, activities such as caretaking, cleaning, and emotional expressiveness are converted into occupational fields such as tending or teaching younger children, lower-paid health-care jobs, janitorial services, and the arts and entertainment. These professions are characteristically given to women, "less manly" men, and/or people of color. At the same time, such activities as caring for dependents, providing emotional nurturing, and doing routine cleaning and physical maintenance also make up the essence of women's domestic chores in the unpaid, invisible economy.

Meanwhile, the privileged individuals at the top of social, political, and economic hierarchies sit around, have meetings, and give orders, looking clean and respectable in their elegant offices. But their privileges, comforts, and power would not be possible without the caretaking, maintenance, and connecting work of all the people below.

Hierarchical systems are maintained because members of the supposedly inferior groups, taught that they are stupid, unimportant, and worthless, often suffer from lack of belief in their own abilities and value and may not realize that they do have power to make changes. At the same time, the superiors must put on a constant show of omnipotence and invulnerability, never able to admit that they, too, are only human, with all the fears, needs, and weaknesses this includes. The superior groups bear the burden that they cannot fully express their human or caring side, cannot express their need for human connection. They are not allowed to admit that they, too, may be in pain.[4]

I don't mean to imply that the suffering caused by hierarchical systems is purely psychological, or that it is borne equally by superiors and inferiors. Despite their inner pain, those in the superior categories control the resources and institutional power of the system. They are therefore able to do far greater damage—to other people, and to the Earth—than the inferiors can possibly do. Furthermore, without significant power over material resources and institutions, the inferiors can suffer real physical harm, often lacking such basic needs as food, shelter, caretaking, and protection from violence.

Nevertheless, in any hierarchical system, whether based on supposed differences related to gender, race, nationality, or other artificially imposed criteria, both superiors and inferiors have had to give up parts of themselves, have been denied their full humanity. Emotionally, psychologically, and spiritually, both groups are suffering. This dynamic is a constant, unrecognized threat to the stability of any hierarchical system.

The Vulnerability of Systems Maintained by Invisibility

The modern economic paradigm is also vulnerable to change because it is sustained by making essential aspects of reality invisible. Its hierarchical systems are maintained by making invisible

— the weaknesses of, and harm caused by, those categorized as superior;

— the strengths and positive contributions of those categorized as inferior;

— the suffering of those categorized as inferior;

— the suffering of those categorized as superior; and

— the possibility of alternatives to the existing system.

Likewise, its addictive systems are maintained by denying that the system promotes addictions, the addictions are harming the addicts, and the addicted individuals and institutions are harming others.

Any system maintained by invisibility is inherently vulnerable to breakdown because at some point in time its dysfunctional and destructive consequences finally become too obvious to be ignored any longer. As more anomalies become visible, people begin to reexamine their assumptions about who they are and how the world works. And that's what's happening in modern economies today.

Not only are all kinds of hierarchical assumptions and structures now being challenged but, increasingly, people are seeking to uncover destructive secrets, are admitting to long-denied abuses and addictions, and are bringing important realities long hidden back into personal—and public—awareness. Much of this uncovering work has been done in the context of the addiction-recovery movement, which has a strongly individualistic bias. Nevertheless, such phenomena as abuse, denial, addiction, and recovery also apply to larger social and economic realities. Now it is time for us to extend this awareness to our economic lives, to make visible the hidden addictions that shape, and the abuses that are generated by, the modern economic paradigm.

The old paradigm has long been able to promote its superiority because it has made alternatives invisible. Meanwhile, numerous alternatives for a more humane, just, personally fulfilling, and environmentally supportive economy have been hidden away in the invisible economy. But now, as the beliefs and structures of the modern economic paradigm break apart, these alternatives are beginning to emerge and to shape the postmodern economic paradigm.

NOTES

1. On the hidden psychological dynamics of patriarchal society, see Jean Baker Miller, *Toward A New Psychology of Women*, 2d ed. (Boston: Beacon Press, 1986), esp. chap. 3, "The Importance of Unimportant People."

2. On the assumptions of the white, male paradigm, see Anne Wilson Schaef, *Women's Reality: An Emerging Female System in A White Male Society* (New York: Harper & Row, 1985), chap. 1.

3. Miller, *Toward A New Psychology of Women*, 23.

4. The psychological injuries to and suffering of the male/superior group in hierarchical systems is noted by many feminists. See for example Miller, *Toward A New Psychology of Women*, chaps. 2 and 3; and Schaef, *Women's Reality*, 7–15. African-American feminist bell hooks notes that men at the bottom of economic, racial, or other hierarchies suffer extreme emotional pain; see bell hooks, *Feminist Theory: From Margin to Center* (Boston: South End Press, 1984), chap. 5.

Beyond the Textbooks: The Economics of Daily Life

Chapter 10

LESSONS FROM THE INVISIBLE ECONOMY

CHARACTERISTICS OF ECONOMIC SYSTEMS: THE QUESTION OF CHOICE

Destructive systems maintain their dominance by making alternatives unattractive, or invisible. The modern economic paradigm says that the market system, which supposedly promotes both maximum productivity for businesses and maximum free choice for consumers, is the ultimate economic form. Ironically, by insisting on the superiority of market economies, with their near-infinite choices among products and services, the modern economic paradigm actually denies us the possibility of real choice.

According to conventional economics, societies throughout history have chosen from among three basic economic models to meet people's needs: tradition, command, and the market system.[1]

Tradition. According to the conventional view, economies run by tradition follow rigid modes of production and distribution, handed down from the distant past and strictly maintained by law and custom. Tradition is assumed to characterize primitive agrarian and other nonindustrial societies, or caste systems in which one's social and economic position are determined by birth. Societies that follow traditional economic modes are assumed to be static, do not allow for economic change, and therefore inhibit progress.[2]

Command. In command economies, people's economic activities are determined by imposed authority. Command economies include the ancient despotic empires of the East, where hordes of slaves painfully built the pyramids or the Great Wall or, more recently, centrally run Communist economies. The command mode is occasionally applied in democratic societies during emergencies such as wartime. Although command economies may not be fair or enjoyable, they get things done.³

The market. According to a standard economics textbook, the market system "is a complex mode of organizing society in which order and efficiency emerge 'spontaneously' from a seemingly uncontrolled society." Each individual has complete free choice as to the type of work he will do and the goods he will buy. The market automatically coordinates individuals' choices so that society produces what people need and distributes the various forms of wealth appropriately.⁴

Of course no economic system is perfect. But given the alternatives—the rigidity and limitations of old-fashioned traditional economies, or the lack of freedom and initiative in the command economy—what choice do we have? Obviously the dynamic market economy, which combines limitless choices, individual freedom, and incentives to produce abundance, offers the best of all possible economic worlds. However, this familiar typology—tradition, command, or the market system—is both logically flawed and factually inaccurate. Perhaps most important, it makes invisible the numerous and infinitely varied choices that actually exist. It ignores the wide variety of economic modes that people naturally create in their daily lives as they meet their needs and the needs of those they care about.

For one thing, the tradition/command/market model is based on faulty assumptions about traditional economies. It uses "traditional" as a code word to imply inefficient, even irrational economic actions and institutions based on superstitions, ritual, and other supposedly primitive forms. But historians and anthropologists now recognize that there are really endless varieties of so-called traditional economic systems. Some are bustling, others are low-key. Some are based on class differences, others on equality. Some are tied to religion, others to private gain. Traditional economies can be individualistic, communally oriented, patriarchal, matriarchal, or any other form or combination of forms imaginable. The automatic lumping together of all preindustrial societies as static and inferior was a common practice of Western social scientists until the 1950s and 1960s. Since then, scholars and activists have increasingly come to recognize the broad diversity among nonmodern cultures, their many functional and adaptive characteristics, and the fact that there is much that modern cultures can learn from them.⁵

Besides, it's illogical to compare tradition—what people have always done—with the market system. After all, for at least two hundred years the United States had a market system. U.S. leaders think it's great and don't intend to change it. So couldn't we say that the market system is the traditional U.S. economy?

The command system is also a code word, making us think of cruel, despotic systems far removed from free, modern economies. But up until one hundred forty years ago, a thriving command economy—slavery—flourished right in the U.S. Ironically, the slaves were sold to their owners according to the principles of the market system, highest prices for the most desirable. And the cotton, tobacco, and other crops the slaves produced were also sold through the market system, according to the laws of supply and demand.

And what about our lives today? We may be operating in the market system when we go to the shopping mall, when we buy our food or clothes or entertainment. But when we go to work, the minute we step through our employer's door, we may have entered and must obey a hierarchically structured, centrally run command system. The fact that a society exchanges its goods and services through a market system is no guarantee that the people in that society are free.

Accepting this simplistic and misleading typology of tradition/command/the market limits our ability to recognize the emerging postmodern economy. In reality, there are many more economic forms than just these three conventionally recognized modes, and people regularly utilize a variety of economic modes in their daily lives. All the different modes operating within a society, and the various combinations of economic modes that individuals and institutions utilize, can be identified and studied. To observe how people actually meet their economic needs would provide us with valuable and empowering information about the range of economic choices available to us.

THE EMERGENCE OF THE INVISIBLE ECONOMY

Many of these unrecognized economic modes are now becoming visible. Some of them have been around long before industrialization, but lost their legitimacy with the dominance of industrial production and the modern market system. Some of these economic forms have been hidden away in the informal, unpaid sectors of the economy. Still others represent consciously developed new models, created out of the urgent need to find alternatives to the modern economic paradigm. Together, they are bringing about the postmodern economy.

Major sources of these formerly invisible economic models include the following:

1. Unpaid domestic activities for home and family, such as cooking, cleaning, child care, nursing the sick, commonly known as women's work (although men are increasingly participating in these activities);

made invisible because the work is unpaid; done primarily by women; serves our most vulnerable physical and emotional needs; and because it could be attributed to women's so-called natural instincts;

now becoming recognized because of the increasing stresses on women both at home and in the paid workforce, and because of women's growing self-awareness.

2. Women's biological activities of pregnancy, childbirth, and breastfeeding:

made invisible because they represent some of the most frightening, vulnerable, and powerful aspects of life; because they are done only by women; and because they could be defined as part of nature;

now becoming recognized because women have increasingly fought for the right to choose if, when, and how they will participate in these activities.

3. Household production and neighborly exchanges of goods and services;

made invisible because they do not involve the use of money; because they are primarily done by women in their homes; and because they are especially characteristic of poorer communities;

now becoming recognized because of women's increased empowerment; and because with a failing visible economy, more people are forced to develop non-monetized alternatives.

4. Volunteer activities for the community and the public good;

made invisible because they are unpaid; are often (although not exclusively) carried out by women; and because they are sponsored by non-profit and community organizations, not by businesses;

now becoming recognized because they support our deepest values; offer the opportunity to make a difference; and because they deal with pressing economic, social, and environmental problems which cannot be solved by, and are often caused by, the visible economy.

5. Innovative new economic models and institutions, such as worker-ownership, consumer cooperatives, land trusts, community money systems, etc.;

made invisible because they have other purposes in addition to—or instead of—the conventional business goal of profit maximization;

now becoming recognized because people realize we need new economic models; and because these innovations continue to multiply in variety and numbers.

6. Economic forms from nonwestern and nonindustrial cultures;

made invisible because they were created by nonwhite, nonmodern people; because it was assumed they had nothing to teach modern people, or that their experiences were not applicable to Western society;

now becoming recognized because modern societies are growing less culturally arrogant, and are learning to honor other cultures and their own traditional roots.

7. The naturally diverse, abundant, generative, self-healing, and self-renewing forms and processes of nature;

   made invisible because they are less controllable, messier, and supposedly less efficient than modern technology;

   now becoming recognized because modern people are becoming less arrogant about the supposed omnipotence and perfectibility of technology; more aware of our need to heal the damage we've done to nature; and more aware of nature's patterns and processes in ourselves.

These formerly invisible aspects of the economy point the way toward the postmodern economic paradigm. They include long-ignored, officially disregarded parts of life and the activities of people who have been defined as unimportant, without value. They represent activities which have been deprived of material resources, social recognition, and/or legal legitimacy, although they are essential to our survival and well-being. But all these aspects of the invisible economy are now gaining recognition and resources in their own right. Furthermore, they are beginning to influence and transform the institutions and values of the conventional, visible, economy. These processes are helping to create the postmodern economy.

A POSTMODERN WORLDVIEW: THE NATURAL-SYSTEMS MODEL

Another source of the postmodern economic paradigm is a new scientific model of how the world works, based on such principles as individual integrity, mutuality and interdependence, and rhythmic cycles over time. This postmodern worldview, coming out of the latest discoveries of the physical and biological sciences, stands in distinct contrast to modernism, which came out of a hierarchical, fragmented, mechanistic view of the world and of human nature.[6] I believe that as we learn more about the emerging postmodern economic paradigm, we will discover that in many ways its structures and relationships resemble the patterns that characterize natural systems.

In this ecological or natural-systems model, several key phenomena are assumed to shape the interactions and well-being of every participant. One is the existence of complex, multilevel but nonhierarchical structures in which we all participate. Another is the role of time, since cyclical, repeating rhythmic patterns of activity characterize both all living beings and the processes of the universe.

According to the natural-systems model, every living being is made up of smaller and smaller units—organs, cells, molecules, and atoms—each with their own unique properties, although they all participate in promoting the survival and well-being of the larger entity of which they are part. Every living being is also part of increasingly larger systems of connection and interaction—a social community, an ecological or bioregional community, and a planetary ecosystem—each with its own unique properties, although they all influence and are influenced by each individual member.

One crucial point about this ecological, natural-systems model is that it is not hierarchical. No level of organization is superior to any other. Each individual depends on and is supported by both the smaller entities that comprise it and the larger systems in which it participates. And all levels affect each other, not through top-down control but through mutually beneficial interactions based on the interchange of information, energy, and nutrients, and shaped by the constantly recurring rhythms of growth and decline, activity and rest, birth and death and rebirth.

The role of cyclical activity is crucial in this model. It appears that every aspect of the world, every living being, and every organ and cell, is shaped by regular rhythmic cycles of activity, such as breathing and heart rate. These cycles do not represent a flaw or abnormality, nor is any part of a cycle (for example, an expanding phase) better than any other part. In their wholeness, as they continually play out phases of rising and falling, these rhythms and cycles determine the health of every being and system. For example, when a person is hungry, more food is better—up until the moment when you have eaten enough. Beyond that point, more food can cause pain, discomfort, illness, eventually even death. However, once you have eaten enough to satisfy your hunger, you have only to wait a few hours and hunger will return, at which point in time more food again becomes better. In other words, our rhythmic patterns and cycles over time determine the natural limits that affect our well-being.

Because of its simplified, mechanistic view of life, which says that more is better, and less is worse, the modern paradigm fails to recognize that time is a central factor in well-being. By pretending that such cycles and limits do not exist, and assuming that only the expanding (growth) phase of a cycle is beneficial, the modern economic paradigm has created an economy which promotes addiction, stress, disease, and destruction. But in the postmodern paradigm, awareness of these constantly fluctuating natural cycles, rhythmic patterns, and limits leads to economic activities that also fluctuate naturally, rising and falling over time, and that do not require stress or addictions to assure society's well-being.

The natural-systems model also recognizes the integrity and wholeness of every individual system, including of every human being. It acknowledges that mind, body, intellect, and emotions are all interconnected, and that to treat people as if these so-called parts are separate from each other is pathological, and a cause of disease and dysfunction. It assumes that we can improve our health and well-being by reintegrating the fragmented parts of our lives. This perspective can help us recognize that the modern economy may appear to have increased the choices available to us, but it has done so by breaking the wholeness of life into increasingly fragmented pieces, offering us an increasing number of fragments to choose from. So in the postmodern economy, the most important choices become those that help us make our lives more whole.

TOWARD AN ECONOMICS OF MUTUALITY AND EMPOWERMENT

If the modern economic paradigm could be summed up in one central principle, it might be this: More is better: Take the most that you can for yourself.

By contrast, the emerging postmodern economic paradigm might be characterized by *the principle of balance* (Whenever you take, always give back) and *the principle of mutuality* (By honoring yourself and each other, everyone gains).

Balance requires that we recognize when we are taking too much, and when we are taking too little; when we are giving too much, and when we need to take more. Mutuality reminds us that while each individual is unique and each of us needs to affirm our inner wholeness, we also need to build relationships that honor the wholeness of other people and of the natural world around us. These two principles of balance and mutuality are shaping what I call a new economics of empowerment.

The term "empowerment" refers to individuals and communities gaining the ability to shape their own development. The new economic paradigm could be called "the economics of empowerment" because the process of individuals and communities taking more control over their economic activities is one of its central characteristics. However, in the new paradigm, empowerment is shaped by balance and mutuality. These new principles lead to an economics of accountability and responsibility, of individual respect combined with interdependence; to an economics that challenges false categories of superiority and inferiority; to an economics of natural limits, whose goal is to maintain balance in all activities and relationships, rather than allowing them to become distorted by hierarchy, inequitable accumulation of resources, or addictions. As we participate in new kinds of economic institutions and relationships, which are designed to honor each person's uniqueness, to respect our natural cycles and limits, and to restore our wholeness, we become more in touch with ourselves and enhance our ability to make a difference.

NOTES

1. On the tradition-command-market typology, see Robert L. Heilbroner, *The Making of Economic Society*, 5th ed. (Englewood Cliffs, N.J.: Prentice-Hall, 1975), 13–21.

2. Ibid., 13–16.

3. Ibid., 16–18.

4. Ibid., 18–21.

5. Changing attitudes of Western social science toward traditional societies are described in Allan Hoben and Robert Hefner, "The Integrative Revolution Revisited," *World Development*, 19, (January 1991), 17–31.

6. The natural-systems model is described in Fritjof Capra, *The Turning Point: Science, Society, and the Rising Culture* (New York: Bantam, 1983), chap. 9. I am indebted to Capra's emphasis on the role of cyclical rhythms as an essential aspect of health and wholeness.

Chapter 11

NOT BUSINESS-AS-USUAL: NEW DIRECTIONS FOR ENTERPRISES

Over the last twenty-five years, in response to the inadequacies and destructive effects of the modern economic paradigm, there has been a little-publicized but amazing explosion of new kinds of economic institutions, in both modern and developing societies, as alternatives to conventional business. They are meeting the economic needs of individuals and communities while at the same time recognizing that people have physical, emotional, intellectual, social, and spiritual aspects. They promote democratic participation in their operations and recognize the dependency of human well-being upon the well-being of the natural environment.

Some of these new economic institutions are businesses, although their structures and/or goals differ from the conventional ones. Others are not businesses, because they do not sell goods or services, or they do so for reasons other than to make a profit. Since these institutions come in a wide range of forms, and meet the needs of individuals, communities, and/or the Earth through a diverse range of activities, and since they empower people as an integral part of their economic activities, they could be called generically "empowering enterprises."

Organizationally, empowering enterprises may be very small or quite large; privately owned, owned cooperatively by their participants, or run on behalf of a larger community. They may be profit-making or not-for-profit; organized by private individuals, community or neighborhood groups, religious organizations, government agencies; or combinations of these or other forms.[1]

THE ECONOMIC SIGNIFICANCE OF EMPOWERING ENTERPRISES

In the old paradigm, "the economy" is defined by the activities of businesses in producing and selling goods and services, and by customers' activities of buying, accumulating, and consuming goods and services. Success for both businesses and individuals is measured by increasing accumulations of money and material wealth. But this model has led to enormous waste, imbalances, and inequities in modern societies.

In the emerging postmodern economy, enterprises use resources more carefully and constantly seek ways to recirculate resources so they go where most needed. The resources which these new enterprises create, or which flow through them to individuals and communities include money, natural resources, land, tools and technology, technical skills and information, communication networks, organization-building skills, and power and decision making. The underlying goal of empowering enterprises is to restructure the accumulation and use of resources in order to empower individuals and communities, while continuously balancing and restoring the larger system.

As empowering enterprises shift the accumulation of resources, they redefine the activities that make up the economy. Their activities reveal that a healthy economy includes much more than merely production and consumption. Other crucial economic functions performed by empowering enterprises include aligning economic activities with noneconomic values; using resources more carefully to minimize waste and prevent environmental damage; building collaborative and community relationships to increase wealth and enhance people's well-being; and redistributing resources for greater equity and individual and community empowerment.

VALUES-ORIENTED ENTERPRISES

Many of the enterprises in this category are profit-making businesses that demonstrate that they can produce and sell goods and services while serving goals other than profit maximization, and that they can make a good profit while respecting employees, suppliers, and customers, supporting the local community, and honoring the natural environment. It should be noted that values-oriented businesses could more fully express their socially and environmentally responsible values if larger societal assumptions about and legal restrictions on business activity were altered. Needed changes include reducing the pressure on businesses to grow and maximize profits and allowing them to engage in more cooperative, less competitive forms of operation. These issues are discussed later in this chapter and in chapter 19.

Socially Responsible Businesses (SRBS)

In modern market economies, businesses are legally allowed, to greater or lesser extents, to abuse their employees, manipulate their suppliers and customers, eliminate their competitors, destroy plant and animal species, disrupt ecosystems, and abandon their local communities, leaving widespread economic and social devastation when other locales appear more lucrative. At the same time—within the limits allowed by law—caring, concerned business owners, managers, and other employees can also use their positions and companies to actively promote more ethical, humanitarian, participatory, environmental, and other desirable policies. While some companies have a long and well-known history of such commitment, interest in socially responsible business has blossomed dramatically since the 1970s, especially in the United States.

SRBs express their values through innovative practices, often pioneering employee-friendly policies such as on-site child care, generous family leave, gender and ethnic diversity, flattened hierarchies and employee participation in shaping the workplace. Some encourage—even pay—employees to take time off from the job to do community work. They may also set aside a regular portion of their profits as donations to community and environmental causes.

SRB policies often run counter to conventional business practices. For example, some SRBs limit the range in employees' salaries. In many conventional businesses, especially in the United States, the Chief Executive Officer or other top executives may earn up to 1,000 times as much as the lowest paid employees. Some SRBs have limited this ratio to 5:1 or 7:1, on the grounds that this improves overall worker morale and productivity. Other SRBs make their financial records open to the public.

Many SRBs are privately owned, and their innovative policies reflect the beliefs of their owners or managers. They can also be owned directly by those who work in them or have some other unconventional ownership structure.[2]

Worker-owned Businesses

The unique structure of worker-owned businesses allows them to be more responsive to workers' well-being, local community needs, long-term economic goals, and to promote other beneficial and empowering values. In the United States, interest in worker-owned businesses has increased over the last two decades, particularly because they offer a way to save jobs and keep firms in local communities when an outside owner wants to shut down a local branch, or when the existing owner has to retire. Supportive state and federal legislation, growing union interest, and the development of technical assistance groups with experience in helping people organize and run successful worker-owned businesses have all contributed to this trend. By the end of the 1980s, there were over three hundred worker-owned businesses in the United States of various ownership structures, ranging from enterprises of twenty workers or less to large corporations with thousands of employees. They produced a variety of goods and services, and their combined sales totaled nearly $10 billion annually.

Worker-owned firms have several unique advantages. Since employees have both financial ownership of and decision-making participation in the places where they work, their morale and empowerment are enhanced. As a result, research shows that worker-owned firms average 20 percent higher productivity than conventional businesses. In addition, they are not under the control of distant owners, nor are they under pressure from outside stockholders to produce short-term profits. Because the workers and owners are one and the same, they can direct resources to the company's long-term benefit, improving the work environment and performance for the long term. And when the owners are workers who live in the same communities where their companies are located, worker-owned businesses are going to stay in their communities, providing jobs and economic opportunities in the long term. Thus, worker ownership is a win-win solution that simultaneously benefits workers, customers, and local communities.[3]

Supporting Values-oriented Enterprises

Increasingly, people are choosing what to buy not just on the basis of price, but by taking into account the values and actions of the businesses they buy from. And many people are no longer content to invest their money solely on the basis of where they can get the highest return, but are actively seeking to lend or invest with companies that adhere to those investors' social, political, environmental, or other values.

In response to this interest, various businesses and nonprofit organizations now offer services or resources to assist socially conscious consumers and socially conscious investors to locate and interact with values-oriented businesses. Some groups publish guidebooks, such as *Shopping for a Better World* and *Rating America's Corporate Conscience*, which evaluate thousands of products and businesses by their employee, community, environmental and other policies to assist people in making product choices that express their values. The newly developed Green Cross in the United States, and similar symbols established by environmentally concerned groups in other nations, are helping consumers identify products that make the least environmentally harmful impact.[4]

Many investment advisors, companies, and publications now assist socially responsible investors. Through organizations such as the Social Investment Forum, advocates of socially responsible investment inform and support each other and further promote socially responsible business and socially responsible investing. Advocates of socially responsible investing have documented that by investing in environmentally clean, ethical, and employee-friendly companies, the investor not only promotes more just and sustainable values, but may make as much money, if not more, than by investing in greedy, exploitative companies.[5]

Any discussion of support for values-oriented enterprises must include Co-op America, even though it is a one-of-a-kind enterprise in the United States. It is a national nonprofit membership organization that integrates and promotes the values-aligning trends described here, utilizing publications and organizing campaigns to advocate more widely for a just and sustainable economy. In addition to its yearly national directory of over one thousand socially responsible businesses, it also publishes a quarterly magazine that reports on many aspects of a more-empowering economy, including environmentally responsible tourism, community economic development, boycotts against abusive businesses, and much, much more.[6]

RESOURCE-PROTECTING ENTERPRISES

By using resources more carefully, new kinds of enterprises not only reduce pollution and protect the natural environment and human health but also produce wealth more efficiently and protect it from exploitation.

Materials-conserving Enterprises

Many new enterprises emphasize the conservation of material and natural resources. Green, or environmentally responsible businesses (also known as eco-businesses), are an important branch of the socially responsible business movement. Some of them solve environmental problems such as pollution and the generation of toxics. Others use resources in more environmentally responsible ways, such as making products out of recycled materials.[7]

Reducing energy waste is a goal of many resource-protecting enterprises. Examples include energy-conserving design and construction businesses, and utilities that promote energy conservation among their customers or that replace fossil fuels with less environmentally harmful, renewable energy sources.[8]

Both businesses and community-based enterprises are reclaiming, reusing, and recycling materials, and some enterprises assist them in setting up such programs.[9]

Market-exempt Enterprises

Resources needing protection include not only natural and material resources but also socially and economically beneficial organizations and relationships. The goal of market-exempt enterprises is to remove valuable material and organizational resources from the market so they cannot be sold off to the highest bidder. Instead, they are preserved under the direct control of present or future users.

Housing cooperatives (Resident-owned multiple housing units). Although each apartment is the private property of its inhabitants, all residents agree that if they move they will not sell to speculators or absentee landlords, and they will keep the price within moderate guidelines regardless of current market value. Through these mechanisms, housing co-ops keep property owner-occupied and affordable for future residents.[10]

Land trusts. A land trust is a nonprofit organization that owns land in order to keep it from being sold and assures that it is used only for a specific designated goal. Its purpose may be to protect scenic, historic, or wild land from future development, or to preserve working farmland, often near urban or suburban areas. In land trusts designed to protect affordable housing, residents own their own dwelling units, and can resell them if they move, but lease the land under their homes from the land trust.[11]

Worker-owned businesses. Using a structure called the "internal capital account," worker-owned businesses can be designed to assure that the business will always remain in the hands of those who work there. This legal mechanism specifies that when worker-owners retire or quit, they cannot sell their shares to outside buyers, but only to the company itself. This protects worker-owned companies from takeover and ravaging by outside buyers.[12]

COMMUNITY-BUILDING ENTERPRISES

The whole economy consists not only of the interactions of businesses and consumers but also of communities that support people as they go about the activities of meeting their needs. Community-building enterprises enhance collaborative relationships and communities as a way to maximize people's wealth, empowerment, and well-being.

Linking Enterprises

Linking enterprises demonstrate that competing with others in order to maximize one's accumulation of wealth and power is not the only model by which our economic institutions can operate. By promoting communication and cooperation among businesses, or between producers and consumers, linking enterprises empower people while more fully meeting their needs.

Consumer cooperatives (Enterprises owned and run by, or on behalf of their customers). They include food co-ops, child care co-ops, and other enterprises of all sizes and levels of formality or informality, which offer various products or services. Sometimes they offer lower prices or regular refunds to their member-owners. Even more important, their activities can respond to members' needs and values. For example, many food co-ops support local farmers and environmental practices through their food purchases.[13] In the United States today there are more than 30,000 consumer co-ops. They include 4,000 consumer goods co-ops, 13,000 member-owner credit unions, nearly 100 cooperative banks, nearly 5,000 housing co-ops, 100 cooperatively owned insurance companies, 1,200 user-owned rural utilities, and 115 telecommunication and cable TV co-ops.[14]

Community-supported agriculture (CSA). CSAs link people directly with their food source. Members (shareholders) contract yearly with a local farmer, paying in advance for the food they will receive during the subsequent growing season. Members travel to the farm or other designated location regularly to pick up their food. Some CSAs invite members to participate in planting and harvesting. CSA farmers benefit by receiving cash up-front and can concentrate on growing food, freed from the need to find a market. Members are guaranteed fresh, healthy food, know exactly how it is grown, and can have input into the crops is offered. The direct connection with a farm is also an empowering educational experience for many CSA members.[15]

Seikatsu Club. Perhaps the most fully developed of a new-paradigm enterprise that directly links customers with producers is the Seikatsu Consumer Cooperative Club of Japan. Founded in 1965 as a buying club to obtain lower-cost, high-quality milk products, Seikatsu now includes 225,000 households that collectively purchase about $700 million worth of food and other household products each year. Emphasizing an anti-consumerist ethic, Seikatsu offers only basic products that are beneficial to human and environmental health, and through its own farms produces what it cannot obtain commercially. Also, in the Seikatsu network are 161 worker-owned businesses, including retail stores and home health care service for the elderly. Over 90 percent of Seikatsu's consumers and workers are women, and the organization emphasizes a grassroots-run, democratic structure.[16]

Linked Businesses

Some linking enterprises are replacing the business competition model with more collaborative relationships among businesses to better serve both the enterprises and their customers. This is not as easy as it sounds, especially in the United States, because the market model assumes that any attempt by businesses to cooperate with each other is "collusion"—that is, companies scheming together in order to take advantage of their customers. In other words, the modern paradigm may force businesses to compete against each other, even when this is unnecessary or harmful, because it assumes that it is unlikely for businesses to cooperate for their customers' benefit. Ironically, with increasing global economic competition, the United States has recently legalized some forms of business cooperation—in order to increase U.S. competitiveness against other nations.[17]

Within the limits of the law, several models of positive business cooperation, either for informal support or as active co-participants in business ventures, have already emerged in modern nations.

Supportive small business networks. The Briarpatch Network in the San Francisco is an important model of constructive business cooperation. Its members, representatives of 150 separate small businesses, agree to a statement of ideals thath includes environmental responsibility, commitment to quality rather than profit maximization, and making financial records open to the public. Briarpatch has sponsored parties, classes, workshops, and technical assistance, and over 800 local businesses, both members and nonmembers, have utilized its services. Briarpatch has inspired similar networks throughout the world.[18]

Active cooperation among autonomous businesses. Especially in Europe, independent small businesses are developing innovative forms of cooperation, such as temporary alliances among distinct firms to carry out specific ventures. A prominent example is the network of independent but regularly affiliating small textile companies in the Prato area of Italy.[19] Another important example is the Mondragon network of thriving worker-owned industries in the Basque region of Spain. These enterprises assist each other in a variety of ways. For example, instead of being laid off, workers who are no longer needed in one company can move to another company within the network that needs more staff.[20]

Community-based Economic Development

Many communities in modern nations remain poor because the wealth of their inhabitants is taken out of the community and redistributed to wealthier people who live in wealthier communities. In *Reclaiming Capital: Democratic Initiatives and Community Development*, an innovative study of community economies, Christopher and Hazel Dayton Gunn describe how wealth flows out of poor communities in the form of rents to outside landlords; mortgage payments to outside banks; wages, rents, and profits from local stores paid to employees, landlords, and owners who live outside the community; and high energy costs paid to outside utilities.[21]

It is widely assumed that bringing new businesses into an economically depressed community will revive its economy. That's why many poor neighborhoods without an adequate economic base, and many municipalities that have lost their economic base, are seeking to attract new businesses. But much of the wealth such businesses generate also leaves the local community. In an impressive case study, the Gunns analyze the flow of money generated by the local branch of a fast-food chain. They conclude that about three-fourths of the money that local people spend at their neighborhood burger franchise will leave the community! Most of that money goes out to regional and national banks, insurance companies, outside advertising agencies, large corporations that supply raw materials or intermediate products, and to outside utilities, owners, and stockholders.[22]

Such problems have led to the recent innovation known as community economic development (CED). Whether implemented in a locale within a modern nation, or in the Third World, the goal of community economic development is to create locally controlled wealth-producing institutions and to assure that locally generated wealth remains in the local community so it can be recycled and reinvested for further local wealth creation.

Varieties of Community Economic Development

A community in need of economic development may be defined socially—for example, the members of a specific racial or ethnic group or a group of mothers on welfare. Or geographically—for example, a specific neighborhood, town, city, rural area, or larger region. CED programs integrate the experience, culture, and skills of the community's members into the process of identifying local needs and resources and creating the plans and new enterprises that will be developed. The CED process can be initiated by a community on its own behalf, or by concerned nonprofits, religious groups, business associations, and labor unions, often in cooperation with consultants or organizers experienced in CED.[23] Various locally-controlled institutions can accumulate and recirculate locally-generated wealth as part of CED.

Community development credit unions. These are lending organizations, owned by their depositors, that target loans for specific purposes, such as housing rehab or development of minority-owned businesses. There are over one hundred community development credit unions in the U.S.[24]

Community development corporations (CDCs). Originated in the United States in the late 1960s, CDCs are community-run nonprofit corporations in low-income, urban neighborhoods or rural areas, specifically designed to stimulate local economic development. Many CDCs coordinate construction or renovation of affordable housing. Others start new local businesses and channel the profits back to the CDC, to be used for further CED programs.[25]

Regional Community Economic Development

As modern nations continue to lose once-thriving industries, entire cities, towns and even larger regions encompassing several cities and towns begin to need economic redevelopment. Regionwide CED approaches include:

Community-labor coalitions. Catalyzed by the recent devastation of former industrial areas in the northeast and midwest United States, local coalitions made up of unions, community organizations, religious groups, and other interested parties have been organized to stimulate local economic development that can more fully serve the needs of local residents, workers, and their communities. Similar coalitions have also been formed in response to the shut-down of former military facilities to explore new uses for their resources, a process known as economic conversion.[26]

Rural community economic development. In the United States, several organizations have as their goal the rebuilding of this nation's agriculture-based rural communities, while maintaining a uniquely rural way of life. They promote independently owned small farms and other locally owned agriculture-based enterprises and environmentally sustainable practices; and they connect interested new farmers with available land. Their activities often have a political component as well, by exposing and opposing the increasing domination of the rural sector by large agribusiness corporations.[27]

Sustainable CED. Increasingly, CED programs emphasize environmentally responsible enterprises in order to improve the community's environmental and economic well-being simultaneously. CED advocates are promoting environmentally healthful projects both for urban and rural areas.[28]

Community economic development is an empowering approach to economic improvement because it identifies the residents of a materially poor community not as dependent clients but as economic actors with their own skills and cultural resources. And rather than identifying the community as an inadequate area which can only be improved through the intervention of superior economic institutions, it builds on the community's own potential for wealth creation.

RESOURCE-REDISTRIBUTING ENTERPRISES

Within the modern economic paradigm, resources are constantly being redistributed, but they move in the wrong direction: from those at the bottom of society to those at the top. Typically, resources move from individuals and small businesses to big corporations, from communities of color to more affluent, white communities, from the Third World to modern nations and from those with less power to the more powerful. So one of the most significant innovations of the emerging new economy are institutions that voluntarily redistribute wealth, power, information, and other resources outright, from those with more to those who have less.

In the old paradigm, voluntary redistribution of resources from those with more to those with less can only be understood as charity, benevolent givers helping the needy and inferior. Uplifting media stories occasionally report on resource redistribution by "extraordinary" individuals e.g., ex-President Jimmy Carter building homes for the poor, or a low-income woman who devotes her free time to helping others even less fortunate. This makes voluntary redistribution seem like something unusual, something few of us could participate in on a regular basis or that would have no significant impact on our larger social or economic problems. But as the following examples suggest, resource redistribution can be done by anyone, and it can increase equity and empowerment for both givers and recipients.

Community banks and community loan funds. These enterprises target loans to lower-income communities for empowering purposes, such as construction of affordable housing or community economic development. The South Shore Bank of Chicago was the first full-scale community bank in the United States, with others organized recently in New York City and Vermont. Community banks and loan funds are needed because conventional banks and lending agencies often refuse loans to poorer clients on the grounds that they are poor credit risks. Racism, or the small size of the requested loans, are usually the real reasons for their refusal. So it should be noted that community banks and loan funds have a superior record of loans repaid—especially in contrast to the poor repayment records that led to such debacles as the S&L scandal.[29]

Affirmative or high social-impact investing. A variation of socially responsible investing, affirmative investing places loans or investments not into conventional businesses or stocks but in community-oriented enterprises such as community banks and loan funds, and community economic development projects, among others. Although the return on such investments may be less than conventional rates, investors who choose this route are willing to forego maximum financial return because they support and benefit from the increased social stability, equity, and community empowerment their loans or investments will help create.[30]

Microlenders. Over 200 organizations in the United States now provide loans from a few hundred to a few thousand dollars to budding entrepreneurs. Loans are made especially to residents of low-income communities, helping them turn their interests and skills into successful businesses. Many microlenders also offer business education,   technical assistance, and peer-support groups for loan recipients. Microlending is creating jobs and income for low-income people in both the United States and Third World nations.[31]

Technical assistance. A wide range of consulting enterprises, both not-for-profit and profit-making, disseminate information, skills, and other resources to people seeking greater economic empowerment. Areas of expertise range from hands-on production skills, business, organizational, financial, and political action techniques to community economic development and environmentally oriented community-planning assistance. Such consultants also refer clients to funding sources and larger support networks. Many such groups are included in the endnotes of this chapter.

Voluntary redistribution for personal empowerment. To avoid the pitfalls of anonymous charity, many redistributing enterprises encourage open communication between recipients and donors, and emphasize that both donors and recipients can benefit, learn, grow, and become more empowered when donations go to projects for social and economic change. This process is documented by Christopher Mogil and Anne Slepian in *We Gave Away a Fortune*. Their book discusses the social and psychological barriers to voluntary redistribution and includes the personal stories of individuals who have taken up this challenge. Also described are many organizations that connect donors with empowering projects. For example, the National Association of Community Development Loan Funds lends money at below-market rates to low-income community groups in the United States, and the Ashoka Foundation makes grants to Third-World individuals who are providing creative leadership for social or environmental problems. Mogil and Slepian emphasize that resource redistribution can be done by anyone, whether rich or poor, and that money is not the only resource we have to give.[32]

BUILDING A NEW MODEL OF THE ECONOMY

Empowering enterprises are making visible many crucial economic processes and relationships, such as mutuality, open communication, cooperation, community building, resource protection, and resource redistribution, which are not valued by the old paradigm. Moving beyond business-as-usual, they are demonstrating a rich variety of new models for how an economy can operate.

NOTES

1. The following books provide in-depth information about empowering enterprises, including theory, legal and technical information, contacts and resource lists, and many detailed examples: Susan Meeker-Lowry, *Economics As If the Earth Really Mattered* (Philadelphia: New Society Publishers, 1988); Susan Meeker-Lowry, *Invested in the Common Good* (Philadelphia: New Society Publishers, forthcoming, 1995); Severyn T. Bruyn and James Meehan, eds., *Beyond the Market and the State* (Philadelphia: Temple University Press, 1987); Paul Ekins, ed., *The Living Economy: A New Economics in the Making* (New York: Routledge & Kegan Paul, 1986); and Guy Dauncey, *After the Crash: The Emergence of the Rainbow Economy* (New York.: Bootstrap Press, 1988).

2. On socially responsible business, see Willis Harman and John Hormann, *Creative Work: The Constructive Role of Business in a Transforming Society* (Indianapolis: Knowledge Systems, Inc., 1990); Tom Chappell, *The Soul of a Business: Managing for Profit and the Common Good* (New York: Bantam, 1993); Paul Hawken, *The Ecology of Commerce: A Declaration of Sustainability* (New York: Harper Business, 1994); *Business Ethics* magazine, available from 1107 Hazeltine Blvd., Suite 530, Chaska, MN 55318; Co-op America's *National Green Pages*, 1994 Edition, available from Co-op America, 1612 "K" St. NW, Suite 600, Washington, D.C. 20006; Businesses for Social Responsibility, 1030 15th St. NW, Washington D.C. 20005, (202) 842-5400. On the principles behind—and problems with—a salary ratio of 1:5 at Ben & Jerry's, see Erik Larson, "I scream, you scream....," *Utne Reader*, January/February 1989, 64–75.

3. On worker ownership, see James D. Megson and Michael O'Toole, *Employee Ownership: The Vehicle for Community Development and Local Economic Control* (Boston: The ICA Group, 1993). This and other resources on worker ownership are available from The ICA Group, 20 Park Plaza, Suite 1127, Boston, MA 02116, (617) 338-0010. Also contact the National Center for Employee Ownership, 2201 Broadway, Suite 807, Oakland, CA 94612, (510) 272-9461.

4. On socially responsible consuming, see Rosalyn Will et al., *Shopping For A Better World* (New York: Council on Economic Priorities, 1989) available from CEP, 30 Irving Pl., New York, NY, 10003, (212) 420-1133; Council on Economic Priorities, *Rating America's Corporate Conscience* (Reading, Mass.: Addison-Wesley, 1987); and Green Seal, 1250 23rd St. NW, Washington, DC 20037, (202) 331-7337.

5. On socially responsible investing, see Amy L. Domini and Peter Kinder, *Ethical Investing* (Reading Mass.: Addison-Wesley, 1986), Ritchie P. Lowry, *Good Money: Profitable Social Investing in the '90s* (New York: W. W. Norton & Co., 1991); see also the listings in Co-op America's *National Green Pages* (under "Financial/Investment Services"). The Domini Social Index has documented that socially responsible companies tend to provide higher returns than conventional firms; contact Kinder, Lydenberg, Domini & Co., 129 Mt. Auburn St., Cambridge, MA 02138, (617) 547-7479.

6. Co-op America publishes *Co-Op America Quarterly* magazine and the *National Green Pages:* c/o Co-op America, 1612 "K" St. NW, Suite 600, Washington, D.C. 20006, (202) 872-5307.

7. On green businesses (especially opportunities for small business), see *In Business: The Magazine for Environmental Entrepreneuring*, 419 State Ave., Emmaus, PA 18049, (215) 967-4135. They also issue a yearly directory of green businesses. Also contact EcoExpo, 14260 Ventura Blvd., Suite 201, Sherman Oaks, CA 91423, (818) 906-2700.

8. On energy conservation, see the American Council for an Energy-Efficient Economy, 1001 Connecticut Ave. NW, Washington, D.C. 20036 (202) 429-8873; also the Rocky Mountain Institute, 1739 Snowmass Creek Rd., Snowmass, CO 81654-9199.

9. On sustainable-materials use, see John E. Young, *Discarding the Throwaway Society*, Worldwatch Paper 101 (Washington D.C.: Worldwatch Institute, January 1991); also the Institute for Local Self-Reliance, 2425 18th St. NW, Washington D.C 20009, (202) 232-4108.

10. On housing cooperatives, contact the National Association of Housing Cooperatives, 1614 King St., Alexandria, VA 22314, (703) 549-5201.

11. On land trusts, contact The Land Trust Alliance, 1319 F St. NW, Washington, D.C. 20006, (202) 638-4725; also the Institute for Community Economics, 57 School St., Springfield, MA 01105, (413) 746-8660.

12. On internal capital accounts that keep worker-owned firms in the hands of the workers, see Frank T. Adams and Gary B. Hansen, *Putting Democracy To Work: A Practical Guide For Starting Worker-Owned Businesses* (Eugene, Ore.: Hulogos'i Communications, 1987), 89–91.

13. On consumer cooperatives, contact the National Cooperative Business Association, 1401 N.Y. Ave. NW, Washington, D.C. 20005-2166, (202) 638-6222.

14. Gar Alperovitz, "Ameristroika is the Answer," *Washington Post*, 13 December 1992, sec. C.

15. On community-supported agriculture (CSA), contact the Biodynamic Farming and Gardening Association, P.O. Box 550, Kimberton, PA 19442.

16. Information and bibliography on the Seikatsu Club appear in *Grassroots Economic Organizing Newsletter*, Issue 12, March/April 1994, 1–8, available from GEO, P.O. Box 5065, New Haven, CT 06525. See also Mark Worth, "Community Economics: Cooperatives Can Extend the Democratic Clout of Consumers and Workers into Whole New Areas," *In Context*, Issue 36, Fall 1993, 24–26: or request more information directly from Seikatsu Club Consumers' Cooperative, 3-2-28 Miyasaka, Setagaya-Ku, Tokyo 156 Japan.

17. Barriers to business cooperation, and cooperative alliances among businesses in Europe and Japan which could serve as models, are a major theme of Severyn T. Bruyn, *A Future for the American Economy: The Social Market* (Stanford, Calif.: Stanford University Press, 1991), esp. chaps. 6 and 7. On the trend toward cooperation among businesses locally, nationally, and internationally, see also Jessica Lipnack and Jeffrey Stamps, *The TeamNet Factor: Bringing the Power of Boundary Crossing into the Heart of Your Business* (Essex Junction, VT: Oliver Wight Publications, 1993).

18. For more on Briarpatch, see Dauncey, *After the Crash*, 121–122; and Michael Phillips, "What Small Business Experience Teaches about Economic Theory," in Ekins, ed., *The Living Economy*, 272–280. Phillips is a founder of Briarpatch, and this article summarizes many of its activities and implications.

19. On linked small businesses in Northern Italy, see Michael Piore and Charles Sabel, *The Second Industrial Divide* (New York: Basic Books, 1984).

20. On the Mondragon worker-owned cooperatives, see William Foote Whyte and Kathleen King Whyte, *Making Mondragon* (Ithaca, N.Y.: ILR Press, 1988).

21. Christopher Gunn and Hazel Dayton Gunn, *Reclaiming Capital: Democratic Initiatives and Community Development* (Ithaca, N.Y.: Cornell University Press, 1991), 38–43.

22. On how a community's wealth leaves through a local McDonald's, see Gunn and Gunn, *Reclaiming Capital*, 25–36. See also Hawken, *The Ecology of Commerce*, 144–147, for similar examples.

23. On community economic development, see *Community Economic Development Strategies* (Chicago: Center for Urban Economic Development, University of Illinois at Chicago, 1987); John L. McKnight, *The Future of Low-Income Neighborhoods and the People Who Reside There: A Capacity-Oriented Strategy for Neighborhood Development* (Evanston, Ill.: Center for Urban Affairs and Policy Research, Northwestern University, 1987); *The Neighborhood Works* magazine, published by Center for Neighborhood Technology, 2125 W. North Ave., Chicago, IL 60647, (312) 278-4800; *Geo (Grassroots Economic Organizing) Newsletter*, P.O. Box 5065, New Haven, CT 06525; the annual Management and Community Development Institute (training program), c/o Lincoln Filene Center, Tufts University, Medford, MA 02155, (617) 627-3453; and Gunn and Gunn, *Reclaiming Capital*, chaps. 3 and 4.

24. On community development credit unions, see Gunn and Gunn, *Reclaiming Capital*, 62–66.

25. On community development corporations (CDCs), contact the National Congress for Community Economic Development, 1875 Connecticut Ave. NW, Washington D.C. 20009; also Gunn and Gunn, *Reclaiming Capital*, 89–94.

26. On community-labor coalitions, see Dan Swinney, Miguel Vasquez, and Howard Engelskirchen, "Towards a New Vision of Community Economic Development" (1991), available from the Midwest Center for Labor Research, 3411 W. Diversey Ave., Suite 14, Chicago, IL 60647, (312) 278-5418; also

Jeremy Brecher and Tim Costello, eds., *Building Bridges: The Emerging Grassroots Coalition of Labor and Community* (New York: Monthly Review Press, 1990).

27. On rural community economic development, contact the Center for Rural Affairs, P.O. Box 406, Walthill, NE 68067, (402) 846-5428.

28. On environmentally sustainable community economic development in small towns, contact Economic Renewal Program, Rocky Mountain Institute, 1739 Snowmass Creek Rd., Snowmass, CO 81654-9199. In urban areas, see publications by the Center for Neighborhood Technology, 2125 W. North Ave., Chicago, IL 60647 (312) 278-4800, including *Sustainable Manufacturing: Saving Jobs, Saving the Environment;* and *Environmental Business Opportunities for Low-Income Neighborhoods.*

29. On community banks and loan funds, contact the South Shore Bank, 7054 and Jeffery Blvd., Chicago, IL 60649-9989, (312) 288-1000; the Self-Help Credit Union, P.O. Box 3619, Durham, NC 27702 (919) 683-3016; and many other organizations, listed in Co-op America's *National Green Pages* under "Financial/Investment Services."

30. Many organizations that practice high social-impact investing support organizations that make below market-rate loans, such as the National Association of Community Development Loan Funds, 924 Cherry St., Philadelphia, PA 19107, (215) 923-4754; and the National Federation of Community Development Credit Unions; 121 Wall St., 10th Floor, New York, NY 10005, (212) 809-1850.

31. For more on microlending, contact Association for Enterprise Opportunity, 320 N. Michigan Ave., Suite 304, Chicago, IL 60601, (312) 357-0177.

32. On voluntary redistribution for personal empowerment, see Christopher Mogil and Anne Slepian, *We Gave Away a Fortune* (Philadelphia: New Society Publishers, 1992).

Chapter 12

THE FUTURE OF WORK: SEEKING MORE EMPOWERING OPTIONS

Over the last few decades, modern economies have been experiencing enormous changes in the nature of work. For example, the shift from industrial production to service and information jobs has accelerated. Women and Third-World residents are entering the paid work force in increasing numbers. And fulltime, high-paid jobs are being replaced by marginal, low-wage, parttime, and temporary jobs, while unemployment continues to rise.

One response to such changes is to cling to old-paradigm explanations and solutions: to insist that full employment can be achieved through new technological inventions or new markets; to characterize the degradation of paid work as "restructuring" that improves business' profitability; or to blame certain groups, such as women, people of color, or immigrants, for taking "our" jobs.

Another alternative is to assume that these changes signify a transition to a different kind of economy—from an industrial to a postindustrial, postmodern economy. This means that we must explore how we can take advantage of these changes in order to create an economy that offers more fulfilling work opportunities and a more balanced life. This chapter describes some of the ways in which people are responding to these changes in order to create more empowering work and life options.

Individuals and Communities Are Taking More Control over Their Jobs

In the old paradigm, people who need paid work depend for employment on businesses, which depend upon business cycles and the health of the larger economy. Not only are businesses considered the main source of job opportunities, but employers make the rules about what each job entails, and employees have to accept these rules or go find new jobs. In the new paradigm, in response to the degradation of paid work and rising unemployment, many communities are actively creating jobs that will better meet the needs of their members.

One method is through community economic development. In *After The Crash: The Emergence Of The Rainbow Economy*, British community-development consultant Guy Dauncey describes the self-initiated renewal of economically depressed communities in the United States, Canada, Great Britain, Germany, and other Western nations. Residents of these communities discovered unrecognized skills and resources and founded community-development corporations or other community organizations that supported the growth of new businesses. These initiatives have been successful because they utilize a combination of profit-making, cooperatively owned, and not-for-profit enterprises, and because they build on local culture and enhance community and social life along with their economic-development projects.[1]

Many individuals are now taking more control personally over their paid work lives. One example is the increase in home-based work. In the old paradigm, there was a sharp separation between paid, productive work and the home. Increasingly today, people are earning a living by working in their homes rather than going out to work. Home-based work can offer a variety of advantages, including more time because commuting is unnecessary and more flexibility in regard to work schedules, activities, and attire. For many parents—both women and men—home-based work allows them to care for their children while earning a living.

A new form of home-based work today is telecommuting: business or government employees who work part- or fulltime in their homes while maintaining regular communication with their employers through electronic technologies. In 1992, 6.6 million U.S. employees were telecommuters, and the numbers will continue to rise.[2] Incidentally, because telecommuters do not drive to work they save energy and reduce pollution. As a result, a number of localities, including the city of Los Angeles and the state of Massachusetts, are promoting telecommuting as an environmental measure.[3]

Self-employment is another way that people can take control of their work, and many home-based workers are self-employed. In the United States in 1992, 11.7 million people ran their own home-based businesses parttime, and 12.1 million ran a business fulltime from home. However, neither home-based work nor self-employment guarantee either greater empowerment or economic success, and both can have a downside.[4]

The trend to greater worker control over one's paid work is also extending to conventional workplaces. Employers are now discovering that workers who have more control over their job tasks and workplace environments are physically and emotionally healthier and more productive. Many forward-looking businesses are flattening job hierarchies, providing opportunities for workers to enhance their skills, and increasing employee participation in workplace decision making. Some nations, such as Sweden and Norway, now have national legislation that requires employers to give workers some decision-making power in shaping their jobs and workplace environments.[5]

The Empowerment of Women

The increasing number of women entering the paid workforce has conflicting effects on their quality of life. Women are systematically segregated into lower-paid occupational areas, and most work a double day, first on the job and then in the home. As a result, many women wage-earners suffer physical and emotional stress and are overworked, yet they and their families remain economically disadvantaged.[6] Nevertheless, the opportunity to earn an income and to work outside the home is also an empowering experience that can benefit both women and their families.[7] In order to optimize these gains, women need more economically and socially supportive work environments.

One approach is women's economic development. A growing network of nonprofit economic-development programs in the United States and around the world is training women—especially those on welfare, the very poor, and women of color—to start and run their own businesses. Some socially responsible loan funds are focusing their lending to women-owned enterprises.[8]

Feminist activist and writer Gloria Steinem describes the results as "women's economic empowerment." She notes that these women-initiated enterprises have unique characteristics. They integrate traditional economic activities such as job training and management with innovations such as flexible work schedules, child care, assertiveness training, and cultural celebrations. They emphasize participatory decision making; many of these enterprises are worker-owned. And they are challenging the assumptions of conventional economics, empowering women even more through economic literacy and political action.[9]

Advocates for women's economic empowerment also note that because conventional community economic development programs assume that men are the primary breadwinners, they focus on job creation for unemployed men. Since women with children actually constitute the largest group of the poor, women's advocates are promoting gender-oriented community economic analyses that specifically look at women's economic situations and the effects of proposed development programs on women. And they are urging economic development programs tailored specifically for women.[10]

Another aspect of women's economic empowerment is described by Patricia Aburdene and John Naisbitt in their book *Megatrends For Women*. These new-paradigm business consultants say that as more women rise within corporations or start their own businesses, women's less hierarchical, more democratic leadership styles are humanizing the workplace and empowering those with whom they work.[11] (See chapter 13 for more on women-owned businesses.)

Women also are demanding that their unpaid work be included in measures of the economy. Following the 1985 International Women's Conference in Kenya, the United Nations passed a resolution urging national governments to recognize the value of women's unpaid production. Since then, several European and Third World nations have found ways to count women's unpaid work, while the United States and Canada have not yet figured out how to implement this resolution. Toward this end, African-American Congresswoman Barbara-Rose Collins (D-MI) is currently sponsoring the "Unremunerated Work Act of 1993" in the U.S. Congress, and other women around the world are participating in a range of initiatives, both organized and spontaneous, to get unpaid work acknowledged.[12]

Recovering from Job Addiction and Work Addiction

As unemployment rises and modern nations experience increasing pressures from the global economy, the debate over work-time has once again moved into public prominence. In Europe, which is suffering severely from sustained high unemployment, many government leaders, economists, union representatives, forward-looking businesspeople, and others are now proposing that work hours officially be shortened in order to reduce unemployment, share the existing jobs more widely, and improve the quality of people's lives by allowing them more time for family and personal needs.[13] And as this is being written, the U.S. Congressional Black Political Caucus is sponsoring a bill to institute a 30-hour workweek in the United States for the same reasons. [14]

It might be argued that we already have shorter work-time, in the form of poorly paid parttime jobs without benefits. It makes no sense to argue for shorter work-time unless all jobs, especially parttime jobs, have regular benefits and pay enough for earners to support their families. Workers also need to have more control over their work schedules in order to benefit fully from reduced work hours.[15] Supporters of shorter work-time who are considering these and other related issues include economist Juliet Schor, author of *The Overworked American*, and groups such as the Society for the Reduction of Human Labor.[16] A comprehensive and lively study of work addiction and job addiction, with practical steps for personal and community recovery, is *Working Harder Isn't Working*, by Canadian therapist and shorter work-time activist Bruce O'Hara. O'Hara has also founded the Workwell Network, a grassroots organization in Canada actively advocating shorter work-time policies and lifestyles.[17]

The debate over work-time is just beginning. In the next few months and years it will spread more widely, and will involve many more people, perspectives, and new experiments in shorter work-time and greater flexibility in people's paid-work arrangements.

THE NEED FOR EMPOWERING WORK OPPORTUNITIES

Many people are dubious about shorter work-time because they fear that others would only use their additional free time to watch TV or get into trouble. This fear that people would misuse their unsupervised time is challenged by the reality of what many individuals actually do outside of their jobs. In their free time—as hobbies, recreation, or community volunteer work—millions of people freely perform all kinds of productive, creative activities, and even all kinds of mundane activities essential for life. In self-chosen activities—from handicrafts to home remodeling; from vegetable gardening to gourmet cooking; from volunteering in schools, youth centers, nursing homes, hospitals, and hospices; in recycling and environmental restoration programs; to roughing it in country cabins or on camping trips—people voluntarily seek out opportunities to do those activities that have always constituted the basic, everyday work of life.

It's ironic that so much destruction—of people's lives, health, and relationships, and of the natural environment—is done in the course of or as the result of paid work. And so much of the healing and restoring work is done by unpaid volunteers, often by people who are seeking more meaning in their lives, often in addition to their paid work.[18] The new paradigm acknowledges that the desire to do work is an innate human need when that work is creative, empowering, self-enhancing, and enjoyable; when it allows us to connect with and enjoy other people; and when it makes a positive, recognizable contribution to the world. People don't want to avoid such work, they want to participate in it. And they don't need to be forced to do it—they need to be allowed to do it.

THE TRANSFORMATION OF WORK

Modern economies are going through difficult times, and many individuals, families, and communities are suffering from the inequitable distribution of work. However, there are discernible trends characterizing a more desirable postmodern economic paradigm. In the postmodern economy, both women and men will participate in a mix of activities: paid work for others, unpaid work for oneself and one's family or household, and unpaid participation in community activities. Work will become more diversified and self-directed and will offer greater opportunities for personal fulfillment and empowerment. We can also assume that people will spend much less time at paid work and will have much more time that they can devote to caring for each other and for the Earth.[19]

These changes are summarized in Figure 12.1.

TABLE 12.1:   THE TRANSFORMATION OF WORK IN MODERN ECONOMIES: FROM DISEMPOWERING JOBS TO EMPOWERING WORK

Disempowering Jobs (The old—modern—paradigm)	*Empowering Work (The emerging postmodern paradigm)*
Provided by:	
An employer: someone who pays you and controls your work.	A range of options: working for a socially-responsible employer; a worker-owned enterprise; yourself; your community; or various combinations.
Role of jobs:	
Jobs are equated with productive work.	Jobs are only one form of work. A better balance between earning money and doing needed work (paid and unpaid).
Purpose:	
Making money for the employers, the investors, and those at the top of the workplace hierarchy. Enhancing the employer's power and/or ego. Earning some income ("It's just a job...").	Meeting real needs in a way that is enjoyable and empowering for all involved. Promoting personal and environmental health and community betterment. Serving both worker's material needs and non-material values.
The work structure:	
Hierarchical. Emphasizes power and superiority of those on top over those below.	Flattened or non-hierarchical structure, participatory or egalitarian.
Decision-making criteria:	
Whatever will bring the owner(s) and top executives the most money and power.	What will lead to the best win/win solutions for workers, their larger community, and the natural environment.
Relation to existing social structure:	
Reinforce existing divisions: gender, racial, economic, age.	Encourages participation and self-development by all, regardless of gender, ethnicity, economic status, age...

Disempowering Jobs	*Empowering Work*
Gender roles:	
Divided into "men's work" and "women's work."	Everyone participates, both leading and following, both producing and caring.
Relation to the environment:	
Destroy the environment by turning it into excessive products and waste.	Sustains the environment that sustains us, with low-impact activities, recyclable materials, and ongoing environmental restoration.
Role of technology:	
Used to control and de-skill workers.	Designed with worker input, to make work more enjoyable and educational. (Appropriate technology).
Skill distribution:	
Extreme specialization. Those at the bottom confined to narrow, routine, unpleasant tasks, with little opportunity to use or expand skills.	All workers share a mix of mental, physical, routine, and complex tasks. Experimentation, skill-enhancement, and worker-redesign of work encouraged.
Access to resources (material, financial, informational):	
Controlled by employers. The most resources go to those on top.	Determined by participants together. Open access to resources for all, hierarchical differentiation limited.
Time perspectives:	
Short-term perspectives. Speed-ups and technological control of time. Work times and total hours determined by employer. Job takes precedence over all other needs.	Long-term perspectives. Work shaped by natural rhythms and cycles. Work times arranged to fit workers' needs. Overall work time limited, allowing ample time and energy for the rest of life.
Employment/Unemployment:	
Overwork for some, not enough work or unemployment for others.	Access to resources for everyone to meet their needs, regardless of whether or not jobs are available.

NOTES

1. On community-initiated economic renewal, see Guy Dauncey, *After the Crash: The Emergence of the Rainbow Economy* (New York: Bootstrap Press, 1988), chaps. 6 and 7.

2. Figures on telecommuting are from Robert E. Calem, "Working at Home, for Better or Worse," *New York Times*, 18 April 1993, sec. 3.

3. On promotion of telecommuting for environmental reasons, contact Massachusetts Office of Energy Resources, Telecommuting Project, 21 Ashburton Pl., Boston, MA 02133, (617) 727-4732.

4. Figures on home-based self-employment from Calem, "Working at Home, for Better or Worse," p. 1. Other resources on home-based businesses include the *National Home Business Report*, P.O. Box 2137, Napierville, IL 60567, and *Micropreneur: The Newsletter for the Kitchen Table Entrepreneur*, Micropreneur Assistance Center, Upper Deerfield Rd., Northwood, NH 03261. On the downside, feminist economist Teresa Amott notes that many home-based workers are sub-contractors, sometimes unreported, who toil for long hours, under intense pressure, for miserably low pay. All family members, including young children, may be pressed to work in such sweatshop conditions in order to produce enough to help the family survive. Many home-based workers in this category are women, especially immigrants who cannot speak the prevailing language or lack other supportive institutions. And the isolation of home-based workers in their homes may prevent them from communicating with each other, seeking shared solutions to their problems, or connecting with labor unions that could help improve their status. On the underside of home-based work and self-employment, see Teresa Amott, *Caught in the Crisis: Women and the U.S. Economy Today* (New York: Monthly Review Press, 1993), 67–72.

5. On the growing trend toward increased employee participation in workplace decision making and other characteristics of more empowering workplaces, see John Naisbitt and Patricia Aburdene, *Re-Inventing the Corporation* (New York: Warner, 1985); Willis Harman and John Hormann, *Creative Work: The Constructive Role of Business in a Transforming Society* (Indianapolis: Knowledge Systems, 1990); and *Inc.*, the magazine for growing companies, available on newsstands or for $19/year from P.O. Box 51534, Boulder, CO 80321-1534. On legislation in Sweden and Norway requiring worker participation in decision making, see "Preventing Stress at Work," *Conditions of Work Digest*, 11 (1992), 18–19 and 139–141.

6. On wage-earning women's overwork and inadequate income, see Amott, *Caught in the Crisis*, chaps. 3, 4, and 5. On reasons for wage-earning women's stress, see "Preventing Stress at Work," 10–13.

7. See Faye J. Crosby, *Juggling: The Unexpected Advantages of Balancing Career and Home for Women and Their Families* (New York: Free Press, 1991).

8. On women's economic development in the U.S., see Mary Kay Blakely, "Quilting New Networks," *Ms.*, March/April 1992, 19–23.

9. On unique characteristics of women' enterprises, see Gloria Steinem, "Creating Jobs We Can't Be Fired From," *Ms.*, March/April 1992, 21–23

10. On the exclusion of women from conventional economic development projects in poor communities, see Nancy Nye, "Putting Women in the Picture: Gender Analysis in Economic Development Planning" (1992), and Nancy Nye, "A Proposal to Enhance the Role of Women in Community Development" (1992), available from Nancy Nye, Community Development Consultant, P.O. Box 61, Taftsville VT 05073. Considerable work has been done on women's economic development issues in the Third World. Nye's articles represent a growing interest in gender-oriented development in modern economies.

11. On how women's leadership styles are transforming the workplace, see Patricia Aburdene and John Naisbitt, *Megatrends for Women: From Liberation to Leadership* (New York: Fawcett, 1992); and Pat Barrentine, ed., *When the Canary Stops Singing: Women's Perspectives on Transforming Business* (San Francisco: Berrett-Koehler, 1993).

12. On the movement to count women's unpaid work, see Gloria Steinem, *Moving Beyond Words* (New York: Simon & Schuster, 1994), chap. 5.

13. On the shorter work-time debate in Europe, see Roger Cohen, "Europeans Considering Shortening Workweek to Relieve Joblessness," *New York Times*, 22 November 1993, sec. A.

14. See Peter T. Kilborn, "U.S. Unions Back Shorter Week, But Employers Seem Reluctant," *New York Times*, 22 November 1993, sec. A.

15. For a study of different types of reduced work-time, how they enhanced or diminished workers' lives, see Cynthia Negrey, *Gender, Time, and Reduced Work* (Albany: State University of New York Press, 1993).

16. For a comprehensive study of overwork in the United States with proposals to relieve it, see Juliet B. Schor, *The Overworked American: The Unexpected Decline of Leisure* (New York: Basic Books, 1991). An organization which provides the latest information on the shorter work-time movement, both in the U.S. and around the world, is the Society for the Reduction of Human Labor, c/o B. K. Hunnicutt, 1610 E. College St., Iowa City, IA 52242, USA; their newsletter costs $25/year.

17. A comprehensive study of overwork in Canada, with concrete suggestions that apply to the United States also, is Bruce O'Hara, *Working Harder Isn't Working: How We Can Save the Environment, the Economy and Our Sanity by Working Less and Enjoying Life More* (Vancouver: New Star Books, 1993), available at bookstores or from New Star Books, 2504 York Ave., Vancouver, B.C. V6K 1E3, Canada, (604) 738-9429, for $19.00 postage paid.

18. In the United States, the growing interest in volunteering for community service and social-change projects is documented by the recent publication of a new magazine, *Who Cares: A Journal of Service and Action*, available from Who Cares, Inc., 1511 K St., NW, Suite 1042, Washington D.C. 20005, (202) 628-1691. It is available on newsstands or by subscription, $15 individual rate, $20 institution, for 4 issues/year. The most recent issue (Spring 1994) includes a directory of over fifty national organizations that sponsor or can direct interested people to service and social-change opportunities.

19. For more on the future of work, see James Robertson, *Future Work: Jobs, Self-Employment and Leisure After the Industrial Age* (New York: Universe Books, 1985); Melissa Everett, *Careers with a Conscience* (New York: Bantam, forthcoming 1995); the *Utne Reader*, July/August 1991 (see the special section entitled "For Love or Money: Making A Living vs. Making a Life," pp. 66-87); the *Co-op America Quarterly* special issue entitled "What in the World are We Working For?" (Summer/Fall 1993); or contact the Center for New Work, 2200 Fuller Rd., Suite 1204B, Ann Arbor, MI 48105.

Chapter 13

THE RESTORATION OF CARING: NEW ROLES FOR WOMEN AND MEN

Caregiving is one of the most troubling problems in modern economies, both because caring is so strongly identified with women and because it is so often part of the invisible, unpaid economy. It is not surprising that many modern nations are experiencing a crisis in care, and that this crisis is forcing people to reexamine both the value of caring and their assumptions about gender roles.

WHY CARING IS DEVALUED

Caregiving individuals assist others to attain well-being. The recipient of care is dependent to some extent on the caregiver. For example, young children can not survive without caregivers who regularly make sure they are fed, cleaned, kept warm, and protected from harm. Likewise, seriously ill or injured people, who may be weak, unconscious, paralyzed, or otherwise incapacitated, may be dependent upon others, temporarily or permanently, for necessary care, as may be frail elders.

Because such dependence is a natural part of every individual's life cycle, caring is an essential activity of daily life. Thus, it's ironic and tragic that because of its hierarchical and patriarchal biases, the modern economic paradigm inherently devalues caregiving.

Because women are biologically designed to give birth and nourish infants out of their own bodies, women as a gender are automatically associated with caregiving. Thus, caring is automatically devalued by patriarchal societies.[1] The need for care is also devalued by any hierarchical system that glorifies the power and invulnerability of the dominant group. Good caregiving requires that the more powerful caregiver respect, rather than dominate, the dependent recipient of care. The fact of dependence is also uncomfortable to those who seek the illusion of invulnerability, since it reminds us that each of us has at one time been, and may again become, helpless, vulnerable, and dependent. In social systems based on domination, both care recipients and caregivers are an embarrassment to be devalued, shoved out of the public gaze, even made invisible.

Furthermore, although caregiving provides the recipient with a service of immense value, it is unique among economic activities in that the recipient is inherently unable to pay for this service. The infants, young children, frail elders, ill or injured people, and others needing care are usually unable to earn money to pay for their care—yet they must receive care in order to live. Sometimes, someone other than the recipient pays for the caregiver's work. Often no one pays, but the care is given anyway, because it must be given. Since the modern economic paradigm only values people who have money and activities which make money, caregiving is inherently devalued. And since the recipients of care are considered unproductive, the modern paradigm further devalues the act of caring for them.

For all these reasons caring in modern economies is systematically degraded, and both caregivers and the recipients of care often lack resources and respect. This harms women, professional caregivers such as health workers, teachers, and child-care workers, and dependent recipients.

Poor People and the Problem of Care

Receiving adequate care is especially difficult for poor people. Since the low incomes of poor households make it difficult for them to hire caretakers for their own children, elders, or ill family members, such dependents may often go without adequate care altogether. This is especially ironic since members of poorer, ethnically or socially disadvantaged groups often make their living by caring for the dependents of those who are more socially and economically privileged. It's also ironic that in the United States, poor mothers who seek government support for themselves and their children are increasingly expected to go out and work, while considerable public anguish is expressed over the plight of middle-class children when their mothers advance their careers instead of staying home to take care of their offspring.

Such inequities are even being reproduced at the global level. In many predominantly white modern societies, children, elders, and ill people are increasingly being cared for by low-paid immigrants, usually women, from Third-World nations.[2]

Is Caring an Innately Female Activity?

The devaluation of caring and the resulting crisis of care in modern economies is rooted in the division of gender roles. It is justified by the belief that men are naturally active, competitive, and creative, and therefore belong in the productive paid economy, while women, being naturally nurturing, dependent, and self-sacrificing, belong in the supposedly noneconomic sector of home and family.

Many people believe that because women are biologically designed to nurture developing human beings in their wombs and to feed infants out of their own bodies, that it is women's innate nature to be emotionally empathetic, nurturing, and instinctively want to care for dependent people—that is, that caring is inherently feminine. This belief is further reinforced by the assumption that gender-related traits are, or should be, polar opposites. For example, if being able to think logically is defined as characteristic of males, then being illogical becomes feminine. Or if caring for others is defined as an inherently feminine trait, then caring for oneself and being self-assertive becomes unfeminine, the prerogative of males.

But such divisive categories harm both women and men. If only women can be caring, then it is right that they should be restricted to household duties or lower-paid caretaking jobs. And if men naturally lack the ability to care, this implies that men can never be truly human and truly humane. Yet caring, as well as most other supposedly gender-linked traits exist as potentials in almost all of us, regardless of gender, and both women and men can benefit from realizing the universality of the ability to give care.

Evidence that both men and women are naturally caring comes from anthropological studies. In numerous tribal societies, fathers and other males actively participate in child care, regularly holding, fondling, talking baby talk, and singing to even the youngest babies. Anthropologists have also found that societies with the highest male involvement in child care tend to avoid warlike activities and value women for work other than bearing and rearing children.[3] Studies of modern men have demonstrated that they, too, are able to bond with their newborns if given the opportunity during or immediately after birth.[4]

GENDER TRAITS AND WHOLENESS

The possibility that so-called gender traits are not confined to just one gender is further supported by a series of tests performed by psychologist Sandra Bem, who designed a measure that defined masculine and feminine characteristics as merely different, not opposite. When she tested male and female subjects in a variety of activities, she found that while some women tended to display predominantly feminine traits, and some men displayed predominantly masculine traits, others—both women and men—ranked high in expressing both so-called masculine and so-called feminine traits. Perhaps most interesting, she found that women and men who combined both strong masculine and strong feminine traits—for example, individuals who were both highly nurturing and highly self-assertive—were most successful in her tests. Subjects whose behavior favored the characteristics assigned to only one gender—that is, the more strictly masculine males and feminine females—tended to be more limited and less successful in tested activities.[5]

Another perspective, which also suggests that supposedly gender-linked traits such as caring are really universal, comes from the work of biologist and Congregationalist minister Genia Pauli Haddon. In her remarkable book *Body Metaphors*, Haddon explores the physical characteristics on which so-called typical masculine and feminine character traits are based. She notes that so-called masculine characteristics—such as being potent, penetrating, initiating action, forging ahead into virgin territory, being goal oriented, strong, or firm—are all related to the image of the active, erect penis. And so-called feminine characteristics—such as being welcoming, sustaining, nourishing, embracing, nurturing, and connected to others—are related to the image of the encompassing, nurturing womb.

But Western culture selectively chooses the physical characteristics it recognizes, and makes invisible other equally important physical gender characteristics which could lead us to different images of what it means to be masculine or feminine. Haddon describes the active, expulsive womb, which women experience during birth, menstruation, and orgasm. This can become the grounding image for feminine characteristics such as organic transformation, exertion, birthing, becoming, initiating growth, urging toward completion, and ecstasy. Likewise, for men, she reminds us of the abiding and resourceful testicles, whose constant presence is conveniently forgotten because they are a major source of male vulnerability. The testicles can symbolize masculine characteristics such as patience, grounding, steadfastness, and generativity (and, I would add, being protective of life).[6]

Haddon's imagery demonstrates how we can honor both gender similarities and gender differences, moving beyond the destructive divisions of superiority and inferiority. And her new models suggest that both women and men can actively participate in the larger economy and society, providing creative leadership, just as both women and men can be caring and nurturing in more intimate and personal relationships.

CHANGING WOMEN, CHANGING MEN

In her hard-hitting book *Prisoners of Men's Dreams*, feminist author and labor activist Suzanne Gordon details the crisis of care in the United States: the continued cuts in government expenditures for education, the continuing exodus of professionals out of caring fields such as teaching and nursing, and the declining well-being of the nation's children. She agrees that the traditional patriarchal devaluation of caring as women's work is partly responsible for this problem. However, she also makes the controversial assertion that as more women have sought to become successful in the visible economy, they too have learned to give up humane values such as caring and are replacing them with typically masculine values such as trying to get the most for oneself. Meanwhile, Gordon claims that women who remain in caring professions such as nursing, teaching, and social work (that is, the typically female professions) are frequently criticized by more successful women for being unliberated and are made to feel ashamed of their job choices.[7]

As Gordon and other observers of this crisis of care point out, one key to establishing a more caring society lies in a broader affirmation of traditionally feminine values, such as caring, along with new workplace policies and financial commitments that provide concrete support for such values. The transition to a more caring society also requires that men challenge their traditional masculine roles and values and incorporate more so-called feminine activities into their daily lives.

MEN REACHING FOR WHOLENESS

The incorporation of the feminine into all aspects of men's lives is now slowly taking place. For example, many men are beginning to challenge their conventional roles as money-makers and are seeking more time for family and personal relationships. In a 1989 U.S. poll by Robert Half International, over 50 percent of the men questioned said they would be willing to reduce their income to get more free time. Seventy-four per cent said they would be willing to switch to a slower career track in order to have more family time. A 1990 poll by Yankelovich, Clancy and Schulman found that more than half the male respondents between the ages of 18 and 24 wanted to spend less time at work.[8] And in a 1990 survey of two-earner families in California, 39 per cent of the mothers and 51 per cent of the fathers felt their work interfered with family responsibilities. Seventy-nine per cent of the mothers and 39 per cent of the fathers said they would quit their jobs if they could stay at home with their children.[9] Such responses on the part of men would have been culturally unacceptable just ten years ago.

A growing number of books and articles describe men who have chosen to give up high-powered careers and are instead working and earning less so they can spend more time with their families. Such men often emphasize that being with their children, caring for them, and watching them grow is one of the greatest benefits of this new life direction.[10] It should be noted that this transition is not necessarily easy for men. Traditional definitions of male identity and the fear of being labeled "unmanly" still inhibit many men from taking advantage of shorter or more flexible work-time options or switching to less prestigious, less stressful jobs.[11]

Nevertheless, more men are experimenting with taking on so-called feminine activities, relationship styles, and values. And still others are outspokenly seeking to redefine the meaning of masculinity. In an impassioned article titled "A Time for Men to Pull Together," Andrew Kimbrell claims that in the United States, the typical male obsession with aggressive macho images such as the Wild West cowboy or Rambo is really a compensation for the powerlessness that most men feel in their everyday lives, especially in their paid work:

> In real life most men lead powerless, subservient lives in the factory or office—frightened of losing their jobs, mortgaged to the gills, and still feeling responsible for supporting their families. Their lauded independence—as well as most of their basic rights—disappear the minute they report for work.[12]

Kimbrell urges men today to acknowledge the painful nature of their lives and to seek positive rather than illusory solutions. "Men can no longer afford to lose themselves in denial," he says. "We need to experience grief and anger over our losses and not buy into pseudo-male stereotypes propagated by the male mystique."[13] In particular, Kimbrell urges men to acknowledge and mourn the fact that so much of their lives has been channeled toward the destruction of the Earth and its inhabitants. He calls for men to reclaim their traditional roles as protectors of family and of the Earth, the generative role of men. Growing numbers of men throughout North America and the rest of the world are reexamining their lives in this way, seeking new identities and new ways to build more caring relationships—with each other, with women, children, their surrounding communities, and with the Earth.[14]

WOMEN REACHING FOR WHOLENESS

The challenge for women is somewhat more complicated. On the one hand, women need to escape the confines of their stereotype as weak, passive, dependent, less-competent individuals who are qualified only to change diapers, wash dishes, and wipe away tears. On the other hand, as women become more active, successful, and influential in the visible economy and in other public realms, they must beware the trap of taking on the exaggerated masculine and destructive values of hierarchy and patriarchy. That is, if being a man is defined as remaining isolated from one's feelings while dominating and exploiting other people and the Earth, then successful women must avoid becoming like men.

In response to this double challenge, many women today are exploring a new model in which they are gaining and exercising power in the larger economic and political world while using their newfound power to express more humane, egalitarian, empowering, and caring values.

Women Changing the Workplace

Since the 1970s, as women in modern economies have been entering the paid workforce in unprecedented numbers, their increased presence has gradually been forcing the workplace to change. Perhaps most important, the realization that workers have lives outside of their job, and need time to pursue the rest of life has been exemplified by a growing interest in such innovations as shorter work hours, more flexible work schedules, child-care programs in the workplace, and alternatives to long commutes.

While such changes are sometimes inaccurately identified as serving the special needs of women, the fact is that both men and women want, and are expressing more interest in achieving, a better balance between their jobs and personal lives. However, women in the workplace—as union activists, concerned managers, enlightened business consultants, and through other new roles—deserve credit for most strongly keeping up the demand for meeting these needs through more caring solutions that we are now realizing can improve the lives of both women and men.[15]

In *Our Wildest Dreams*, a study of women entrepreneurs in the United States, business innovator Joline Godfrey claims that many women business owners are organizing their companies around rules that differ significantly from traditional masculine models. Godfrey claims that many women who have started their own businesses in recent years did so after rising as far as they could in large corporations, then leaving in disgust. Deciding that "I'm not going to do it their way, I'm going to build a different kind of company" motivates many women entrepreneurs, she says.[16]

Godfrey has found that women-owned businesses tend to

— recognize that employees have lives outside of work and promote policies that enable workers to achieve a balance between paid work and the rest of life;

— utilize networks rather than pyramidal structures and encourage employee participation and creativity rather than rigid hierarchical obedience;

— serve a deeper meaning, such as meeting people's emotional needs or helping solve a social problem, in addition to making money; and

— be more aware of reducing waste and respecting the natural environment.

Recent studies suggest that in the United States, approximately 5,000,000 businesses are now owned by women, constituting about 30 percent of all U.S. businesses, and it is estimated that by early in the next century perhaps 40 to 50 percent of all businesses will be woman owned.[17] As the numbers of women-owned businesses grow, their influence will increasingly transform the lives of people directly involved with these companies as suppliers, employees, or customers. They will also bring more caring models and values to the larger public consciousness.

Women Changing the Health Care System

Suzanne Gordon describes how nurses are demanding the right to be more than machine-watchers and health technicians. In hospitals throughout the United States, nurses today are taking the lead in instituting programs that provide more integrated and supportive connections between staff and patients. For example, at Beth Israel Hospital in Boston, the nursing staff has promoted the concept of "primary nursing." Each patient is assigned one nurse, who provides daily direct care. In addition, the primary nurse is in charge of developing a round-the-clock caring plan for the patient and coordinates the other nurses and hospital departments that will assist in carrying out the plan. Not only does this system give each patient a consistent one-on-one caring relationship and allow for more individualized caring. Because nurses now have more decision-making authority, they receive increased respect within the hospital hierarchy, and consequently play less of a subordinate, and more of a collaborative, role in relating to doctors.[18]

Women Caring for Their Communities and the Environment

Women throughout the world are fighting against toxic pollution and environmental degradation, for the health of their communities. Lois Gibbs, a former housewife now active with the grassroots environmental network Citizen's Clearinghouse for Hazardous Waste says that in the United States alone, hundreds of local and regional organizations for environmental justice are typically led by women, working-class people, and people of color. Many of these women have never previously been politically active, becoming involved primarily out of concern for their children's safety.[19]

Women in the Third World are leading many struggles against environmental destruction in their societies. Indian scientist and ecofeminist Vandana Shiva says that because they are daily involved with producing the necessities of life in direct cooperation with nature, Third-World women can provide more useful ecological insights than the technological experts of industrialized nations. Standing up to addictive corporations and misguided governments, women-led movements in both industrialized and Third-World nations are taking the lead in the struggle for clean and healthy places to live and work.[20]

FROM THE MARTYRED MOTHER TO THE CARING COMMUNITY

The recent large-scale entry of women, including many mothers of young children, into the visible economic and political realms has led to one of the most painful controversies of our times: Who should take care of our children? Since in many households all adult members must go out to work in order to bring in enough income, the establishment of widely available, affordable child-care programs for the children of working parents seems an obvious societal necessity. Yet the number of such programs is still far from adequate. Besides, the low status and low pay of child-care workers hinders the quality of such programs, and many parents feel uneasy about leaving their children with strangers whose only connection to the child comes out of an impersonal monetary obligation.

Some parents have decided that being able to care for their own children is a priority and are able to arrange their lives so that the mother (or sometimes the father, or a combination of both parents) can provide the bulk of child care. However, many women are discovering that they feel best about themselves, and have the most to offer their children, when their lives include some or even a substantial amount of outside work.[21] Mothers with outside jobs are a frequent target of concerned traditionalists, who claim that children's need for strong values and a secure family life can best be met by mother as a fulltime, stay-at-home caregiver. Such claims are often justified by reference to studies of "maternal deprivation." It has been found that when children were institutionalized at an early age and deprived of regular physical and emotional affection, many of them did not grow normally, and some died.[22] Although these studies describe extreme situations, they can cause women who enjoy working in the larger world to feel guilty, wondering if they are harming their children by meeting their own needs.

This controversy about the proper role of mothers is often framed in terms of "What is best for the child?" But when women's needs to participate in the larger world are seen as depriving their children of adequate love, guidance, and stability, then both mothers and their children lose. If any problem today needs a new, win-win solution, this one does. We can find such solutions by looking beyond the modern ideal of mother and child, bound together in intimate union while isolated from the rest of the world. Other cultures offer alternative models. For example, up until the Industrial Revolution the child's world was the adult world. From their earliest years, children were regularly involved, first as observers, then participants, in adult activities of work and play. Furthermore, preindustrial families usually included people of many different generations, various relatives, and even unrelated individuals, such as servants or apprentices. As a result, women with children were rarely isolated, and child care was often shared among members of the extended family.[23]

This pattern of communally supported child care is even more common in tribal societies, where all adult women, even those with newborns, actively participate in economic production and adult socializing. But as many anthropological studies have demonstrated, children in such societies are certainly not neglected. If anything, they often receive more attention and affection—from their mothers, fathers, and other caregivers, both female and male—express greater contentment, and eagerly participate in adult activities, compared with children in modern societies.

What are the real needs of the child in all this controversy? One answer comes from writer Jean Liedloff, who for two and a half years lived with and studied the child-rearing techniques of the Yequana, a Stone-Age tribe in the Venezuelan rainforest. In her challenging and richly detailed book *The Continuum Concept*, Liedloff claims that until infants crawl—usually by six to nine months—they need constant physical contact. During these earliest months, Yequana children are constantly held, rocked, lean or lie against a caregiver, whether awake or asleep. The act of providing this contact is shared by a community of caregivers. Among the Yequana, as in many other nonmodern societies, precrawling infants are constantly in someone's arms or against someone's body, although the caregiver may change throughout the day from mother to father to grandparent or older sibling to other relatives or neighbors.

Liedloff also observes that among the Yequana, since infants and young children receive the constant physical contact and social stimulation they need, they do not fuss or demand other kinds of attention (except to be fed or cleaned). As a result, neither children nor their caregivers are isolated from the activities of daily adult life. And rather than being spoiled by this constant holding, Liedloff observes that such children are eager to learn from adults and to cooperate socially as their physical independence increases.[24]

Liedloff's model, which is gaining increased attention from parents, psychologists, child-care workers, and educators, suggests that both children and their caregivers can have mutually satisfying solutions. Her conclusions imply that we need to heal the isolation of martyred mothers or other caregivers who, supposedly in the best interests of the child, are left alone with their young charges. Just as children thrive in a community of caregivers, so too will caregivers thrive from participating fully in a larger, caring community.

A NEW DEFINITION OF CARING

As we increasingly acknowledge that the giving and receiving of care are both essential human needs, the following rights will gradually become publicly accepted parts of daily life:

1) the right of both women and men to be caring people;

2) the right of both women and men to express their caring in larger economic and political arenas, and in relation to the natural environment, as well as in their more personal, intimate relationships;

3) the right of every individual, regardless of gender, to express both traditionally masculine attributes (being active, effective, and self-assertive) as well as traditionally feminine attributes (being emotionally expressive, nurturing, and connected to others);

4) the right of children to receive all the physical and emotional affection, social involvement, and creative, intellectual stimuli they need as part of receiving care;

5) the right of children not to be confined constantly with one isolated caregiver;

6) the right of caregivers to receive the emotional and social support they need, and to be able to share their caregiving responsibilities with other caregivers; and

7) the right of both recipients and caregivers to be respected for their roles and to receive adequate material as well as emotional resources.

NOTES

1. On the patriarchal devaluation of caregiving worldwide, see Nancy Folbre, *Who Pays for the Kids? Gender and the Structures of Constraint* (London and New York: Routledge, 1994).

2. The increasing utilization of Third-World people to care for the dependents of Western societies is described in Allan R. Meyers, "Global Development and Personal Dependency: The High Cost of Doing Well," *World Development*, 19 (January 1991), 45–54.

3. On the extent and importance of males doing child care, see Caryl Rivers, Rosalind Barnett, and Grace Baruch, *Beyond Sugar and Spice: How Women Grow, Learn, and Thrive* (New York: Ballantine Books, 1979), esp. chap. 2.

4. Rivers et al., *Beyond Sugar and Spice,* 22–28.

5. Ibid., 108–113.

6. See Genia Pauli Haddon, *Body Metaphors: Releasing God-Feminine in Us All* (New York: Crossroad Publishing Co., 1988), esp. chap. 2, for her schema of more liberating body metaphors for women and men.

7. On the crisis of care in the United States, see Suzanne Gordon, *Prisoners of Men's Dreams: Striking Out for A New Feminine Future* (Boston: Little, Brown, 1991), esp.chaps, 3, 4, and 5.

8. Suzanne Gordon, "Men, Women, and Work: Job Dissatisfaction Knows No Gender," *Boston Sunday Globe*, 28 July 1991, 68.

9. "California Poll Finds A Wish for More Family Life at Careers' Expense," *Boston Globe*, 13 August 1990, 6.

10. Men who have chosen to work and earn less so they can spend more time with their families are described in Carol Hymowitz, "Trading Fat Paychecks for Free Time, "*Wall Street Journal*, 5 August 1991, sec. B, and Amy Saltzman, *Downshifting: Reinventing Success on A Slower Track* (New York: HarperCollins, 1991).

11. Men's reluctance to take advantage of less stressful work options is described in Alan Deutschman, "Pioneers of the New Balance," *Fortune*, 20 May 1991, 61–68.

12. Andrew Kimbrell, "A Time for Men to Pull Together," *Utne Reader*, May/June 1991, 66–74.

13. Ibid.

14. Contacts for the men's movement include the National Organization of Men Against Sexism, 54 Mint St., #300, San Francisco, CA 94103; Men's Stuff: Working to End Men's Isolation Since 1985, P.O. Box 800, San Anselmo CA 94979; *Changing Men* magazine, 306 N. Brooks St., Madison, WI 53715; and *Wingspan* magazine, P.O. Box 23550, Brightmoor Station, Detroit, MI 48223. All these contacts can provide information about networking, publications, and events.

15. Joline Godfrey, *Our Wildest Dreams: Women Entrepreneurs Making Money, Having Fun, Doing Good* (New York: HarperBusiness, 1992).

16. Statistics on women-owned businesses in the United States are cited in Godfrey, *Our Wildest Dreams*, 209–218.

17. On primary-care nursing, see Suzanne Gordon, "The Crisis in Caring," *Boston Globe Magazine*, 10 July 1988, 22–73.

18. Lois Gibbs, in Richard Hofrichter, ed., *Toxic Struggles: The Theory and Practice of Environmental Justice* (Philadelphia: New Society Publishers, 1993), ix–xi.

19. On women leading the environmental movement worldwide, see Vandana Shiva, *Staying Alive: Women, Ecology and Development* (Atlantic Highlands, N.J.: Zed Books, 1989); and Vandana Shiva, ed., *Close to Home: Women Reconnect Ecology, Health and Development Worldwide* (Philadelphia: New Society Publishers, 1994).

20. On benefits of women combining family and paid work, see Faye J. Crosby, *Juggling: The Unexpected Advantages of Balancing Career and Home For Women And Their Families* (New York: Free Press, 1991).

21. The implications of "maternal deprivation" studies are discussed in Rivers et al., *Beyond Sugar and Spice*, 68–83; and Ann Dally, *Inventing Motherhood: The Consequences of an Ideal* (New York: Schocken Books, 1983), 87–123.

22. Historical data on nonisolation of mothers and shared child care is given in Rivers et al., *Beyond Sugar and Spice*, 15–16, and Dally, *Inventing Motherhood*, chap. 7.

23. See Jean Liedloff, *The Continuum Concept* (New York: Alfred A. Knopf, 1977); or contact The Liedloff Continuum Network, P.O. Box 1634, Sausalito, CA 94965.

Chapter 14

HOUSEHOLD AND COMMUNITY WEALTH: FROM CONSUMERS TO CREATORS

In the modern economic paradigm, businesses are considered the primary producers of wealth, while people in their lives outside of paid work, in the home or community, consume wealth. This rigid division, formalized in the models of professional economists, also affects people's self-image. Many individuals in modern society identify so thoroughly with their paid work that they find it difficult to recognize that they have creative skills, or can perform any productive activities, other than what they do for their jobs.

Our discussion of the informal economy documented that considerable production takes place outside the visible, monetized economy even in modern societies. As part of the emerging postmodern economy, interest in household- and community-based production is increasing. This chapter explores in more detail the wide range of goods and services that people are producing directly for themselves, in their homes or in collaboration with fellow community members. And it explains why—whether you call them doing-it-yourself, grassroots self-help, or self-reliance—such activities enhance and empower both individuals and communities.

BASIC AREAS OF SELF-RELIANCE

Worldwatch researcher Bruce Stokes, in an extensive study of grassroots self-help efforts, found that providing food and shelter readily lend themselves to do-it-yourself approaches.[1] With regard to food production, Stokes describes how for many people in the United States, vegetable gardening has recently shifted from a casual activity to a significant do-it-yourself food-producing operation. He notes that an intensively worked backyard garden can produce a pound of vegetables per square foot, which means that the average U.S. resident could meet his or her annual vegetable needs with a 10-by-30 foot plot.[2] The National Gardening Association estimates that in 1993, approximately 25 million U.S. households (one-quarter of the population) had vegetable gardens, producing a total of approximately $500 million worth of vegetables per year.[3]

As to shelter, although we can easily imagine someone adding on decks or remodeling the rec room, it seems unlikely that doing-it-yourself can be applied to building a complete home. Nevertheless, examples abound of owner-built housing in both rural and urban areas of North America, sometimes as an individual project and sometimes with outside assistance. Stokes reports that in the United States, individual owner-occupants build more homes than the government. Owner-built housing accounted for one-third of all new homes built after World War II, and for one-fifth of all new homes built between 1964 and 1976. In *Freedom to Build*, author William C. Grindley estimates that owner-builders save one-quarter to one-half on construction costs over developer-built housing.[4]

Other reports document the viability and unrecognized frequency of self-help housing in modern cities and towns. For example, a study of self-reliance in Canada interviewed "Michael," a Portuguese immigrant. He explained that relatives and other members of the immigrant community help each other purchase and remodel old houses. Many of these people work for building contractors during the day. Because their employers support their initiative, they often lend trucks and donate extra building supplies to these weekend self-help projects.[5] Michael goes on to describe how his countrymen in the "new world" are also extremely self-reliant when it comes to food production:

> Portuguese families are largely self-sufficient for food. They do not grow grass in the backyard. . . . They grow vegetables like they used to back home. "Freezers are a good place for keeping vegetables." Michael said that he had two gardens, the upper garden had produced seventy-five gallons of wine from his own backyard, and in the lower garden there were flowers, and vegetables that are now in the freezer.[6]

The organization Habitat for Humanity, founded by U.S. businessman and philanthropist Millard Fuller, brings together groups of volunteers to help poor people build themselves new homes. Although this group is perhaps best known by the image of former President Jimmy Carter helping out in rural Georgia, Habitat has organized self-help throughout the world, including inner-city Boston.[7] In the low-income, predominantly African-American rural community of Four Corners, Louisiana, women worked together to build or renovate their homes and community buildings, through a women-run nonprofit organization called the Southern Mutual Help Association. As part of their project, participants agree to teach women in another community the self-help skills they have learned, explains founder Lorna Bourg.[8]

The Peruvian architect and economic theorist Alfredo L. de Romaña has devoted much of his life to making owner-built housing in urban Canada more feasible. He works on community organization and legal issues, since government regulations often prevent rather than encourage self-help efforts. He also develops new designs and construction components that support owner-building. De Romaña notes that buying a house from someone else and then paying a mortgage for twenty or thirty years is a great source of insecurity. In a society where loss of income can mean loss of shelter, he sees owner-built housing as an extremely important source of security and empowerment, especially for people in precarious economic situations.[9]

Closely related to self-reliance in housing is energy production, especially for heating, hot water, and electricity. Many energy conservation measures, as well as some solar heating systems, are relatively simple and can be implemented on a do-it-yourself basis with readily available materials and a few basic construction skills. Considerable information and equipment is available for individuals and communities interested in making more extensive use of natural and renewable energy sources. Another approach is to cut energy waste, one of the most accessible ways to make more wealth available for other purposes.[10]

SELF-RELIANCE IN EDUCATION, RECREATION, AND OTHER SERVICES

Self-reliance can apply to the nonmaterial as well as to the physical aspects of life. Many of the services which people buy in modern societies can be created at least as well, if not better, by individuals, families, friends, or neighbors. I'm not recommending do-it-yourself surgery, of course. But many health-care activities, particularly health maintenance and illness prevention, are most effectively carried out as part of one's daily living. Self-help groups for a variety of physical and emotional problems are also an important, growing trend in the United States today.[11]

And then there's do-it-yourself education. A formal version is home-schooling one's children, an option that several hundred thousand families of widely diverse backgrounds are pursuing, for widely diverse reasons. Studies of home-schooled young people show that they are far better educated and more self-confident than their peers who have gone through the conventional education system.[12] Equally as important, children are always learning from the environment and activities around them. Imagine how much more they can learn from living in a home or neighborhood in which people regularly engage in creative, productive, interesting, stimulating, meaningful skills and activities, compared with those whose leisure activities consist primarily of watching television or going to shopping malls.

Finally, for most of human history people have been entertaining themselves, expressing themselves artistically and creatively, and participating in spiritually deepening experiences and rituals. Although many traditional arts, crafts, songs, and musical abilities have become lost in as little as one generation through exposure to modern culture, such skills can be restored if one is willing to devote time, patience, and focused attention. Throughout modern societies one can find a growing interest in community-based arts, cultural festivals, neighborhood and regional celebrations honoring people's ethnic heritages or local environments. Through such activities, people are reasserting their artistic and creative abilities and bringing more artistically and spiritually meaningful expressions back into their homes and communities.[13]

EMPOWERING YOUNG PEOPLE IN THE HOUSEHOLD AND COMMUNITY

In traditional tribal or agricultural societies, children as young as three begin learning adult skills and taking some responsibility for essential tasks such as food gathering, preparation, and care of younger children. Economic participation by individuals of such young age may sound cruel, or even impossible, to many inhabitants of modern societies. A familiar modern image of young people is of rude, awkward kids stuffing themselves in front of the TV set or hanging around the shopping mall, and occasionally, grudgingly doing a few chores such as making their beds or taking out the garbage. This image has come about because the modern paradigm gives children into their teens little opportunity to exercise their inherent skills and maturity. When the home and community are seen primarily as places for consumption, young people in particular suffer from a loss of self-esteem, since they have little opportunity to make any important contributions to the life around them. Such feelings can lead to aimlessness and even to socially destructive behavior.

In the United States, the current crisis in the educational system and the low self-esteem so widespread among students has recently stimulated innovative programs that allow young people to express their maturity, competence, and creativity. Many communities now offer community-service programs for students of all ages, that are sometimes optional but frequently integral parts of the school program. Activities include redeeming recyclables and using the money to fund community centers; tutoring younger children; planting trees and other environmental restoration projects; collecting food and clothing for, or bringing firewood to people in need; and volunteering in nursing homes or with handicapped individuals. It turns out that community-service programs offer myriad benefits for kids, schools, and communities. Not only do young people who participate gain in self-esteem and reduce negative behavior, but their classroom learning also improves.

The director of Youth Service Charleston, South Carolina, which has involved over 2,000 young people in 23,000 hours of community service since 1987, comments, "High school and college students have a need to belong. . . . And they're either going to fulfill that need in a constructive manner or a destructive manner." Even much younger children have something to give and the need to interact with and affect the larger world. Comments the director of another such program, "Imagine an 8- or 9-year-old helping out in a nursing home, The kids find out that they *can* make a difference in someone else's life."[14]

Sometimes, young children in modern economies are given the opportunity to make a real contribution to their families' well-being. Examples include children as young as six or seven who, with great competence and pride, help in a family business; grow food, care for animals, or sell produce from their family's farm; or help care for younger or older relatives. They demonstrate how responsible and capable even young children can be.

I'm not suggesting that children spend all their free time on child care or household chores, as does happen in some families, or that they should take on dull, low-skilled jobs in order to help bring in income, although many young people today do that, too. These are oppressive activities that neither children nor adults should have to do. What I am urging is that young people's desires and ability to make a real contribution to their family and community be recognized and that they be empowered as important participants in their households and community.

EFFECTS OF INCREASED HOUSEHOLD AND COMMUNITY-BASED PRODUCTION

In modern economies, where almost any conceivable product or service can be produced and purchased commercially, even the smallest act of producing directly for oneself, one's family, or community is an expression of a different, postmodern, paradigm. Furthermore, because self-reliant production can be applied to so many diverse areas of life and may contribute anywhere from a tiny to a significant portion of one's needs, household and community production have a variety of effects.

Saving Money

Baking one's own bread, sewing one's own clothes, other forms of making things from scratch, or doing one's own household repairs rather than hiring outside service people, can significantly reduce monetary expenses. Indeed, many lower-income people are forced to rely on their do-it-yourself skills in order to obtain goods and services that more affluent families purchase as a matter of course. For such people, self-reliance is an economic necessity.

Others shift to a more self-reliant lifestyle as a way of escaping the rat race; by doing for themselves, they can cut expenses and spend less time earning money, or working at an undesirable job. Some people utilize self-reliance to make the most of existing incomes, a strategy exemplified by the Dacyczyn family of Leeds, Maine. These self-proclaimed tightwads—Amy, Jim, and their six small children—rely on household production, doing-it-yourself, and creative utilization of others' throwaways to keep their expenses as low as possible. This has enabled them to devote the salary from Jim's fulltime job to such luxuries as purchasing a sprawling farmhouse on seven acres of land, and donating money to others who are less fortunate. The Dacyczyns also publish a newsletter, *The Tightwad Gazette*, which shares ideas on creative frugality, both from their own experiences and those sent in by their readers.[15]

Incidentally, doing-it-yourself does not automatically equal frugality. Any project can use expensive luxury materials and be costly in time, money, or both.

The needs and resources of the creators will determine if self-reliance is being carried out in order to save money or for other reasons.

Expressing Creativity and Individuality

Self-reliance in any area of life can be a satisfying way to express one's innate creativity or to exercise artistic impulses. Since you are not producing to meet someone else's standards, you can shape a project or creation exactly to your liking. The discovery that one can make beautiful, useful things is a frequent surprise result of self-reliance.

Increasing Self-Esteem and Empowerment

Learning new skills or discovering that you can meet various everyday needs directly and that you can create beauty or solve problems without having to rely on outside experts, all contribute to self-esteem. Self-reliance also helps people discover that expensive equipment or lengthy and expensive formal education is not always necessary in order to do useful, important work. As people gradually acquire a range of skills, which can serve as an antidote to overspecialized paid work, feelings of self-esteem and wholeness grow. Such activities also help people in modern economies to realize that we are not totally dependent on large, unresponsive, or uncaring institutions for our survival and well-being. They remind us that *we* create the economy.

Strengthening Local Communities

As individuals and households gain new skills and expand their productive activities, they discover that they have more to share with their neighbors. As William Nicholls and William Dyson observed in their comprehensive study of self-reliance in Canada:

> The process is one that begins with self-reliant activities within the household, and moves from there to other face-to-face relationships in the community. In effect, these relationships become informal social and economic networks of mutual support and cooperation—a pattern of inter-reliant activities made up of exchanges and gifts of goods, skills and services.[16]

BENEFITS OF SELF-RELIANCE

By participating in community self-reliance—joining a community gardening program, helping in a barnraising-style construction project, or taking part in community cultural activities such as musical or theater groups—people get to know their neighbors better and build a base for other community activities. Especially important, many forms of community production and creativity bring together individuals of diverse ages, skills, and backgrounds who might otherwise never have the opportunity to meet, certainly not in such positive and mutually empowering circumstances.

As individuals and households become more self-reliant and empowered, they lay the groundwork for new community responses to larger social and economic problems. When plant closings, layoffs, loss of local stores, or other large-scale economic hardships afflict their communities, such empowered, creative individuals may be more able to develop new solutions to these problems. And the new community ties they have been forming through their shared activities serve as a base for building new economic structures and enterprises that more fully meet their community's needs.

Many publications, classes, workshops, and networks are now available to help people learn skills in self-reliant production. Important aspects include sharing information, learning by doing, and obtaining emotional support for those embarking on this new adventure.[17]

NOTES

1. See Bruce Stokes, *Local Responses to Global Problems: Meeting Basic Human Needs*, Worldwatch Paper 17 (Washington, D.C.: Worldwatch Institute, 1978) and Bruce Stokes, *Helping Ourselves: Local Solutions to Global Problems* (New York: W. W. Norton & Co., 1981).

2. Stokes, *Local Responses to Global Problems*, 20.

3. Figures for 1993 are from the National Gardening Association, 180 Flynn Ave., Burlington, VT 05401, (800) 538-7476.

4. Stokes, *Local Responses to Global Problems*, 12–13.

5. William M. Nicholls and William A. Dyson, *The Informal Economy: Where People Are The Bottom Line* (Ottawa: Vanier Institute of the Family, 1983), 123.

6. Ibid.

7. On Habitat for Humanity, see Millard Fuller, *No More Shacks!* (Waco, Tx.: Word Books, 1986); or contact Habitat for Humanity International, 121 Habitat St., P.O. Box 1167, Americus, GA 31709-9951.

8. On the Southern Mutual Help Association of New Iberia, Louisiana, see Claire Safran, "The Women Who Helped Themselves," *Good Housekeeping*, May 1993, 40–47.

9. Information about Alberto de Romaña's work in self-help housing is available through the Intercultural Institute of Montreal, 4917 St. Urbain St., Montreal, Quebec H2T 2W1, Canada.

10. Information and materials for do-it-yourself energy conservation and household energy production are available from Real Goods, 966 Mazzoni St., Ukiah, CA 95482-3471.

11. On self-help health care, see Stokes, *Helping Ourselves*, chap. 6. An important example of this trend is the guide written by the Boston Women's Health Book Collective, *Our Bodies, Ourselves*, 2d ed. rev. (New York: Simon & Schuster, 1992).

12. Benefits of home-schooling are documented in "A List of Selected Research on Homeschooling," (1991), available from Holt Associates/Growing Without Schooling, 2269 Massachusetts Ave., Cambridge MA 02140. Holt Associates, which is a national information and resource center on home-schooling, estimates that in 1994 approximately 500,000 families in the United States are involved in home schooling.

13. On people actively creating their own culture and celebrations, see Evan Imber-Black and Janine Roberts, *Rituals For Our Time: Celebrating, Healing, and Changing Our Lives and Relationships* (New York: Harper Collins, 1992); Milo Shannon-Thornberry, ed., *Alternate Celebrations Catalogue* (New York: Pilgrim Press, 1982); and Gay-wynn Cooper, "Beyond Ordinary Time," *In Context*, 37, (January 1994), 48–51.

14. Community-service programs for young people are described in John B. Thomas, "Kids Who Care," *Better Homes and Gardens*, March 1992, 37–39; also contact Youth Service America, 1319 "F" St. NW, Suite 900, Washington, D.C. 20004.

15. The creatively frugal lifestyle of the Dacyczyn family is described in Brad Lemley, "How to Save a Buck," *Co-Op America Quarterly*, Winter 1991, 16–17. *The Tightwad Gazette* is available from RR 1, Box 3570, Leeds, ME 04263 (sample copies $1.00).

16. Nicholls and Dyson, *The Informal Economy,* 34.

17. Information sharing, skills, and resources for household production and local self-reliance are available through Rodale Press, Book Division, Emmaus, PA 10849; or *Back Home* magazine, P.O. Box 70, Hendersonville, NC 28793.

Chapter 15

A SENSE OF PLACE: DEVELOPING AN ECONOMY ROOTED IN THE EARTH

The modern Western scientific paradigm fragmented nature, destroying the long-recognized connections between human beings and the natural world. As the Industrial Revolution, with its continued advances in science and technology, added increased riches to the visible economy, the power of money and industrial machinery came to represent the productive forces of life, overshadowing nature's constant contributions.

Defining the natural world as without life or spirit, modern societies were free to exploit nature ruthlessly to achieve ever-increasing production and monetary return. Forests were chopped down, animal species made extinct, rivers and lakes poisoned. Formerly diverse ecosystems were transformed into monocropped agriculture—thousands of acres of land devoted to growing a single crop. Meanwhile, natural areas that had not been developed economically were turned into passive, picturesque parks and landscapes, where overstressed workers could go for renewal. But all these uses of nature are distorted. They deny that nature is inherently productive and self-renewing and that for most of history, human life has been sustained by people who carefully harvested and nurtured the Earth's ceaseless production of wealth.

The global environmental crisis has recently forced people to rethink the relationship between our economic activities and the natural world. Programs such as recycling and pollution reduction, which conserve resources and reduce harm to the natural environment, are a step in the right direction. But new-paradigm economic activities are pointing toward an even more comprehensive redefinition of the economic relationship between humans and the Earth. They are suggesting that in order to assure the continued health of the planet and of human well-being, we must allow our economic activities to more directly mirror the productive processes, structures, and dynamics of the natural world.

RECONNECTING TO NATURE'S WEALTH: NATURAL ECONOMIC SECTORS

Throughout modern nations, people are seeking to bring recognition of our innate economic connections with nature back to conscious awareness through direct experience. People are finding ways to interact directly with the productive powers of nature in what I call "natural economic sectors"—physical locations where the processes of the Earth combine with human effort to generate, nurture, harvest, and replenish wealth.

A natural economic sector can be as small as the flowerpot on one's balcony or windowsill, growing a few herbs, or an urban or suburban backyard with a vegetable plot, some fruit trees and berry bushes. It can be a small farm in the suburbs where people come to "pick your own," or a municipally sponsored project, such as Boston's recent "Fruition" program, through which berry bushes and fruit trees were planted in parks and other public areas for any resident to harvest. Other examples include turning a junk-filled lot into a community garden, or bringing an old farm or orchard back to life.

Natural economic sectors can strengthen communities by bringing together people of all ages in shared activities. They are also of enormous educational value in that they provide a constant lesson in the life-giving abundance of nature, while allowing participants to experience how human involvement can enhance or destroy natural wealth. They demonstrate the multitude of connections within natural systems, the abundance and magic power inherent in every seed, the inevitability of death, and the regular regeneration of new life as part of the natural processes of the Earth.

And they help us to discover new resources and potential abundance where formerly we may have seen only poverty, emptiness, dirt, and mess. The person excited by urban gardening, for example, discovers that even in packed urban areas there is usually plenty of space available, tucked next to sidewalks, on empty lots, in tiny front or backyards or in urban parks, that can be transformed into gardens.[1]

In more spacious urban neighborhoods, and in the suburbs, where each individual home has its own, often large plot of land attached, an interest in natural economic sectors can lead people to rethink conventional land use patterns. Any drive through a typical U.S. residential suburb, for example, will reveal the existence of thousands of acres of available land in the form of lawns, where their owners spend countless hours a year seeding, watering, and mowing. (It has been observed that grass is the only crop which people grow in order to throw the harvest away into the trash!) As long as a lawn has not been poisoned with pesticides and herbicides to achieve that golf-course perfection, it can be transformed into a natural economic sector right outside one's front or back door. Perhaps the major barriers to such projects are the neighbors' fears' that property values will fall if one's yard is used for growing useful crops rather than just a conventional lawn.

Natural economic sectors run counter to the trajectory of modernism, which assumes that only in primitive societies do people spend significant time and energy producing in direct contact with nature. Modernization means moving production away from nature, away from the human body, and into factories, offices, and laboratories, or under the control of massive fossil-fuel or electrically powered technologies. In this vision, the most successful economy imports its mundane necessities from more backward societies, while becoming ever richer by producing and selling high-tech goods and services to others.[2]

This assumption has been challenged by economic development consultant David Korten, who promotes what he calls "people-centered development." Korten analyzed the experiences of Taiwan, South Korea, and Japan, three recently industrialized nations that have achieved remarkably rapid success in the modern global economy.

The conventional wisdom holds that these three societies became so successful because they emphasized the production and international sales of electronic goods, automobiles, and other industrial and high tech products. Korten disagrees. He explains that in each of these nations, recent and radical land reform first created numerous small family-owned farms whose primary purpose was to meet their society's domestic needs. In each nation, widespread government-sponsored educational programs and active local organizations, such as member-run cooperatives, irrigation societies, farmers' associations, and rural youth and women's groups, were formed to support and energize their rural sectors. Once each nation had achieved a strong, domestic-oriented agricultural base, it then added local industries, also designed to serve primarily domestic needs, on top of that. Only after their internal economies were strong did these three nations add export-oriented industries.[3]

Korten's analysis suggests that well-established, locally controlled, natural economic sectors that abundantly meet local needs are the basis of a society's economic well-being, with high-tech, export-oriented industries the mere icing on the cake. Incidentally, other observers note that in the last few decades, South Korea and Taiwan have been allowing their family-owned agricultural base to erode, thereby threatening these societies' larger economic viability.[4]

Many new organizations reflect the growing interest in natural economic sector activity. In the United States, groups such as the Center for Rural Affairs in Nebraska promote the social and economic revitalization of local agricultural communities. Networks such as the Midwest Sustainable Agriculture Working Group, a coalition of farm organizations, environmentalists, and religious groups, are working for a healthy, economically viable regional food system that meets the needs of both farmers and consumers. The National Family Farm/Ranch Transition Network links beginning farmers with retiring farm and ranch owners. And a growing number of activist farms sponsor educational or social-change programs in addition to their practical agricultural work. Examples include Genesis Farm in New

Jersey, run by an order of Dominican sisters, which educates people about appropriate technology, bioregionalism, and Earth-based spirituality, and the Earthwise Education Center/Cornerstone Farm in upstate New York, which trains homeless people from New York City to become self-sufficient homesteaders.[5]

A SENSE OF PLACE: DEVELOPING LOCALLY ORIENTED ECONOMIES

One of the most important trends of the postmodern paradigm is a growing interest in the development of more locally based economies in which people try as much as possible to use locally obtained and/or produced resources to meet local needs. This approach comes from the recognition that the Earth is naturally organized into distinct ecological regions, each with its own unique character and resources, and that a healthy economy depends upon honoring the unique needs and resources of the local environment.

This direction is surprising in view of the increased globalization of modern economies. But paradoxically, the increased global awareness and international economic connections of the past few decades have stimulated people to reconsider the value of local economies.[6]

Environmental Issues and Economic Security:
Beyond the Fossil Fuel Economy

Enormous amounts of fossil fuels are required to transport agricultural and manufactured products across nations and around the world from producers to consumers. The oil embargoes of the 1970s reminded people that the supply of such fuels is precarious, due to changing political and economic factors. In addition, the wide-scale burning of fossil fuels for transportation, heating, and many other needs causes air pollution, acid rain, and other damage to human and environmental health. And since oil, coal, and natural gas are not self-renewing, our constantly increasing dependence upon them brings us ever closer to the time when these resources will be depleted.

Such problems have encouraged people to begin questioning an economy and life-style in which a major portion of its fuels and other essentials come from distant suppliers, and which causes severe environmental damage in the process of transportation and power generation. The environmental problems of a fossil-fuel based economy, coupled with the constant threat of interruptions in access to energy sources, and the severe economic and societal damage such disruptions could cause, have led analysts such as U.S. energy economist Amory Lovins to propose more self-reliant national and local energy policies. In his many writings and demonstration programs with energy-producing utilities, Lovins advocates extensive energy conservation and efficiency measures, combined with increased development and use of locally obtainable, renewable energy sources.[7]

Issues of Justice

Following World War II, a stated goal of the United States and other Western nations has been to assist Third-World countries in achieving economic modernization. Billions of dollars in loans from the World Bank have been made to developing nations, while the United Nations and other national and international agencies have advised on countless economic development programs in the Third World.

But disease, poverty, unemployment and inadequate economic opportunity, hunger, and starvation still characterize much of the Third World. Increasingly, people in both modern and developing nations who are concerned about equity and self-determination are concluding that many conventional economic-development programs, loan programs, and the economic policies of Western nations and multinational corporations have actually exacerbated these problems, and have kept most Third-World nations politically and economically inferior.[8]

A powerful example of this kind of analysis is the hard-hitting book *World Hunger: Twelve Myths*, by author-activists Frances Moore Lappé and Joseph Collins. They assert that millions of people go hungry not because of overpopulation, inadequate land, or backwards technology but because of local and international political and economic structures. They point out that in many Third-World nations, agricultural land that formerly supported self-sufficient families and villages has increasingly been converted to raising luxury products, such as chocolate, beef, exotic flowers or fruits, for export. In other words, where local resources were once used to meet the needs of local people directly they are now diverted to serve a wealthy domestic and international elite. The authors cite many examples of more empowering food production and distribution policies through which Third-World people have restored their ability to grow food for their own local and national use. Their local food crops do not necessarily replace crops for export but often grow alongside them.[9]

Empowerment and Accountability

Researchers such as Bruce Stokes and Alan Durning emphasize that in both modern and Third World nations, basic economic needs such as for food and energy can be met effectively through production at the local level. They and many other advocates for environmental sustainability combined with social justice recommend that governments promote and develop partnerships with local grassroots organizations as a key to lasting, community-based economic development rooted in the local environment.[10]

Locally based economic development has many unique advantages. Perhaps most important, as people learn more about the specific natural environments where they reside, they become aware of the distinct qualities, needs, and gifts of their locales. They discover how their actions affect the environment for better or worse, and learn to read the signs that nature is ailing and needs to be restored to health. Locally based development also increases the potential for both individual and community empowerment. When people become more aware of the resources and processes of their own specific locales, they are better able to participate in decision making about the utilization and care of such resources. They are also in a better position than many outsiders, even many so-called experts, to directly observe the effects of their activities on the local community or environment and to make the necessary adjustments, as needed, in an informed manner.[11]

Some of the most impressive examples of environmentally sustainable, locally controlled economies today can be found in nonindustrial communities around the world, where local tribes or villages are seeking alternatives to the disempowerment and environmental, cultural, and economic destruction generated by modernism. Such groups are learning how to combine the most up-to-date scientific knowledge, appropriate technologies, international economic and informational networks, and cross-cultural input, with their own cultural traditions that have long sustained both community values and the natural environment. Sustainable, community-based economic development projects are being created in forested areas, in fishing or agricultural communities, and even in city neighborhoods.[12]

The creation of more locally based economies does not mean that there would be no more trade between communities or regions. People would find many opportunities to trade their local specialties with each other. But in communities that are trying to build more local economies, such trade would emphasize luxuries rather than the basic necessities of the community. Nor do more locally oriented economies mean that the communities involved must become culturally narrow and parochial, afraid of outsiders. While emphasizing the development and use of local material resources to meet local needs, every community can simultaneously take advantage of ever-increasing global communications and connections to share and enhance their intellectual, cultural, and spiritual development.

Incidentally, many economic analysts have noted that the mass markets of industrialism are now breaking up, being replaced by many smaller, specialized "niche" markets for small runs of custom products.[13] What could better exemplify this postmodern trend than the development of more locally oriented economies, each producing goods and services to meet its unique needs by using its own locally available resources?

LOCAL DIVERSIFICATION: A KEY TO NATURAL WEALTH

Increased diversity of locally produced resources is essential to the viability of more locally based economies. Local economic diversification begins with restoring the diversity of the natural environs. Not only is diversity the basis of environmental health, but people exploring the possibilities of the new economic paradigm are discovering new ways to benefit economically from increased natural diversity.

It may be possible to derive most, if not all, of the materials needed by complex modern economies from naturally occurring and plant-derived sources. For thousands of years human beings have survived completely on foods, fibers, flavorings, medicines, chemicals, building materials, tools, and many other gifts they found or processed directly from plants. With today's sophisticated technologies and scientific knowledge, we should be able to utilize nature's diversity and abundance at least as effectively. David Morris, a consultant on sustainable-materials use, writes:

> Anything made out of hydrocarbons, or fossil fuels, can also be made out of carbohydrates, or living fuels. And once upon a time, probably was. In the late 19th century, the first plastic was made out of cotton. A few years later, the first synthetic fiber was made out of wood. Even 75 years ago, paints, varnishes, pharmaceuticals and industrial chemicals were largely derived from vegetable matter, not from minerals.[14]

Morris notes that plant matter is especially bulky, and therefore expensive to transport over long distances, compared with petroleum, which flows easily through pipelines. Therefore, a plant-based economy more readily lends itself to a system of local agriculture, processing, and use. This also implies that growing a diversity of plants in each community or region for local use is more efficient and economical than monocropping single varieties of useful plants in one part of the nation and transporting them to distant regions.

Parallel to this interest in more locally based economies is an increased interest in modern nations in products and production processes that are more compatible with nature. This interest is being stimulated by the harmful effects of many modern technologies, products, and production processes. For example, in agriculture, the continued use of artificial chemical fertilizers, herbicides, and pesticides has gradually eroded soil fertility, damaged the surrounding environment, and threatened human health. The practice of monocropping makes the crop even more vulnerable to pests and diseases. As a result, both farmers and consumers are becoming interested in organic farming methods, which utilize natural materials and growing practices in order to restore the soil, protect the environment, and produce safer, healthier crops. Diversification is an integral part of organic growing, which utilizes such practices as crop rotation and interplanting in order to vary the nutrients that are removed from and returned to the soil.[15]

Other problems are also increasing people's interest in the great variety of plant species that might be grown in our communities. The increasing use of synthetic materials, which are unable to biodegrade, is causing enormous harm to the environment.[16] And many people are now suffering from debilitating allergies and even more severe illnesses because of overexposure to synthetics. Such problems have stimulated an interest in products derived from a diversity of natural material for home furnishing and building materials, for soaps and cleansers, paints, glues, and numerous other everyday items.[17]

Preindustrial societies based on gathering, hunting, and small-scale agriculture have much to teach modern societies about recognizing and benefiting from nature's local diversity and abundance. The Penan tribe of Borneo, in the southeast Asian rainforest, is just one of many:

> For the Penan the forest is alive, pulsing, responsive in a thousand ways to their physical needs and their spiritual readiness. The products of the forest include roots that cleanse, leaves that cure, edible fruits and seeds, and magical plants that

empower hunting dogs and dispel the forces of darkness. There are plants that yield glue to trap birds, toxic latex for poison darts, rare resins and gums for trade, twine for baskets, leaves for shelter and sandpaper, wood to make blowpipes, boats, tools, and musical instruments. For the Penan all of these plants are sacred, possessed by souls and born of the same earth that gave birth to the people.

Identifying both psychologically and cosmologically with the rainforest and depending on it for all their diet and technology, it is not surprising that the Penan are exceptionally skilled naturalists. . . . Not only do they recognize such conceptually complex phenomena as pollination and dispersal, they understand and accurately predict animal behavior, anticipate the flowering and fruiting cycles of the edible forest plants, know the preferred foods of most forest animals, and may even explain where any animal prefers to pass the night. A recent and cursory examination of their plant lore suggested that the Penan recognize over 100 fruiting trees, some 50 medicinal plants, 8 dart poisons, and 10 plant toxins used to kill fish. These numbers probably represent but a fraction of their botanical knowledge.[18]

Increasingly, modern scientists and other modern people interested in a more sustainable way of life are trying to learn from such scholars and harvesters of natural abundance.

However, many regions of the world do not enjoy such diversity and abundance of resources. And in many areas, monocropping and other forms of economic exploitation of nature have destroyed the former natural diversity. One response to this problem is permaculture ("permanent agriculture"), a new science and hands-on practice that seeks to create or restore diverse natural environments that can meet human needs richly while respecting the cycles, processes, and limits of nature. Permaculture practitioners design and plant diversified land-use plans, including food crops, flowers, trees, and many other varieties that when nurtured and harvested with care can continue to meet human needs for food, fuel, and fiber over the years. Permaculture can be applied in urban, suburban, rural, or wild areas, and designers always allow wild elements to coexist along with human planning.[19]

COMMUNITIES IN HARMONY WITH THE EARTH

The new paradigm recognizes that human well-being is directly dependent upon the health of the natural environment and that a healthy environment is characterized by a rich, vibrant, and constantly self-renewing abundance of numerous diverse resources. These two principles are now being expressed in such activities as the sustainable-cities movement, eco-villages, and bioregionalism.

The goal of the sustainable-cities movement is to bring existing cities into greater harmony with nature. All aspects of urban life are examined: land-use patterns, transportation, education, energy use, neighborhood needs, industry and economic development. Also, these activists seek to lessen the harmful impact on the natural environment (both in and around the city) while better meeting residents' economic, community, cultural, and other needs. Diverse cities throughout the world are participating, developing a wide variety of innovations and approaches.[20]

Eco-villages, also called eco-communities, are smaller-scale developments that strive to be ecologically sound, socially just, and economically viable. They may be parts of existing cities or new communities to be built in as-yet-unpopulated areas. Whether rural, suburban, or urban, they are designed to promote local self-reliance as much as possible, while minimizing damage to natural systems.[21]

One of the most pressing needs of modern societies is to create a culture that honors our interdependence with nature. A vibrant new movement with this goal is bioregionalism. Bioregionalism defines the land on which we live not according to political boundaries but on the basis of natural regions as defined by innate ecological and geological features. Thus, a bioregion may be described as " . . . a life region. A geographic area whose rough boundaries are set by nature, not humankind, distinguishable from other areas by characteristics such as flora, fauna, water, climate, rocks, soils, landforms and the human settlements and cultures shaped by these characteristics."[22] Bioregionalists have identified nesting bioregions, named for key natural characteristics. Gene Marshall, a leading U.S. proponent of bioregionalism, explains:

> I live on the planet Earth, on the bio-continent I call Turtle Island [conventionally called "North America"], in the biome I call The Great Prairie, in an Ecoregion containing parts of Oklahoma and Texas, in the Georegion I call the Upper Blackland Prairie. Further, I live in the blackland prairie part of the Trinity River Watershed, and on White Rock Creek . . . we can also discern our local neighborhoods: perhaps the watershed of our local creek or the valley that contains our town.[23]

Supporters of bioregionalism have developed a variety of resources, including maps that show the Earth's bioregions, practical exercises for becoming better acquainted with one's local bioregion, and theoretical discussions that explore the concept's numerous implications and applications. Bioregionalism is a natural organizing principle in relation to which we can orient our economic, political, community, and cultural activities. By inviting us to reconnect with and learn from the distinct area of the Earth in which we reside, bioregionalism offers us an organic basis for making our daily lives richer and fuller while honoring the planet that supports us.[24]

NOTES

1. On community gardening, see Boston Urban Gardeners, *The Handbook of Community Gardening* (Boston: Charles Scribner's Sons, 1982) available for $$7.95 plus $2.90 postage from Boston Urban Gardeners, 46 Chestnut St., Jamaica Plain, MA 02130.

2. One of the most influential visions of economic success through a disembodied high-tech economy with no connection to local environments appears in Robert B. Reich, *The Work of Nations* (New York: Random House, 1992).

3. The importance of locally controlled, community-oriented agricultural sectors in the economic success of Japan, South Korea, and Taiwan is documented by David C. Korten, *Getting to the 21st Century: Voluntary Action and the Global Agenda* (West Hartford, Conn.: Kumarian Press, 1990), 74–77. The importance of local agriculture in the United States and other modern nations is addressed in Trauger

Groh and Stephen McFadden, *Farms of Tomorrow: Communities Supporting Farms, Farms Supporting Communities* (Kimberton, Penn.: Bio-Dynamic Farming and Gardening Association, 1990), available for $12.00 plus $3.00 postage from BDFGA, P.O. Box 550, Kimberton, PA 19442. See also Marty Strange, *Family Farming: A New Economic Vision* (San Francisco: Institute for Food and Development Policy, 1988).

4. Destruction of locally controlled agriculture is causing economic decline in South Korea and Taiwan, say Walden Bello and Stephanie Rosenfeld, *Dragons in Distress: Asia's Miracle Economies in Crisis* (San Francisco: Institute for Food and Development Policy, 1990), chaps. 4 and 11. Available from IFDP, 398 60th St., Oakland, CA 94618, (510) 654-4400.

5. Center for Rural Affairs, P.O. Box 406, Walthill, NE 68067-0406, (402) 846-5428; the Midwest Sustainable Agriculture Working Group, c/o Center for Rural Affairs; National Family Farm/Ranch Transition Network, c/o Farm On, 10861 Douglas, Suite B, Urbandale, IA 50322; Genesis Farm, 41A Silver Lake Rd., Blairstown, NJ 07825; Earthwise Education Center, P.O. Box 91, Camden, NY 13316.

6. In addition to the economic-related issues mentioned here, the interest in more locally based economies also reflects the larger postmodern trend from centralization to decentralization. See John Naisbitt, *Megatrends: Ten New Directions Transforming Our Lives* (New York: Warner, 1982), chap. 5.

7. A comprehensive discussion of the political, economic, environmental and other benefits of a renewables-based, self-reliant energy policy in the United States is found in L. Hunter Lovins, Amory B. Lovins, and Seth Zuckerman, *Energy Unbound: A Fable for America's Future* (San Francisco: Sierra Club, 1986), available from Rocky Mountain Institute, 1739 Snowmass Creek Rd., Snowmass, CO 81654-9199, (303) 927-3851.

8. On how Western nations and multinational corporations have kept Third-World nations economically and politically inferior, see Arjun Makhijani, *From Global Capitalism to Economic Justice* (New York: Apex Press, 1992); or Walden Bello with Shea Cunningham and Bill Rau, *Dark Victory: The United States, Structural Adjustment and Global Poverty* (Oakland, Calif.: Institute for Food and Development Policy, 1994).

9. On political and economic reasons for hunger, see Frances Moore Lappé and Joseph Collins, *World Hunger: Twelve Myths* (New York: Grove Press, 1986), available from the Institute for Food and Development Policy (see note 4).

10. On the effectiveness of local grassroots economic development, see Bruce Stokes, *Local Responses to Global Problems*, Worldwatch Paper 17 (Washington, D.C.: Worldwatch Institute, 1978); Alan B. Durning, *Action at the Grassroots: Fighting Poverty and Environmental Decline*, Worldwatch Paper 88 (Washington, D.C. Worldwatch Institute, 1989).

11. On the environmental sophistication of Third-World women who work directly with nature to produce life's necessities, see Vandana Shiva, *Staying Alive: Women, Ecology and Development* (Atlantic Highlands, N.J.: Zed Books, 1989).

12. On environmentally sustainable, locally controlled community economic development, see Christine Meyer and Faith Moosang, eds., *Living with the Land: Communities Restoring the Earth* (Philadelphia: New Society Publishers, 1992); and Alan B. Durning, *Action at the Grassroots: Fighting Poverty and Environmental Decline*, Worldwatch Paper 88 (Washington, D.C.: Worldwatch Institute, 1989).

13. On the emergence of niche markets in the global economy, see Reich, *The Work of Nations*, chap. 7.

14. David Morris, "Good Stewardship Encourages Local Self-Reliance," *Co-Op America Quarterly*, Winter 1991, 6.

15. On organic agriculture, contact the Biodynamic Farming and Gardening Association (note 3); or the Organic Foods Production Association of North America, P. O. Box 1078, Greenfield, MA 01302, (413) 774-7511. The *National Organic Directory*, a 356-page guide to United States and international organic farmers, distributors, and other organic agriculture-related businesses, support, and political action groups is available for $34.95 plus $5.00 postage from Community Allicance with Family Farmers, P. O. Box 464, Davis, CA 95617, (800) 852-3832.

16. On synthetic chemicals causing environmental damage, see Barry Commoner, *The Closing Circle: Nature, Man, and Technology* (New York: Knopf, 1971).

17. Characteristics of and access to more naturally derived products and materials is described in Debra Lynn Dadd, *Nontoxic, Natural, and Earthwise: How To Protect Yourself And Your Family From Harmful Products and Live In Harmony with the Earth* (Los Angeles: J. P. Tarcher, 1990).

18. Wade Davis, *Penan: Voice for the Borneo Rainforest* (Vancouver: Western Canada Wilderness Committee, 1990), 98. An updated edition of this book will be available shortly from the Western Canada Wilderness Committee, 20 Water St., Vancouver, B. C. V6B 1A4, Canada, (604) 683-8220.

19. *The Permaculture Activist: A Quarterly Voice for Permanent Culture In North America*, provides resources, networking, and information exchange and is available from *The Permaculture Activist*, Rt. 1, Box 38, Primm Springs, TN 38476. Permaculture publications are also available from Arrow Point Press, P.O. Box 14754-0, Portland, OR 97214, (503) 236-7359.

20. Contact the Sustainable Cities Movement, Institute for Resource and Security Studies, 27 Ellsworth Ave., Cambridge, MA 02139, (617) 491-5177.

21. On eco-villages and sustainable communities, contact the Eco-village at Ithaca, Anabel Taylor Hall, Cornell Univ., Ithaca, N.Y. 14853; or see *Co-Op America Quarterly*, Spring 1993, issue on sustainable communities, available from Co-op America, 1850 "M" St. NW, Washington D.C. 20036, (202) 872-5307. Another good contact is the Community Sustainability Resource Institute, P.O. Box 11343, Takoma Park, MD 20913, (301) 588-7227.

22. "Announcement for Turtle Island Bioregional Congress-V, May 17–24, 1992."

23. Gene Marshall, *Realistic Living*, November 1991, Issue 15, 3 available from Realistic Living, Rt. 3, Box 104-A 5, Bonham, TX 75418.

24. For more on bioregionalism, see Kirkpatrick Sale, *Dwellers in the Land: The Bioregional Vision* (Philadelphia, PA: New Society Publishers, 1991); Van Andruss, Christopher Plant, Judith Plant and Eleanor Wright, eds., *Home! A Bioregional Reader* (Philadelphia: New Society Publishers, 1990); Doug Aberley, ed., *Boundaries of Home: Mapping for Local Empowerment* (Philadelphia: New Society Publishers, 1993); and Doug Aberley, ed., *Futures by Design: The Practice of Ecological Planning* (Philadelphia: New Society Publishers, 1994).

Chapter 16

ENRICHING CONNECTIONS: COMMUNITY MONEY SYSTEMS

It might be said that an addiction to money is the root of much evil. However, when money is used wisely, in the roles for which it was intended—as a medium for the exchange of and a stimulus for the production of real wealth—it is a convenient resource, among many others, to help individuals and communities improve their well-being.

Ironically, the modern economic paradigm often prevents people from using money to produce and distribute wealth. In response to this problem people are developing new kinds of money systems that help increase local wealth while strengthening individual self-esteem and enhancing community connections.

LOCALLY AND CENTRALLY CREATED MONEY

Although money systems can be created by local communities to meet their needs, a monarch, national government, central bank, or other centralized power often issues the money that will be used by the rest of society. In the United States, centrally issued money is actually a fairly recent development. Up until the 1860s, banks chartered by either the federal government or by individual states were legally allowed to issue money, and states liberally chartered private banks, which issued their own monies to customers seeking loans.[1] By the 1860s, more than 10,000 different kinds of locally issued bank notes were in use simultaneously![2] But during the Civil War, the U.S. government established a federally regulated system of national banks. It also placed a ten percent tax on notes issued by state-chartered banks, making locally issued money unprofitable, so banks no longer created it. Since that time, individuals and enterprises have instead received bank loans in the form of accounts against which the loan recipient writes checks.[3]

With the Great Depression of the 1930s, thousands of banks around the United States closed, and the deposits they held disappeared. Farmers were still producing food, municipalities and individuals still had needs, and plenty of people without jobs had skills and were willing to work. But there was no money to reconnect these various elements of the economy. So in numerous communities, local governments, business associations, or charitable groups began to create their own money systems for local use. Local Depression money came in many variations: vouchers that could only be traded in specific stores, or for specific items, and printed currencies (often called "scrip") on paper, cardboard, even wood, which had to be spent within the community a certain number of times, or before a certain date, or which were backed by, and under certain conditions could be redeemed for fresh produce, canned goods, or even conventional money. By 1933, the *New York Times* reported that one million Americans in three hundred communities were using barter or scrip systems to keep their economies going.[4] But as new national economic policies, and eventually World War II, lifted the nation out of the Great Depression, local money systems were no longer needed and centrally issued money again became the norm.

PROBLEMS WITH CENTRALLY ISSUED MONEY

Since in modern economies money is created and issued by centralized institutions, other alternatives are labeled by those in power as impractical or economically harmful, or have been made invisible. The modern economic paradigm fails to teach us that because money is simply an information technology based on trust and community—a system of promises to be returned—it is a system that local communities can create to meet their own needs, and to express and promote their members' values.

At this point, you might be wondering about the legality of individuals or communities creating their own money. To clarify: It is illegal to counterfeit government money and try to pass it off as the real thing. But according to people who have done it, it is perfectly legal to make up your own distinct money (not an imitation of the government's), and to use it for your own purposes, either public or private. All that the government cares about is that you pay taxes on it—in government money—when that is required.[5]

But why would people want to create their own money, when the government already goes to all the trouble of printing and distributing it? There are a number of reasons why money issued by a centralized government or bank may fail to enable people to exchange goods and services and stimulate the production of more wealth.

In a Hierarchically Organized Society, Centrally Issued Money Tends to Go to Those on Top, and to Those Who Serve the Dominant Values

In modern economies, the official national currency is distributed through regional and local banks and put into circulation by being loaned out to businesses, other institutions, and to individuals. Hierarchical structures and assumptions mean that already rich individuals and large, wealthy businesses are most likely to get more money. For example, it's easy for a very rich individual or a big corporation to get a loan of millions of dollars from a bank. But a poor person who has a vision, a skill, and the willingness to work hard, but no property to back it up, may be unable to get a bank loan or even $500 or $1,000 in order to start their own modest enterprise. Money is also distributed in the form of salaries and wages. But individuals who meet the criteria of the dominant groups are most likely to get and keep jobs and earn the highest wages, while members of supposedly inferior groups are either restricted to lower-paying jobs or are less likely to find paid employment at all. So centrally issued money can systematically be kept out of the hands of individuals and communities that do not have power or that do not fit the prevailing mainstream criteria of worthiness.

Wealthy and Powerful Individuals and Institutions Can Remove Centrally Issued Money from Local Communities

Within an economically empowered community, money represents the wealth that people create, increases the circulation and exchange of wealth in that community, and can be reinvested in new local enterprises in order to create even more wealth for the community. But when wealth leaves a local community, either in the form of material resources or in the form of money, and if no corresponding wealth comes back in, the well-being of individuals and of the community overall will suffer.

In chapter 11 I cited the book *Reclaiming Capital: Democratic Initiatives and Community Development*, by Christopher and Hazel Dayton Gunn, which describes how the monetary wealth of individuals and enterprises in poor communities is systematically taken out of these communities and redistributed to wealthy individuals and institutions outside.[6] As we shall see, community-based money systems are one strategy for preventing the removal of money from, or restoring money to, poor or economically depressed communities.

Outside Events Can Change the Value or Availability of Centrally Issued Money

The value of money can easily change, and during the last few decades of the twentieth century it has continued to decline as modern nations experience constantly rising inflation. A dollar today will not buy what a dollar bought twenty or fifty years ago, and who knows what a dollar will buy tomorrow? As money loses its value, the purchasing power of our wages, salaries, savings, pensions, and Social Security also declines.

External trends and larger events, such as inflation, recessions, or depressions, are always changing the value and availability of centrally issued money. On top of that, governments regularly change the value and availability of money through their fiscal and monetary policies (e.g., by altering interest rates). Their purpose in so doing is to keep the economy stable or promote needed economic activity, but there is no guarantee that will achieve the desired goals. Besides, government policies to manipulate the money system or control the economy invariably help some groups while hurting others. As a result, individuals and local communities can suffer, through no fault of their own, when money is devalued due to inflation, when high interest rates make it hard to get, or when it disappears from circulation due to government policies or other, larger events.[7]

Reasons for Community-Based Money Systems

Because an economy that utilizes centrally issued money is subject to the problems described above, people today are once again turning to locally created money systems in order to empower themselves and their communities. Community-based money systems usually have one or more of the following purposes:

— to keep money in a local community to retain and build locally created wealth;

— to keep the local economy going even when the larger economy falters (e.g., due to inflation or depression);

to allow all members of the community to obtain goods and services—whether or not they have conventional money, income, or jobs;

— and to keep the value of the local money stable by basing it on locally available, readily accessible sources of real wealth, such as natural resources, people's skills, and their connections to each other.

One of the most comprehensive and up-to-date studies of community money systems is *New Money for Healthy Communities*, recently written and published by community economist and consultant Thomas H. Greco, Jr. In extensive, documented detail, he presents the history and theory of community money systems, describes current examples, and discusses their strengths, limitations, and flaws.[8] This book is required reading for anyone wishing more in depth information.

The rest of this chapter describes several of the most popular systems. It should be noted that some of these systems utilize paper money, while others keep accounts of how much value people have created and exchanged without physical money passing from hand to hand.

LOCAL CURRENCIES

Local currencies are physical money, usually pieces of paper with their value printed on them, which are issued by a local institution and circulate within a limited geographical area. This limited circulation is actually a benefit, because it assures that the money does not leave the area but continues to recirculate within it, facilitating more exchanges.

After the Depression, the next notable use of community currencies in the United States took place in 1972 in the town of Exeter, New Hampshire. Long-time community-economics advocate Ralph Borsodi issued a local currency called "Constants," based on a standard of value using thirty commodities in an index similar to the Dow-Jones Average. Local people and businesses used these Constants, and they were written about in *Time* magazine. After a year, Borsodi, who was then 88 years old, discontinued the experiment, but he was pleased with its success.[9]

Since the early 1990s, Bob Swann and Susan Witt of the E. F. Schumacher Society (an organization that promotes sustainable community-based economies) have been working on a community currency for their rural, small-town community in the Berkshires region of western Massachusetts. In 1991, popular deli owner Frank Tortoriello wanted to expand his business, but could not get a bank loan. Swann and Witt encouraged him to issue "Deli-Dollars," notes sold for nine dollars, which Tortoriello would redeem after six months for ten dollars worth of food. Not only did he raise enough money to expand, but Deli-Dollars soon began to be accepted in place of cash by residents and other local businesses. Next, Swann and Witt assisted two local farms in printing "Farm Notes" (with a head of cabbage instead of the head of George Washington and the words "In Farms We Trust"). More than $8,000 worth of Farm Notes were sold in the winter, when cash income was scarce, helping tide the farms over until the following summer, when the notes were redeemed for fresh produce.[10]

Having gained community confidence (and both national and international media publicity) through these projects, Swann and Witt are now planning to issue a county-wide currency through the local banks. To be called "Berkshares," they will be valued at the rate of ninety cents for one dollar worth of the local currency. Their appeal is that they will recirculate within the community, stimulating the local economy. Other community currencies have been implemented in other parts of the United States.[11]

EXCHANGE-TYPE SYSTEMS

Informal Barter

Barter, or one-on-one exchange, is a time-honored way for people to meet their needs and is especially helpful when money is short. It can be found in communities throughout the United States.[12] Individuals set up informal arrangements with each other as necessary. For example, "I'll trade my typing services for a sweater you knit for me"; "I'll give you singing lessons in exchange for you cleaning my house";"I'll repair your bicycle, and in exchange you watch my child sometime."

Neighborhood Exchange Networks

Neighborhood exchange networks utilize the barter concept to bring neighbors together and enhance the quality of neighborhood life both materially and nonmaterially. Economic innovator Anne Slepian recently founded such a system and encourages others to do similar projects in their neighborhoods:

When Slepian began knocking on doors . . . her neighbors were extremely positive, but some were also unable to see that they might have something to offer. "They would say, 'I don't have anything to contribute.' I remember pointing to a person's guitar and asking if they played," Slepian says. "Just looking around a room gave me a chance to talk about their interests."

With twenty people in her three-block area participating, the exchange opportunities were great. "Margie brought us morning glories, we watered Peter's garden when he was away, and Alice helped Christopher with his bookkeeping." Slepian added, "Two people even developed a romance."

"Those who are active get to know people who live in the area, save money, and create a safer neighborhood," Slepian says. "The neighborhood is safer when you know who lives there and have some sort of relationship with them."[13]

Slepian offers an information packet for others wishing to organize their own neighborhood exchanges.[14]

Formal Barter Networks

One limitation of the tit-for-tat exchange is that when I need word-processing services, I may not find anyone who can give them to me who wants the singing lessons I offer in exchange. To solve this problem and facilitate more diverse exchanges, more formal barter networks have been established that utilize a credit system: when I provide you with word-processing services, you do not need to give me anything in exchange. However, the barter exchange records the value of the services I gave you, based on their dollar value if they were sold commercially. I am entitled to receive up to that value in goods or services at some time in the future from other members of the barter network, and you must repay that value in goods or services to other members some time in the future. Keeping track of credits owed and redeemed requires a more formal degree of organization, but it allows more people to be involved and more wealth to be created and exchanged within networks.[15]

A note about barter and taxes: Although participating in a barter network is a way to meet one's needs without spending money, many barter networks collect a fee in conventional dollars to cover their administrative costs or to make a profit. On top of that, the U.S. government has ruled that whenever you provide other members of a formal barter system with goods or services, you must count the monetary value of the credits you receive as income, and must pay taxes on it. The government's rationale is that since barter networks often include businesses as well as private individuals, the members are engaging in commercial exchanges even if they don't actually pay money for the goods or services they receive. However, while any exchange of professional services for which one would normally be paid must be reported as income, the Internal Revenue Service recognizes that people can also exchange nonprofessional services, in simple neighborly cooperation, and it does not require people to report or pay taxes on such nonprofessional, neighborly exchanges.[16]

SERVICE-EXCHANGE SYSTEMS

In service-exchange systems, participants exchange services only (not material items). A central coordinator, either an individual or a sponsoring organization, keeps track of the value of services donated and how many credits donors are owed. The unique aspect of service-exchanges is that services are measured not according to presumed market value but solely on the basis of time. For every hour of service given, a donor is entitled to receive one hour of service. The actual services involved—whether massage, house-cleaning, carpentry, computer programming, teaching, driving someone to the doctor, or whatever—are irrelevant. The implicit philosophy behind such service-exchanges is an egalitarian one: As long as people's needs are being met, my time is of equal value to your time.

According to IRS rulings, because service exchanges trade nonmarketable skills and are designed to advance charitable purposes (see Time Dollars below), they are not considered commercial, taxable transactions.[17]

WOMANSHARE

WOMANSHARE is a service exchange for women in New York City that began in 1991. Its founders, Diana McCourt and Jane Wilson, originally traded their carpentry and cooking skills with each other informally. This worked out so well for them that, after reading about the Time Dollar model (see below), they were inspired to develop a larger network, its goal being to build both greater community ties and economic empowerment with other women in the city. They had barely begun to publicize their idea when dozens of women contacted them about membership. Eventually they decided to close membership at sixty women. Members range in age from twenty to seventy and include both single women and those with families, with and without paying jobs.

In order to encourage member interaction, WOMANSHARE suggests that every member give at least four hours worth of service each month. By 1993, members were offering each other 60 different kinds of instruction—in everything from stick-shift driving and desktop publishing to t'ai chi and conflict resolution—and 130 different services, including career counseling, publicity campaigns, body work, pet sitting, and simply spending time with another member to provide her with emotional and social support. The orientation process for new members is designed to help women discover their undervalued or unrecognized skills, while the network spreads these riches around, enhancing both individuals and the WOMANSHARE community as a whole.

As a pioneering service-exchange, WOMANSHARE has participated in many educational events, and has inspired and assisted in the formation of more service-exchange networks around the country.[18]

Time Dollars

The Time Dollar approach is a more formal version of a service-exchange network in which, for every hour of service given to another member, the donor receives one hour's worth of service credits, recorded as "Time Dollars." This system was developed by law professor Dr. Edgar S. Cahn as a way to meet the needs, take advantage of the skills and experience, and sustain the dignity of the United States's rapidly growing population of elders. The concept behind it is that retired people who are still active can offer services to more needy elders, then when the donors are in need of services themselves, they can draw on the Time Dollars they have built up to receive the services they need.

Some pilot Time Dollar systems were initiated under the federal Older Americans Act, and the State of Missouri has agreed to purchase service credits from holders if no volunteers are available to redeem them later on. Most Time Dollar programs have been started by nonprofits that serve elders, but they often include people of all ages exchanging services. This not only benefits recipients by providing them with needed services, but also increases interactions among different age groups. In 1990 it was reported that over 3,000 participants were providing about 15,000 hours of service a month through Time Dollar programs in nine states and the District of Columbia, and the numbers have been mounting steadily since then.[19]

In many Time Dollar systems, donors can transfer their credits to others in need, rather than redeeming them for themselves. This adds an even greater degree of flexibility to the system. As a program for elders and others in need, Time Dollar systems emphasize such services as providing home care, and running errands, among others. A range of resources, from a simple descriptive pamphlet to sophisticated computer software, is available to assist others in setting up Time Dollar programs.[20]

LETS SYSTEMS

The LETS system, which can stand either for Local Exchange Trading System or Local Employment and Trading System, was invented in the early 1980s by economic innovator Michael Linton, when his rural community in British Columbia, Canada, was devastated by an economic recession. In LETS systems, members trade both goods and services, using a combination of conventional dollars and credits called "Green Dollars." When people give goods or services to each other, they receive credits in Green Dollars, and when they receive goods or services, they owe Green Dollars. A central computer program keeps track of each member's balance.

What gives LETS systems their unique power is Linton's insight that as participants exchange goods and services, thereby building up debits or credits that will facilitate even more exchanges, they are in essence creating money. It makes sense logically to refer to LETS credits as "Green Dollars," and this nomenclature also helps participants understand how to use the LETS system. But in contrast to conventional physical currencies, which are first issued by an outside agency, and then dispersed throughout the community as people use that money to buy and sell, the unique characteristic of LETS-type "money" is that each person is constantly creating his or her own money as needed, and then reabsorbing it by participating in the process of giving and receiving goods and services. In a LETS system, in order to create more money for yourself, all you need do is reach out and help someone else. The more goods or services you give to others, the more money you create. Participants in LETS systems can also receive needed goods and services first, building up credits owed, which they will repay when others need goods or services that they can provide.

The following report, from a woman active with a LETS system in rural Canada, demonstrates the system's personal, economic, and community benefits:

> Without this system our Christmas would have been very bleak. The children were given handcrafted toys, and other family members were given pottery, jewelery, and candles. All of my and my children's clothing now comes through LETS. We get some of our food through LETS. I feel that I am valued in the community for the work that I provide. I like to have my small children exposed to this alternate monetary system; they now check out if goods are available for green or federal dollars. I have met many new people through the LETSystem and feel that our sense of community in the Comox Valley has greatly increased. I have also found that people have skills which they haven't used or thought about in years, and it is all being drawn out and interest re-kindled. People have started to value themselves differently and come alive.[21]

As of early 1994, it was reported that there are at least 486 LETS systems operating around the world, in Canada, the United States, England, Australia, and New Zealand. Some have been organized by nonprofit community groups, others by ad hoc groups of individuals. Background information and necessary computer software can be obtained directly from the founder, and other LETS systems offer information about their own experiences with, and variations of, the concept.[22]

Although people organize LETS systems in order to enhance community and trade both commercial as well as noncommercial goods and services, the IRS considers LETS a form of commercial barter and requires that participants report as income the dollar-value of all credits received and pay taxes on it. I consider this to be an unfair position, and am interested in developing a campaign to convince the government to declare all nonmonetized exchanges free from taxation.

ITHACA MONEY

One of the latest developments in community money systems is "Ithaca Money" in the small city of Ithaca, New York. It combines both hands-on currency and an exchange network. Created by urban designer and community economist Paul Glover, with assistance from a grant from the Fund for Investigative Journalism, the Ithaca Money system has a currency-printing entity, the Barter Bank of Ithaca, which prints up dollar-size "Ithaca HOURS," and publishes *Ithaca Money*, a bi-monthly newspaper that lists hundreds of barter offers from private individuals.

Any Ithaca-area resident can get involved by filling in a coupon stating goods or services he or she wishes to trade or receive and sending it to the newspaper.

Listings cost one dollar each, and the system sends each newly listed individual forty dollars worth of Ithaca HOURS to use in exchanges. Ithaca HOURS are a labor-based currency; that is, each HOUR is equivalent to ten dollars worth of human labor, the average hourly wage in the Ithaca area.

Ithaca Money has also aggressively recruited local businesses that agree to take Ithaca HOURS in partial payment for their goods or services. Participating businesses, which take out paid ads in the newspaper, include a variety of retail and service businesses, such as the cooperatively owned grocery store, a movie theater, restaurants, a bowling alley, a health club, the credit union, and local farmers who participate in the city's farmers' markets.

The Ithaca Money system officially began in fall, 1991. By the fall of 1992 it was estimated that the system had added $150,000 worth of wealth to the economy through barter and use of Ithaca HOURS. HOURS have helped pay for necessities and luxuries, even for rent and loans, and by 1994 have been used by over 1,000 individuals and over 200 businesses.[23] Ithaca Money also makes small grants of Ithaca Hours to local nonprofit organizations. Says founder Paul Glover:

> While the U. S. dollar is a junk bond issued by the world's greatest debtor, backed by less than nothing, the Ithaca HOUR is backed by the time and skills of real people we can shake hands with. . . . Ithaca HOURS cannot purchase Middle East oil by computer transfer, nor can they purchase Malaysian rainforest lumber, cheap Korean labor, or Congressional votes. Instead, they stimulate us to recycle wealth locally, to shop locally, to produce jobs locally, to invest locally, to declare our trust in Ithaca. They give us power.[24]

To help other communities start their own systems, Ithaca Money offers a comprehensive "Home-Town Money Starter Kit," which includes both specifics about the system and lots of background information about other community money systems in the United States.[25]

IMPACT OF COMMUNITY MONEY SYSTEMS

As the above examples suggest, when people create and participate in community-based money and exchange systems, they:

— realize that they have valuable skills to offer, beyond what they do to earn a living, or that they have valuable skills to share even if they do not have a job;

— interact more with their neighbors, and community connections are strengthened;

— support each other in creating and exchanging wealth; and

— become more hopeful, creative, and productive.

As a result, even more wealth is generated and distributed in the community. People may consider starting community-based money systems out of economic necessity. But the personal and social benefits, and the increased individual and community empowerment which results from such systems, become additional reasons to utilize them.

NOTES

1. John Kenneth Galbraith, *Money: Whence It Came, Where It Went* (Boston: Houghton Mifflin, 1975), chap. 7.

2. "The Story of Money," 4th ed. (New York: Federal Reserve Bank of New York, 1984), 15, available from Federal Reserve Bank of New York, Public Information Department, 33 Liberty St., New York, NY 10045.

3. Galbraith, *Money*, 89–91.

4. "One Million Americans Learn to Get Along Without Money," *New York Times*, 12 March 1933, 2. Articles on Depression money are available from Ithaca Money (see note 25, below).

5. Regarding the legality of issuing local money, Bob Swann of the E. F. Schumacher Society, who has been involved in several such projects, including the Exeter, New Hampshire "Constants" in the early 1970s (see note 9, below), says that there is no federal law prohibiting it. He says that when a reporter asked the U.S. Treasury about the legality of the Constants, the Treasury Department replied, "We don't care if he uses pine cones, so long as they can be exchanged for dollars to pay taxes." See Robert Swann, "The Need for Local Currencies" (Great Barrington, Mass.: E. F. Schumacher Society, 1990), 12. The E. F. Schumacher Society can be contacted at P.O. Box 76, RD 3, Great Barrington, MA 01230.

6. On the removal of wealth from local communities, see Christopher Gunn and Hazel Dayton Gunn, *Reclaiming Capital: Democratic Initiatives and Community Development* (Ithaca, N.Y.: Cornell University Press, 1991), chap. 2.

7. The rationale for, and methods through which the federal government manipulates monetary policies, are described in Robert L. Heilbroner and Lester C. Thurow, *Economics Explained*, updated ed. (New York: Simon & Schuster, 1987), chaps. 11 and 12. A strong case for local currencies as a way of protecting local communities from external manipulation of money, keeping wealth in the local community, and expressing local values is made in Robert Swann, "The Need for Local Currencies," available from the E. F. Schumacher Society, P.O. Box 76, RD 3, Great Barrington MA 02130, for $3.00.

8. The most recent and comprehensive discussion of community-based money systems is Thomas H. Greco, Jr., *New Money for Healthy Communities* (Tucson, Ariz.: Thomas H. Greco, Jr., 1994), available for $15.95 plus $3.00 postage from Thomas H. Greco, Jr., P.O. Box 42663, Tucson, AZ 85733, (602) 577-2187.

9. Ralph Borsodi's "Constants" are described in Swann, "The Need for Local Currencies," 12.

10. Deli-Dollars and Farm Notes are described in Michael Specter, *International Herald Tribune*, 21 May 1991, which is available from the E. F. Schumacher Society.

11. For information about Deli-Dollars, Farm Notes, and Berkshares, send $3.00 to the E. F. Schumacher Society, Box 76, RD 3, Great Barrington, MA 01230, (413) 528-1737. Information about other community currencies is available for $3.00 from Amy Belanger, P. O. Box 7132, Milton, FL 32570. Belanger also plans to start a networking newsletter about community currencies ($10/year).

12. Information about informal exchanges is from my own observations and informal reports from other people around the United States.

13. Warren Goldstein-Gelb and Marcy Goldstein-Gelb, "Neighborhood Exchanges Give Credit to Community," *Somerville Community News*, September/ October 1993, 4.

14. To obtain the information packet "How to Organize Your Own Neighborhood Exchange," send $2.00 to Anne Slepian, 21 Linwood St., Arlington, MA 02174.

15. Enterprises that facilitate barter go by a variety of names, including trade exchanges, barter exchanges, barter networks, and barter clubs. Participants may include businesses only, private individuals only, or a combination thereof. For more information, see Roger Langrick, *Barter Systems: A Business Guide for Trade Exchanges* (Montclair, N.J.: Longmeadow Press, 1994); or Annie Proulx, *Back to Barter: What'll You Take For It?* (New York: Simon & Schuster, 1983), a how-to guide that

covers both formal and informal bartering. For information about business barter, contact the International Reciprocal Trade Association, Great Falls, Virginia, (703) 759-1473, or the National Association of Trade Exchanges, c/o Jack Schacht, (708) 390-6000.

16. On barter and taxes, see Proulx, *Back to Barter*, chap. 7, or Edgar Cahn, Ph.D, J.D., and Jonathan Rowe, *Time Dollars: The New Currency that Enables Americans to Turn Their Hidden Resource—Time—into Personal Security and Community Renewal* (Emmaus, Penn.: Rodale Press, 1991), 77–79.

17. On why the IRS does not tax volunteer service-exchanges that promote community service, see Cahn and Rowe, *Time Dollars*, chap. 6.

18. For general information on WOMANSHARE, send a SASE with 52¢ postage; for four newsletters, $1.00 each; for a 10-minute video, $10 plus $2 postage to WOMANSHARE, c/o Diana McCourt, 680 West End Ave., New York, NY 10025.

19. Edgar S. Cahn, "The Time Dollar," P.O. Box 19405, Washington, DC 20036, 1990, p. 3.

20. For more information on Time Dollar and other service-credit programs, see Cahn and Rowe, *The Time Dollar*. Or send $1.00 for an introductory brochure; $12.00 plus postage for a 10-minute video; $15.00 plus $2.00 postage for a detailed manual; or $78.75 for the complete kit, which includes all the above plus computer programs and more, to Time Dollars, P.O. Box 19405, Washington, DC 20036.

21. Experience with a LETS system quoted in Michael Linton, *LETS System Handbook*, "User Reports," p. 1, December 11, 1985, available from Landsman Community Services (see note 22, below).

22. Information about starting your own LETS system is available from Michael Linton, Landsman Community Services, Ltd., 375 Johnston Ave., Courtenay, B. C. V9N 2Y2, Canada, (604) 338-0213. Other perspectives on LETS systems can be obtained from the Co-op Resources and Services Project, 3551 White House Place, Los Angeles, CA 90004, (213) 738-1254; and "Let's Connect," Highland Valley Elder Services, 320 Riverside Drive, Northampton, MA 01060, (413) 586-2000. Both organizations have been sponsoring LETS systems with several hundred members for several years.

23. Reports on Ithaca Money activities are from *Ithaca Money*, Issue #8, December 1992 January 1993, p. 1, and personal communication with Paul Glover, April 15, 1994.

24. Paul Glover, "New Money for Ithaca's Economy," reprint available from Ithaca Money (see note 25, below).

25. The "Home-Town Money Starter Kit," complete with forms and many news articles on community-money systems past and present, is available for $25.00 from Ithaca Money, Box 6578, Ithaca, NY 14851, (607) 273-8025.

PART IV

Beyond Economic Addiction: Making Choices that Empower

Chapter 17

A HUMAN VIEW OF HUMAN NEEDS

According to the modern economic paradigm, human needs are limitless. This belief justifies the addictive economy, in which we must constantly increase our consumption in order to absorb businesses' constantly increasing production. But starting in the 1960s and 1970s, the assumption of limitless needs began to be challenged by a new environmental awareness and by increasing dissatisfaction, in modern nations, with solely materialistic goals. People began to accept that there are limits to the natural environment, which implies that we must place limits on how many resources we can consume and how much waste we can produce. At the same time, a growing cultural interest in greater emotional fulfillment, community regeneration, and spirituality suggests that there comes a point where people want to do more with their lives than merely earn money so they can buy and consume more goods and services. Such new perspectives have been crucial to the emergence of the postmodern economic paradigm.

IS THERE A HIERARCHY OF HUMAN NEEDS?

The recent and startling discovery that people can move beyond the desire for material affluence had to be reconciled with a two hundred-year history of industrialization and economic growth in western societies. One attempt to explain the emergence of this new, apparently nonmaterialistic, more spiritual stage in human history uses the hierarchy-of-needs theory proposed by twentieth-century U.S. psychologist Abraham Maslow. He suggested that human needs are hierarchical and that as each level is satisfied, needs move to the next higher level. According to Maslow, people first seek to satisfy their physiological needs, e.g. for food and warmth; then the need for safety and security; then they are motivated by the need for companionship and affection; next for self-esteem and the esteem of others; and only after all these lower needs are satisfied does each individual seek self-actualization, i.e. being able to realize one's potential to the fullest.[1]

Initially, such a hierarchy of needs may sound quite sensible. But ranking human needs in a hierarchy, with so-called physical or material needs at the bottom and the other needs at the top, is based on the faulty assumption that we can separate our minds, emotions, and spirit from the physical, bodily aspects of our lives. This assumption is destructive to human health and integrity, as the most advanced findings of medical science are now discovering.[2]

Not only does such a hierarchy separate us from ourselves, but it also promotes a hierarchical view of society. It implies that until they have their material needs met, poor people cannot care about others or develop their full human potential and are therefore incapable of developing good values or running their own lives. It also implies that art, spirituality, love, self-respect, and respect from others are irrelevant to the lives and needs of poor people and poor communities. It ignores the fact that creativity, courage, compassion, art, spirituality, and other highly esteemed human qualities exist in even the most materially impoverished communities.

Furthermore, a hierarchy of needs could imply that only people who have satisfied their so-called lower, material needs, are capable of experiencing and expressing higher forms of self-expression such as art, spirituality, love, compassion, or inspired leadership. The deepest implication of such a hierarchical conception of needs is that because modern, white, Western nations have most successfully met their inhabitants' lower—material—needs, they are now the most spiritually evolved societies in the world. And this is obviously an absurd conclusion. A more empowering economy requires a model that acknowledges the variety of human needs but does not place them in a hierarchical order.

A WHOLE-LIFE MODEL OF HUMAN NEEDS

Needs develop, and are satisfied, in relation to time. The cyclical patterns and rhythms of the human body, of human life, shape our needs in very specific ways ignored by conventional economic models. If we acknowledge time as a central organizing principle of human needs, we could develop a much more realistic and empowering conception of how the economy could work. When people are free to develop economic activities under their own direction, rather than to meet the needs of either a hierarchically superior group or of an addiction-driven system, we will discover that their actions meet these following types of needs:

Ongoing survival needs;

Cyclical needs for care;

Ongoing needs for amenities;

Occasional needs for luxuries; and

The ongoing need to replenish the sources that support and sustain us.

These five types of needs are not arranged in any kind of hierarchy but are all equally essential to human survival and well-being. Some of them may become more crucial in emergency circumstances. And some of them can be hidden for long periods of time, with their lack showing up in long-term destruction or displacement onto seemingly unrelated aspects of life. Let us examine these five needs in more detail.

Ongoing Survival Needs

Basic or ongoing survival needs are for such things as food, water, shelter, fuel or energy, and the removal of waste products. Meeting such needs is part of the ongoing work of a healthy economy, because people must have them met on a regular basis—more or less every day—in order to survive.

Cyclical Needs for Care

Every human being goes through stages of being dependent upon the care of others as part of the natural processes of life: infancy, childhood, and sometimes old age. Not only must dependent people have their ongoing survival needs met, but they also require other people to obtain material necessities for them, and provide them with the most intimate bodily services, such as feeding, bathing, or toileting. In addition to our natural stages of dependency, which happen to everyone, people can also become dependent on the care of others due to various traumas, accidents, or illnesses. Such states of dependency may either be temporary (a matter of days, weeks, or months) or more or less permanent. There are also varying degrees of dependency and needs for care associated with such circumstances.

The main point about dependency is that it is not an aberration, not a shameful state. It is a natural, although usually cyclical, part of life. Therefore, the provision of goods and services for dependent people, and the ability of caregivers to administer these goods and services to dependent people, are also essential parts of the ongoing work of any healthy economy.

Ongoing Needs for Amenities

Amenities are simple pleasures needed by everyone on a regular basis, which enhance life physically, emotionally, aesthetically, socially, and/or spiritually. They include beauty and creative expression, physical pleasure, intellectual challenge, and social companionship; a variety of tasty and healthful foods; hugs, massages, and more sensual forms of physical affection; work that enables us to enjoy sensual gratification, intellectual stimulation, and sociability, and that makes us feel good about ourselves; ample opportunities for music, dancing, physical movement, sports, and play; jokes, word-games, good conversation, and poetry; enjoying quietness, nature, exploring spirituality and one's own inner life; learning and expanding one's skills, and feeling self-esteem; and feeling that you can shape your own life to achieve your goals, that you can make a positive contribution to the people you care about and to the larger world around you.

Usually, amenities depend not so much on material affluence but on a minimum of simple material resources. They are shaped by people's time and skills to make life more pleasurable, fulfilling, and inspiring. A healthy economy allows everyone to have the time, resources, and freedom to integrate amenities into all aspects of daily life. Since amenities do not appear to contribute to one's immediate survival, and people often seem to survive for years without them, we can be fooled into thinking that they are not necessary for life. But in fact, a lack of amenities can impair an individual's health, reduce life energy, weaken the immune system, and ultimately shorten one's life span. The lack of amenities can cause emotional and even physical pain, which when turned inward leads to self-destructive and/or addictive behaviors or, when turned outward, can lead to abuse of others.[3]

We can also be fooled into thinking that amenities are luxuries, special pleasures reserved only for special people. But the enjoyment of amenities is really an essential, ongoing need of all people, and the ability of all to enjoy them is part of a healthy economy.

Occasional Needs for Luxuries

As I use the term, luxuries are goods and services needed by everyone, but only in small amounts or on an occasional basis for special times. Luxuries are powerful items and experiences, of which it may be said "A little goes a long way," or "You can have too much of a good thing": e.g., ice cream, chocolate, mood-altering chemical substances, or life-threatening challenges. Such experiences have their place during holidays, cultural festivals, special healing ceremonies, personal celebrations, rites of passage, initiations, sacred times, or spiritual retreats. But if we experienced them in large quantities, or on a daily basis, they could exhaust us or threaten our mental or physical health.

We usually think of luxuries as rare goods or services enjoyed only by special people, such as the rich or powerful. Instead, let us think of luxuries as special things, moments, or experiences, that every one of us needs, and every one of us should be able to have, at special times in our lives. Thus, a healthy economy recognizes that luxuries are a rarity, yet potentially available to everyone.

Ongoing Need to Replenish the Sources
That Support and Sustain Us

According to the modern economic paradigm, we express the most power by taking the most for ourselves. But people feel even more empowered when we recognize that the wealth that makes our life possible comes from ever-revolving cycles of activity—both natural and human-made—and when we are able to participate as nurturers and cocreators in these processes. This innate human need to participate in and replenish the sources that nurture us is an emotional need of both adults and young people.

We can express this ongoing need to replenish our sources by participating in mutually empowering relationships in which all involved are able to contribute, both giving and receiving; by being part of open, participatory economic institutions, shaping the goals and actions of the institutions that affect our lives; and by supporting and nurturing the environment, rather than just taking and using up resources.

The need to replenish our sources is also a very practical imperative, which may be the only way to ensure that we do not destroy the natural processes upon which human survival ultimately depends. Thus, a healthy economy regularly provides activities and relationships where each of us can give back, where we can regularly participate in nurturing the sources that nurture us.

MEETING ESSENTIAL HUMAN NEEDS

For maximum human health and well-being, all of the needs described above must be met adequately and appropriately. For maximum well-being, they must all be met simultaneously. Ignoring any of them can harm individual and societal well-being, even survival. But harm can also come from overemphasizing any of these needs inappropriately. For example, people who must spend a large majority of their time working just to meet their survival needs may experience life as harsh and oppressive. On the other hand, people whose lives are devoid of amenities or occasional luxuries may experience life as boring or empty. Meanwhile, people who are deprived of the opportunity to contribute to their own survival or to the survival or well-being of others will feel disempowered and resentful, no matter how full of amenities or luxuries their life may be.

Modern economies are riddled with imbalances. Some crucial needs are met, many remain unmet, and many are met inappropriately or excessively. The economic, social, time, and other pressures of modern life mean that we are increasingly being deprived of amenities both at work and at home. And while some people still have to devote most of their time and energy to sheer survival, millions of others are kept out of the productive processes altogether because they are too young, too old, or otherwise ineligible, and because there are not enough paying jobs to go around. At the same time, people in modern economies are enabled and encouraged to overindulge in luxuries. This helps to blot out our feelings of disconnection, emptiness, and disempowerment and momentarily makes us feel special. But overemphasis on luxuries often harms people's physical health and leads to various types of addictions. Meanwhile, the real causes of our emptiness and discontent are never acknowledged.

As the old-paradigm model of limitless needs fades away and people become more able to acknowledge their real needs, they will create different economic goals, relationships, and institutions that more fully meet these needs. In the emerging paradigm, our material, emotional, intellectual, spiritual, social, and other needs are all being recognized as valid and essential.

NOTES

1. Maslow's hierarchy of needs is cited in *Work in America: Report of A Special Task Force to the Secretary of Health, Education, And Welfare* (Cambridge, Mass.: MIT Press, 1973), 12.

2. Many recent publications explain the scientific validation of mind-body connections. One of the best popular works is Joan Borysenko, *Minding the Body, Mending the Mind* (Reading, Mass.: Addison-Wesley, 1987)

3. On the scientific and medical value of amenities, see Robert Ornstein, Ph.D., and David Sobel, M.D., *Healthy Pleasures* (Reading, Mass.: Addison-Wesley, 1989).

Chapter 18

NOT DOWNSIZING, BUT DOWNSHIFTING: RECOVERING FROM THE ADDICTIVE ECONOMY

BEYOND ADDICTIVE GROWTH

The modern economic paradigm says that continued growth is essential for a successful economy and that limits harm economic well-being. But economic growth, as symbolized by a constantly rising GDP, means only a constant increase in the production and sales of goods and services. In the postmodern paradigm, people are discovering that such growth is meaningless as an overall measure of well-being and that limits of the right kind are also essential for a desirable quality of life. This is so because we need more of some things and less of others. We need more skilled and empowered individuals, more coherent and supportive communities, more equitable distribution of resources. And we need less pollution, less environmental degradation, reduced stress at work and at home, and fewer addictions. It is simply not possible to combine all these factors into one meaningful, aggregate measure.

In the 1920s, the need to constantly increase business activity led to the creation of the addictive economy in which economic growth was maintained by promoting all kinds of addictive behaviors. We have now reached the point where our individual, societal, economic, and environmental well-being can only be achieved by freeing the economy from its dependence on addictions. It's ironic that the term "recovery" has a double meaning in this regard: In order to achieve economic recovery, we need to recover from our addictions. And all around us, new approaches are being developed that can make this double recovery possible.

FINDING A NEW MODEL: FROM DOWNSIZING TO DOWNSHIFTING

Whenever a major paradigm shift takes place, as is happening today, a variety of confusing and often mutually contradictory trends occur simultaneously. For example, some people steadfastly resist the change and cling furiously to the old ways. Others jump right into the new paradigm, eagerly throw out the old, and bring the new approaches into every aspect of their lives. Still others adopt some aspects of the new paradigm, but apply it in the service of old-paradigm goals and values.

Such conflicting trends are especially noticeable in the economic realm. The increase of socially responsible businesses, worker ownership, and community economic development represent a welcoming of the new paradigm. Speedups, deskilling, and increased salary differentials between highest- and lowest-ranking employees represent a die-hard attachment to the old. And then there are those complicated events where the diverse elements must be sorted out. Take, for example, some of the innovative management techniques now being utilized by business corporations in order to increase efficiency, profits, and productivity. One such approach, called "reengineering," advocates a return to craft-style production: allowing a single person or a small team to perform more than one task or to carry a whole project through to completion. This requires flattening organizational hierarchies and increasing the information and responsibility given to each employee—a truly radical change from the fragmented, hierarchical, and deskilled workplace of the modern industrial system.

The results achieved by such changes are also dramatic. For example, Bell Atlantic discovered that under its old system, processing orders related to long-distance carriers took 15 to 25 days turnaround time because each order went through twenty-eight separate employees. By establishing teams that followed one customer's order through the entire process, the company was able to cut its processing time by at least half and can now handle some orders in only a few hours! The Cigna Insurance Corporation used such reengineering techniques to cut its policy-processing time by 90 percent, and the increased efficiency enabled them to reduce their staff by 40 percent.[1]

Such results demonstrate how much waste and dysfunction exist in overspecialized, overly hierarchical structures. And they show how efficiency, applied intelligently, can lead to downsizing that is better for customers, better for the remaining employees, and better for the company itself. But such downsizing is disastrous for the many former employees discovered to be unnecessary and who are now on the unemployment lines. And in many companies, increases in efficiency are merely generated on the backs of the remaining employees, who are forced to work faster, take on more tasks, and spend more time at their paid work, often without any compensation other than awareness that they are lucky because they still have jobs.

In the modern paradigm, where more is automatically assumed to be better, the only other alternative is less, which is worse. According to the modern economic paradigm, the way to reduce inefficiency and increase profits is by downsizing, reducing wages and casting more and more people out of the visible economy into joblessness or worse.

The postmodern economic paradigm offers us a new alternative: downshifting. The term comes from a book by Amy Saltzman, *Downshifting: Reinventing Success On A Slower Track*, about professionals who opted out of the rat race. But the concept has a much broader application. I use the term downshifting to mean finding ways to cut back on harmful, addictive, and wasteful economic activities while enabling people to benefit, rather than suffer, from the cutbacks. (The term "downscaling" has also been used in this way, to mean cutting back on wasteful activities in order to improve quality of life.)[2] Some of the new-paradigm methods for achieving downshifting include recognizing true efficiency, setting limits, reducing waste, taking advantage of synergies, increasing diversity, and sharing the benefits.

Distinguishing False and True Efficiency

False efficiency focuses on monetary measures of success, using such criteria as lower expenses and higher profits to create the illusion that waste has been eliminated. But, in fact, it achieves these results because it has reduced quality of life outside of visible economic criteria. For example, false efficiency in business generates lower costs, higher productivity, and higher profits—at least for the short term—because it overstresses employees, harms their physical and emotional health, disrupts their family life, abuses the local community, and harms the natural environment. False efficiency displaces the costs onto the invisible economy. In the long run, more of society's overall resources must be exhausted to cope with the considerable harm caused by false efficiency. Because false efficiency is actually extremely wasteful, one key to successful downshifting lies in recognizing the difference between false and true efficiency.

By contrast, true efficiency actually creates more real wealth because it not only eliminates waste and stress but also transforms destructive goals, institutions, and relationships, restoring wholeness in people's work, communities, and personal lives.

Setting Limits

Our limits determine our identity. They tell us who we are, how much we can give or take, and when we have enough. By not honoring our own limits, by not recognizing when we have enough, we increase waste and pain. Not only are vast amounts of material resources, human skills, time, and energy wasted in producing excessive, addictive goods and services, but the continued stress caused by excessive work, production, selling, and consuming further debilitates us and requires even more resources to combat the destruction and heal the wounds generated by such stress and addiction. For these reasons, the ability to set appropriate limits, to recognize when we have enough, and to say no beyond these limits is a powerful strategy for downshifting the economy. The New Road Map Foundation, a nonprofit organization in Seattle, urges people to reexamine their consumer-oriented life-styles. Their publications, including the book *Your Money or Your Life*, provide concrete steps through which individuals can recover from money addiction, free themselves from unfulfilling jobs and over consumption, and become financially independent in order to achieve a life that is both more personally satisfying and of greater service to others and the Earth.[3]

The Media Foundation, a lively activist group from Vancouver, is committed to deconstructing the North American consumerist-advertising culture. Through their in-your-face magazine *Adbusters Quarterly*, they promote guerrilla anti-ads and demarketing campaigns that tell the truth about harmful products and marketing practices. In 1991 they produced a series of TV "uncommercials" that encouraged viewers to buy less in order to reduce resource use and help save the Earth. Although air time was purchased for these ads several television stations simply refused to run them.[4]

In his book *How Much Is Enough?*, researcher Alan Durning suggests that there is middle ground between the overconsumption of the West and the extreme poverty of the Third World. He describes a materially moderate life-style, or culture of permanence, which can reduce stress on the natural environment while still supporting personal and community well-being and which can meet the diverse needs of people throughout the world.[5]

In the book *Voluntary Simplicity*, which is both deeply moving and eminently practical, Duane Elgin describes how many people in modern economies are choosing to simplify their lives materially, in order to create time and energy for the more heartfelt aspects of life. An active voluntary-simplicity movement has now developed in the Seattle area, with support groups, publications, and classes on how to live more simply and fully.[6]

Recently, the farmers of Sweden declared, "Around the world, people are trying to squeeze ever increasing amounts of food from the environment by using drugs on both the animals and the soil. We do not want to continue in this direction." They have pledged to create "the purest form of farming in the world" for the sake of the environment, for human and animal health, and to allow the land to provide livelihood for future generations of farmers.[7]

Reducing Waste

False efficiency attempts to squeeze more work and higher productivity out of living beings—human workers, plants, animals, and the Earth. By contrast, true efficiency is achieved through more intelligently designed production processes that use fewer material resources, produce less material waste, and decrease harmful effects on human and environmental health.

Energy use is a classic case in point. According to the modern economic paradigm, in order to continue economic growth and constantly improve our standard of living, we constantly need to develop and consume more energy. But since the energy crisis of the 1970s, people have been turning to efficient-energy approaches, which allow us to meet our needs while consuming less energy. Modern nations throughout the world have been introducing more energy-efficient products, processes, and life-styles, demonstrating that ever-increasing energy use is not necessary for a successful economy. For example, both Japan and the former West Germany, two affluent modern economies that have improved their energy efficiency even more than has the United States, now use about half as much energy per capita as does the United States.[8] Of course, this does not mean that their standard of living is half that of the United States, but rather that the West Germans and Japanese are able to use energy sources as much as twice as efficiently.

Nature is the most efficient producer of all, since in nature the waste generated by one life-form eventually becomes a resource for some different variety of life-form. This process, sometimes described as "closing the loops," can be duplicated in human economies through the three R's: repair, reuse, and recycle. For example, to produce recycled aluminum requires only 4 percent the fuel-energy needed to produce new aluminum from bauxite ore.[9] Or consider the difference between repairing a broken chair or car, compared to throwing it away and building a new one. In one sense, repairing an old item is equivalent to producing a new one, but repair uses up less raw materials, energy, and labor than does producing a new one.

By redesigning our products and processes, and using both existing and new resources with much greater care, we can eliminate significant amounts of waste while better meeting human needs. Such approaches to eliminating waste are an important aspect of downshifting the economy.

Taking Advantage of Synergies

As we discover and implement more ways to set appropriate limits and reduce real waste, an amazing result starts to appear: Various methods of downshifting begin to dovetail, to work together, so that the ultimate outcome is even more far-reaching and rewarding than any single solution. This merging of separate solutions is an example of synergy, a natural process whereby the various parts work together to produce a new whole even more beneficial than any of its separate parts. A classic example of such a synergistic outcome results from energy efficiency. In the United States during the early 1980s, then-President Ronald Reagan rejected policies to reduce national energy use. He scornfully described energy conservation as "freezing in the dark." Meanwhile, businesses and homeowners that had introduced such measures as insulation, more efficient heating and lighting systems, and more energy-conscious life-styles were discovering multiple benefits. They were physically more comfortable, and their heating and electric bills were lower. They could also take comfort in knowing that by burning fewer fossil fuels, they were using up fewer resources, while reducing harmful effects on the environment and on human health. Downshifting becomes possible because of such synergies, which naturally occur as we reduce waste and close the loops.

Organic agriculture—producing food in harmony with nature—creates another important set of synergies. By reducing reliance on artificial fertilizers and poisonous chemical pesticides and herbicides, organic farmers reduce their expenses, reuse natural wastes, restore the soil, improve the health of both farmworkers and consumers, and help protect clean water and other natural resources.[10]

Shorter work-time provides another opportunity for synergies. By eliminating truly unnecessary jobs, and spreading the remaining work around more widely, unemployed people can find paying work and everyone can spend less time at work. More time for personal, family, and community life also means less stress, better health, and lower health-care costs.[11]

But, you may object, people working less means people paid less. However, several other, related synergies can ease this problem. For example, by producing better-quality, longer-lasting goods that can be repaired easily, we not only reduce resource use but also reduce the work necessary to keep producing, selling, and disposing of throwaways. Although longer-lasting products may cost more up-front, their cost over time will be lower than the constant purchase and disposal of throwaways, which means that people would not have to earn as much to sustain their life-style. In addition, by reducing the need for planned obsolescence, entire job categories now devoted to thinking up new consumer fads and convincing the public to buy them can fade away. This means even less work to be done and even more free time to be shared by all.[12]

There are many more synergies that could develop as we create more sustainable life-styles and a more sustainable economy. They represent another way in which we can downshift the economy so that we reduce waste and stress and limit unnecessary resource use while actually improving people's well-being.

Increasing Diversity

Industrialization produces cheap goods in large quantities because it takes advantage of a phenomenon that economists call "economies of scale." By bringing together large numbers of workers, raw materials, and powerful mass-production machinery, and by fragmenting the work process to suit the machines, modern businesses can produce more goods more quickly and at lower cost than through the old craft methods. The benefits derived from economies of scale encouraged businesses to grow in size. And as companies became ever larger they had to introduce greater hierarchical stratification and greater simplification of jobs in order to maintain control over the burgeoning workforce. Meanwhile, in agriculture, large-scale production efficiencies were achieved through "monoculture" or "monocropping"—that is, devoting large areas of land to the production of one single crop. Just as overspecialization destroyed the diversity of an individual's work experience, monocropping destroyed the inherent diversity of the natural environment.

Narrow specialization and hierarchical stratification for the sake of greater efficiency gradually became the model for many other aspects of modern life. In modern societies, human communities have gradually been reorganized by separating out various groups of people according to some single, narrow characteristic, such as their age, the type of activity they perform, or their state of mental or physical health. The same kinds of people are then grouped together, often in large institutions, to which they may legally be confined for at least portions of the day, if not for life. I call this phenomenon the monocropping of people.

The monocropping of human beings is a distinctly familiar characteristic of modern life. For many of their activities, children are separated from adults, older adults separated from younger ones. People who are learning are separated from those who are working, and people who are producing are separated from those who are consuming. Not only are all the workers kept together in factories or offices, but all the assembly-line workers are kept together in one building, while all the typists are somewhere else, all the engineers are somewhere else, and all the managers and executives are in still another place. Meanwhile, our children are stuck together in schools, where they are then separated from each other according to age and often by supposed ability. Physically or mentally ill people are grouped in hospitals or residential institutions. And increasingly, the oldest people are placed in retirement communities or nursing homes, where they slowly die together. Furthermore, all these monocropped groups of people are controlled and supervised by their own specialized "experts," just as the workers in the blue- and white-collar factories are controlled by their own special equipment and supervisors.

Because the technical and social organization of mass production brought about such productivity and efficiency, it was easy for people to assume that these forms could be transferred to the rest of life. It seemed only logical that separation, stratification, and economies of scale could also bring about the greatest efficiency in healing the sick, teaching the young, and caring for the old.

But we are finally learning that overspecialization at work is inefficient because it destroys wealth by impairing human well-being. Instead, new models of workplace organization are demonstrating that we can actually improve workplace performance and efficiency and enhance people's well-being by making the work experience more diversified. Also essential for workplace empowerment is reducing the size of the immediate workgroup in which workers participate and over which they have decision-making power. In other words, workers' well-being is enhanced by decreasing the scale (size) while increasing the scope (diversity of activities) of their immediate workplace.

So, too, people are beginning to recognize that the monocropping of human beings in other aspects of life also destroys wealth because it impairs human development. For example, studies of people in hospitals or nursing homes suggest that when the residents are not treated as passive recipients of care, but are actively involved in making decisions about their environment, their spirits, abilities, and health often improve.[13] Such improvements are also observed when institutionalized people participate in creative, productive activities that benefit themselves, such as gardening, or the outside community, (e.g., serving as foster grandparents).

Often, healthier models of social diversity come from preindustrial cultures. Sustainable-development activist Helena Norberg-Hodge describes the benefits of mixed-age communities, based on her experiences in the small Himalayan nation of Ladakh:

> If you have children reacting to people of different ages, you get a completely different sense of identity than if you segregate them into age groups.

If you have a whole room full of children who are all at the stage of learning how to walk, it's physically impossible for one child to reach out a hand and help another one. And inherently, it creates competition [because each child is trying to find a way to be unique]. . . . But if you have a group of people made up of a range of ages from one to sixty, which is how traditional people have lived, you get totally different interactions. In this kind of social arrangement, even five-year-olds will develop a sense of responsibility and caring for an infant or a toddler. It brings out their own sense of nurturance—both boys' and girls'.[14]

Social monocropping falsely emphasizes the differences between one group and another and diminishes each group's wealth of experiences. Individuals are prevented from realizing their uniqueness and value, which can best be discovered by interacting, giving, taking, and learning from people of different ages, backgrounds, and abilities. In other words, monocropping prevents synergies from occurring because it enforces sameness.

Identifying and Sharing the Benefits

By reducing unnecessary resource use, eliminating waste and stress, diversifying our environments and experiences, and taking advantage of synergies, we are actually freeing up new sources of wealth. But it is not always easy to recognize this new wealth, because it usually falls outside of conventional economic criteria. For example, the GDP rises when more people get sick and medical expenditures increase. Yet when people's health care expenditures decline because their health improves, the GDP falls, which supposedly means that society is now producing less wealth. So new kinds of economic indicators, which recognize the real sources of human and environmental well-being and enable us to keep track of them more accurately, are essential to downshifting the economy.

One innovative approach to such measurement is the concept of "emergy," developed by environmental economist Howard T. Odum, which refers to the amount of energy required to create or reproduce something efficiently and incorporates both economic and thermodynamic concerns. Odum has used emergy analysis to evaluate proposed economic development projects. Since his technique recognizes the wealth of the invisible economy, it allows people to analyze the real impact of proposed development projects, not to be misled by narrow bottom-line, purely financial analyses.[15]

Another way to measure real wealth is through the concept of shared savings, a technique developed by people in the energy-conservation field. Although energy-efficiency measures may require some expenditures up front, over time the energy savings they produce will result in reduced energy bills. By comparing estimated energy costs without the conservation measures, the savings from energy efficiency can be calculated. In essence, the money saved through conservation is money earned, a new source of wealth. It can be applied to further improvements or to other desired ends.[16]

DOWNSHIFTING TO A HIGHER QUALITY OF LIFE

Increasing the diversity of human experience not only restores richness but also creates new wealth in the natural world and the human community. By enhancing human wholeness while using up fewer material resources, promoting diversification in our worklives and social interactions, and utilizing new indicators for measuring wealth and waste so we can keep more accurate accounts of our accomplishments—all these are keys to downshifting the economy.

NOTES

1. See Paul Hemp, "Preaching the gospel," *Boston Globe*, 30 June 1992, 35–39 for more on new management approaches such as reengineering.

2. Amy Saltzman, *Downshifting: Reinventing Success on a Slower Track* (New York.: HarperCollins, 1991). See also David Babbitt, *Downscaling: Simplify and Enrich your Lifestyle* (Chicago: Moody Press, 1993), available by calling (800) 678-8812.

3. You can purchase an audiotaped training program from The New Road Map Foundation, P.O. Box 15981, Seattle, WA 98115; see also Joe Dominguez and Vicki Robin, *Your Money or Your Life: Transforming Your Relationship with Money and Achieving Financial Independence* (New York: Penguin, 1992).

4. The Media Foundation, 1243 W. 7th Ave., Vancouver, B. C. V6H lB7, Canada.

5. Alan Durning, *How Much Is Enough? The Consumer Society and the Future of the Earth* (New York: W.W. Norton & Co., 1992).

6. See Duane Elgin, *Voluntary Simplicity: Toward A Way of Life That Is Outwardly Simple, Inwardly Rich* (New York: William Morrow and Co., 1981). See also *In Context,* Issue #26, "What Is Enough?," available for $6.00 from The Context Institute, P.O. Box 11470, Bainbridge Island, Washington 98110, (800) 462-6683. The Seattle voluntary simplicity movement can be reached at Voluntary Simplicity Association, c/o Phinney Neighborhood Association, 6532 Phinney Ave., N., Seattle, WA 98103. (Send them a stamped, self-addressed envelope for more information.)

7. See "The Swedish Farmers Revolt," *Organic Farmer*, Fall 1993, 21.

8. Durning, *How Much Is Enough?*, 53.

9. Kathleen Newland, *Productivity: The New Economic Context*, Worldwatch Paper 49 (Washington, D.C.: Worldwatch Institute, 1982), 25.

10. For more on organic agriculture, contact the Committee for Sustainable Agriculture, P.O. Box 1300, Colfax, CA 95713.

11. For a comprehensive exploration of the overwork/shorter work-time issue, see Bruce O'Hara, *Working Harder Isn't Working* (Vancouver: New Star Books, 1993).

12. The synergies possible through a less wasteful, more environmentally nurturing economy are described in John E. Young, *Discarding the Throwaway Society*, Worldwatch Paper 101 (Washington D.C.: Worldwatch Institute, 1991) and Michael Renner, *Jobs in A Sustainable Economy*, Worldwatch Paper 104 (Washington D.C.: Worldwatch Institute, 1991). Economic activist J. W. Smith estimates that in the United States today, approximately 37 million jobs now being done are essentially nonproductive. If they were eliminated, and the remaining necessary work shared among formerly nonproductive employees and the unemployed, the needed paid work could be done in only 2.3 days per person per week. See Smith, "Wasted Time, Wasted Wealth," *In Context*, No. 37, Winter 1993–1994, 18–21.

13. Benefits of involving institutionalized people in decision making are described in Ellen J. Langer, *Mindfulness* (Reading, Mass.: Addison-Wesley, 1990).

14. From "Preserving Communities for our Children's Sake," an interview with Helena Norberg-Hodge, *Planetary Citizen*, 2, (Spring 1993), 19, published by Stillpoint Institute, Meetinghouse

Rd., P.O. Box 640, Walpole, NH 03608. For more on the benefits of mingling children of different ages, see Helena Norberg-Hodge, *Ancient Futures: Learning from Ladakh* (San Francisco: Sierra Club, 1991).

15. For an example of emergy analysis, see *Emergy Analysis of Shrimp Mariculture in Ecuador*, available from Coastal Resources Center, University of Rhode Island Bay Campus, Narragansett, RI 02882.

16. Some of the most innovative work combining energy efficiency and economics is being done by the Rocky Mountain Institute, 1739 Snowmass Creek Rd., Snowmass, CO 81654-9199.

Chapter 19

FREEING BUSINESS CORPORATIONS FROM THEIR ADDICTIVE GOALS

In the modern economic paradigm, the most common way to measure business success is via profits, the money a business has left over after all its expenses are paid. It's assumed that any company making a high rate of profits is a healthy, productive business deserving community and financial support, while a company with a low rate of return is probably poorly managed, a bad credit risk, and in danger of failing. Such assumptions do not necessarily reflect reality, but they are a basic part of the modern paradigm.

Since profits are so central to modern economies, they constitute one of the most emotional issues in the entire discussion of economics and social justice. Profits have been labeled everything from the generator of modern affluence and the reward for entrepreneurial daring and scientific ingenuity, to the basic cause of inhumanity, environmental destruction, and even wars. My goal here is not to try to resolve this intense and complicated debate, but to apply the insights gained from whole life economics and the postmodern economic paradigm to better understand how profits can be misused and to suggest more empowering and nonaddictive approaches to their creation and distribution.

In modern market economies, profits are produced by business corporations, and the decisions about what to do with those profits are made by those who run the corporations, usually by management executives or in rare cases, private owners who are involved in a company's daily operations. A company's profits can be redistributed to investors who were lucky enough to invest in it, reinvested directly back into the business in order to help it expand further, or usually some combination thereof.

Since profits are assumed to have been created by business corporations, and are disposed on behalf of them, we need to reexamine these unique institutions: why they were created, their distinctive position in modern economies, and their changing role in the postmodern economy.

THE ORIGIN OF THE MODERN BUSINESS CORPORATION

In the modern economic paradigm, conventional community expectations and legal precedents relating to business corporations are based on the assumption that businesses are the basis of the economy and the primary source of modern society's wealth and well-being. It is therefore assumed that society benefits when businesses increase their own wealth and power and that businesses should have special legal protections and privileges that enable them to keep growing in size, power, and wealth. The history of the business corporation over the last four hundred years demonstrates how corporations were continually given more privileges and power in relation both to individuals and to the community at large.

The ancestors of the modern business corporation were the limited-liability joint stock companies established in England and the Netherlands in the late 1500s and, early 1600s to facilitate the colonization and plunder of the newly discovered, resource-rich lands of Asia and the New World. These private companies, financed and run by private investors, hired the ships and recruited the soldiers, sailors, colonists, and traders who would do the actual work of subduing the natives and bringing back foreign riches.[1]

Chartered by royal decree, joint stock companies such as the British East India Company were granted unique privileges. They were monopolies, with exclusive rights to operate in the colonized lands. And they had limited liability, meaning that if a venture failed, the individual investors might lose the money they had already invested, but beyond that they were not responsible for paying back creditors. Such privileges were deemed necessary to get people to invest in such risky ventures. Thus, the early corporations were justified by the investors' hierarchical, racist view of the world, driven by greed, and they promised enormous financial returns to those who risked their money. But they separated money-making from actions, and actions from accountability. This model laid the groundwork for the modern industrial business corporation.

In the newly independent United States of America, each state government had the power to grant charters of incorporation. In the early 1800s it was commonly understood that a corporate charter gave the holders unique privileges and powers. Thus, during the early years of the new republic, charters were granted to only a small number of ventures considered to be in the public interest, such as banks, insurance companies, and canal- and road-building ventures.[2] While these early corporations had limited-liability and monopolistic privileges, they also had limited life-spans (usually twenty to fifty years). This assured that when corporate directors sought to renew their charter, the citizenry could assess the corporation's activities, determine whether it really had served the public interest, and decide if renewal were merited.

During the nineteenth century, as the U.S. economy continued to grow, businesspeople recognized the advantages of limited liability in raising capital for expansion, and gradually it became common for private businesses of all types to seek incorporation. And as business corporations steadily grew larger, richer, and more powerful, the granting of corporate charters became a money-making business for the states. By the late 1800s, New Jersey, Delaware, and several other states had made incorporation a mere formality, available to any individual or group who filled out the necessary papers and paid the required fee.[3]

As the ease of incorporating increased, government's restrictions and public scrutiny of corporate activity were systematically eliminated. Most significant, business corporations were now automatically granted unlimited life-spans.[4] A crucial transfer of power came with a ruling of the U.S. Supreme Court in 1886, Santa Clara County *vs.* Southern Pacific Railroad, in which the Court declared that a corporation was legally entitled to be considered a "person," with all the rights and protections that the U.S. Constitution grants to individual U.S. citizens, such as freedom of speech and freedom of privacy.[5] (It might be argued that this ruling was inherently unfair, since most corporations control considerably more resources and power than individuals. But the power of the corporations blinded the Justices to such inequities. Ironically, while corporations now have the same rights as individual citizens, they may legally deprive the employees who work for them of these very same rights.[6])

So the business corporation gradually became an institution in which resources and power would flow only one way: from individuals and the community into the corporation. And as corporate wealth and size increased, so did corporate influence over communities, governments, and the political process.[7] The new laws gave corporations wide freedom to harm employees, communities, and the environment, while their limited liability assured that the individuals who owned, managed, or invested in them would not be held liable for any harm their corporations caused.

TOWARD A MORE BALANCED RELATIONSHIP BETWEEN CORPORATIONS AND THE REST OF LIFE

The modern ideal of encouraging business corporations to constantly grow in size and wealth, while allowing them to have unlimited life-spans, is inherently harmful. The dysfunctional nature of the conventional model is highlighted by the emerging natural-systems model of postmodernism, which suggests that in a healthy system, the varied parts interact with each other through relationships of mutual interdependence, no part dominates or monopolizes resources or control. Moreover, every part will follow patterns of rising and falling activity within its own overall cycle of birth, life, death, and transformation into new life. Any components that do not allow for a mutual flow of energy and resources with others, and that do not allow the natural cycles of life to occur, are a source of dysfunction and disease in the system.

The conventional model of corporate privilege allows addictive business corporations to direct the flow of resources to themselves and to dominate the rest of the economy. (In medical terms, an entity that acted in this way would be called a cancer.) The conventional model also overemphasizes and overvalues corporate production of goods and services, while ignoring the other essential functions which together make up the whole economy. As we have seen throughout this book, other equally essential activities of a healthy economy besides production include protecting resources, restoring damaged human, community, and environmental wealth, meeting the needs of dependent people who can't pay, redistributing resources to increase equity and empowerment, and closing the loops to eliminate waste.

Many of these needs cannot be met by businesses as conventionally defined. They certainly cannot be met by businesses whose success is defined only in terms of constantly increasing size and maximization of profits. In order to place businesses in a more healthy relationship with the rest of life, we need to allow them to give up their privileged position in society and not require them to pursue addictive goals such as constant growth and constantly rising profits.

Reversing Corporate Privilege

During the 1970s, Ralph Nader and his colleagues proposed a series of legal reforms that would make U.S. corporations more accountable to the public. They proposed that since corporations transcend state boundaries, they should be chartered not by states, but by the federal government. These new charters would require greater corporate democracy, with stockholders and community representatives serving on corporate boards of directors and taking a more active role in deciding corporate policies. Other requirements would include publicly disclosing of corporations' social and financial performance; breaking up large corporations that dominate their industries, and establishing an employees' bill of rights.[8] As usual, Nader was ahead of his time, and his recommendations have not been acted upon.

More recently, economic activists Richard Grossman and Frank Adams have proposed that citizens take back the right to grant corporate charters, recognizing that charters should be given only to companies that really serve the public interest; that limited lifespan and regular public scrutiny should be restored as an integral part of any corporate chartering process; and that the community should revoke the charters of businesses which are harming individuals, communities, the democratic process, or the environment.[9]

"Good Neighbor Campaigns" and "Good Neighbor Agreements" are recent innovations that provide immediate and direct ways for communities to ensure greater responsibility and accountability from corporations. Through such mechanisms, citizens' groups are requiring that companies located in their communities reduce toxic emissions and agree to retain local facilities and jobs. Such agreements can allow residents to obtain access to company records; to periodically inspect local facilities, using technical advisors hired by the community; to allow workers at such plants to organize unions; and to include both employees and local residents in making decisions about the future of such companies. Forming alliances between community residents and employees who work for local corporations is essential to the success of Good Neighbor Campaigns.[10]

Finding New Uses for Profits

In the modern economic paradigm, businesses are expected to maximize their profits so they can provide high returns to investors and so they can finance their own continued growth. If these two goals became less important to society, then businesses would no longer be driven primarily by the need to maximize the bottom line, and they would be free to find new, more healing and empowering uses for the profits they made. For example, rather than assuming that stockholders' only desire is for constantly increasing financial returns, why not give stockholders the option of choosing? Andrew Bard Schmookler suggests that corporate officials could offer stockholders the opportunity to make decisions—for example whether they would be willing to take a percentage or two fewer profits in order that the company could install better health and safety measures for its employees; keep local jobs; and institute better environmental protection programs.[11] It may be that stockholders will welcome the opportunity to invest their potential returns in a healthier community or a restored environment that will enhance their quality of life directly.

Business corporations have actually had to fight for the legal right to put their profits to such nontraditional uses. In 1916, when Henry Ford tried to reduce prices on his cars, his stockholders sued him.[12] Although Ford argued that by lowering prices, he would be able to make his cars available to more customers, and that the increased sales would make up for the reduced prices, the Court insightfully described Ford's plan to lower prices as "sharing [profits] . . . with the public." And it ruled that "since a business corporation is organized and carried on primarily for the profit of the stockholders," Ford's plan would unfairly deprive his stockholders of their right to maximum profits.[13]

But in 1953, in the case of A. P. Smith Manufacturing vs. Barlow, the Court ruled that a company could give some of its profits as a charitable contribution to Princeton University. Although the Court's rationale was that this would ultimately benefit the donor company—presumably by providing more highly educated workers in the future—this ruling legitimized the now-common practice of corporate donations to charitable, community, and other socially responsible purposes.[14] A changed model of what profits are used for would require alteration of any remaining legal restrictions that currently force businesses to maintain their addictive goals.

In a new paradigm, which doesn't press for profit maximization, profits could be put to even more innovative uses. Since many others besides just financial investors have contributed to the success of a profitable business, the other constituencies might also be allowed to benefit from this success. Profits could be shared with employees by offering them higher wages, more workplace amenities, or reduced work-time without loss in pay; with suppliers by paying them more; with customers by charging them less; or with the larger community and natural environment by promoting more environmentally supportive practices both in and outside the workplace.

Allowing Businesses to Experience a Natural Life Cycle

Businesses that are successful often reach all their potential customers, serve them well, and then go out of business because their market has been saturated, their purpose has been fulfilled. This is such a natural cycle that it's remarkable the modern paradigm refuses to accept it as natural. And instead of preparing for it, and allowing it to happen in the least harmful ways, in the modern paradigm failing businesses often die horrible deaths, blamed for incompetence and leaving bankrupt creditors and unemployed workers in their wake. Or else society hysterically tries to prevent the demise of particularly prominent corporations, often by using taxpayers' money to prop up these dinosaurs, which only postpones the day of reckoning.

In the postmodern paradigm, we could acknowledge that there is nothing shameful about a company that has fulfilled its mission and faded out of existence. And as we recognize that cycles of business life and death regularly take place, it becomes possible for each enterprise to prepare, with the support of its employees, suppliers, customers, and the surrounding community, to meet its demise in the most socially and economically beneficial manner. The United States already has a model that recognizes the life cycle of organizations regarding the nonprofit sector. Nonprofits are not expected to constantly expand and bring in steadily increasing incomes. They are legally and morally required to fulfill their charitable, educational, and other purposes. If at some point in its existence a nonprofit decides it has fulfilled its mission, this is considered an admission of success, not failure. It has solved the problem, or met the need for which it was organized, and can end its operations. Any remaining assets are legally required to be passed on to some other nonprofit.

In an economy modeled on the organic cycles of life and death, the requirement to transfer resources to other, more active organizations could also be applied to businesses. Not only could this principle be extended to companies that have satisfied their customers' needs, and have assets left over, it could also be applied to companies that must close down because society has now deemed their activities unnecessary or harmful—for instance, weapons producers or businesses whose products are injurious to human health.

There are numerous possibilities for how the information, technologies, material and financial assets accumulated by declining or dysfunctional businesses might be passed on to other more viable enterprises. These assets could be lent to or invested in other businesses. They could be distributed to former employees, to help them retrain for new jobs or start new businesses. They could be distributed to suppliers, the surrounding community, or other groups that nourished the business during its growth phase, or they could be used to enhance the local environment.

Through these and other innovative mechanisms, businesses may be released from their addictive goals and allowed to develop a more balanced relationship with the rest of life. Such alternatives also provide another key to downshifting the economy.

NOTES

1. See Brian Gardner, *The East India Company: A History* (New York: Dorset Press, 1971).

2. This history of the corporation in the United States comes from Ralph Nader, Mark Green, and Joel Seligman, *Taming the Giant Corporation* (New York: W. W. Norton & Co., 1976), chap. 2; and Richard L. Grossman and Frank T. Adams, *Taking Care of Business: Citizenship and the Charter of Incorporation* (Cambridge, Mass.: Charter, Ink, 1993), available for $4.00 from Charter, Ink, P.O. Box 806, Cambridge MA 02140.

3. On pro-corporate legislation in New Jersey and Delaware, see Nader et al., *Taming the Giant Corporation*, 43–54.

4. After the Civil War, increasingly powerful corporations influenced the legal system, leading to new judicial interpretations and legislation that removed public oversight and served corporations' needs exclusively; see Grossman and Adams, *Taking Care of Business*, 10–21.

5. On corporations granted standing as citizens, see Grossman and Adams, *Taking Care of Business*, 20.

6. Many people do not realize that the protections and rights granted in the U.S. Constitution refer only to freedom from government infringements. Business corporations are not inherently required to grant such rights to their employees, but they have increasingly been forced to do so by individual and union action. See Robert Ellis Smith, *Workrights* (New York: E. P. Dutton, 1983).

7. An impressive recent study of corporate influence over the democratic process is William Greider, *Who Will Tell the People? The Betrayal of the American Democracy* (New York: Simon & Schuster, 1993).

8. Nader et al., *Taming the Giant Corporation*.

9. Grossman and Adams, *Taking Care of Business*.

10. For more information, publications, and consulting services related to Good Neighbor Campaigns, contact the Good Neighbor Project for Sustainable Industries, P.O. Box 79225, Waverley, MA 02179 (617) 489-3686.

11. The "Let the stockholders decide" proposal is from Andrew Bard Schmookler, *The Illusion of Choice: How the Market Economy Shapes our Destiny* (Albany, N.Y.: State University of New York Press, 1993), 190–209.

12. Robert Lacey, *Ford: The Men and the Machine* (New York: Ballantine Books, 1986), 179–184.

13. Norman Bowie, *Business Ethics* (Englewood Cliffs, N.J.: Prentice-Hall, 1982), 18–19.

14. Ibid., 19.

Chapter 20

A NEW MEANING OF ECONOMIC CHOICE: MODES OF EMPOWERMENT

THE MARKET SYSTEM AND THE LIMITS OF CHOICE

Adam Smith is called the father of modern economics because he laid out the principles of the market economy. He described how, as each individual seeks to maximize his own personal gain, economic activities are automatically coordinated "as if by an invisible hand" so that people's needs are met.[1] According to the modern economic paradigm, the market system leads to the best possible economic results because it combines abundant wealth production and optimum distribution with individuals' free choices. In conventional economic thought, market activity is often equated with the economy.

But as this book has shown, the market model has many important limitations. Market systems can not meet the needs of people who do not have money, which means that they are systematically biased against poor people, people without jobs, dependents such as children, sick people, and frail elders, and those who care for them. Nor can they take into account the long-term effects of economic activities, such as the damage they cause to the natural environment, unless such non-monetized "externalities" are consciously included in costs and prices.

Some new-paradigm economic thinkers emphasize that immediate or long-term social and environmental costs can be factored into prices ("true-cost pricing") in order to make market choices more honest and realistic.[2] But while the achievement of true-cost pricing would be an important improvement, it still would not resolve many other problems associated with the market model. It still would not make goods and services sold through the market more available to those without money.

Second, even the market dynamics of supply and demand do not guarantee that market economies will solve problems of overproduction in the most socially and economically desirable way. As we saw in chapter 5, when U.S. businesses thought they had overproduced, they created a new culture of expanded consumption. Rather than business being guided by people's needs and desires, the public's consuming activity was altered to fit business' needs.

Third, there are many other economic forms and relationships that people in modern economies utilize regularly, in addition to the market. Some of these forms, such as cooperation among businesses, are used along with businesses' competitive activities in the market. Others are used by nonbusiness institutions, or by people in their daily lives, and are invisible according to conventional definitions of the economy. But people have created and continue to use all of these alternative models, even in market economies, because they serve specific human needs or solve crucial economic problems in ways that the market cannot. In many cases, these unrecognized forms are more appropriate, more empowering, and lead to better economic outcomes, than do market relationships.

MODES OF AN EMPOWERING ECONOMICS

Some of the most important of these more empowering economic modes include doing it for yourself, giving, exchange, mutual aid, the commons, the sociable market, participatory planning, restitution and restoration, and planting seeds for the future. Some of these modes are monetized, others are not, but they all demonstrate such empowering principles as respecting the uniqueness of each individual, recognizing mutuality in relation to other people and to the natural environment, allowing people to engage their whole selves in economic activity, creating and benefiting from synergies, and utilizing both short- and long-term perspectives.

Doing It for Yourself

This mode includes individual and community self-reliance, where people use their own skills and readily available resources to meet their material, social, cultural, and other needs. It allows the development of each individual's unique abilities, leading to personal fulfillment and self-respect as well as to interaction among people with diverse abilities, enabling them to meet each other's needs and enhance synergies. It is often characterized by entire families, households, neighborhoods, or communities joining together at special times, such as planting or harvest time, or on market or festival days, to work and play together, thereby increasing the energy, interactions, and community support necessary to meet everyone's needs.

Giving

Fundamental to the survival of every human being, giving means freely providing another person with material goods or services, without expecting anything in return. It means caring. You would not be alive today if others had not given to you when you were a helpless baby. Giving is essential whenever members of a society go through any of the naturally occurring dependent stages of life. But it is also a double-edged sword. When done inappropriately, giving becomes a one-way hierarchical relationship that emphasizes the power and benevolence of the giver in contrast to the neediness, dependence, and inadequacy of the recipient. An important challenge for a more empowering economy is to support one-way giving and caring activities when they are needed but to allow them to turn into mutual, two-way giving, which implies equality, as soon as appropriate.

Exchange and Exchange Networks

Direct barter is a simple and useful economic form, especially among strangers or others trying to get to know each other better to build community. Exchange, or barter, is different from one-way market transactions, in which an isolated consumer purchases a product or service from a rich and powerful producer or seller. Exchange encourages both participants to see themselves as producers or creators of wealth. I trade my legal skills for your art work, my home cooking for your carpentry. I give you a massage, you give me a massage. Exchange and exchange networks encourage people to discover their skills and other unrecognized forms of wealth and to interact as creative, valued equals.

Mutual Aid

Throughout the world mutual aid is both a simple and highly sophisticated economic form that allows participants to meet their material, social, and spiritual needs simultaneously. Modern Westerners sometimes interpret mutual-aid systems as variations of market-based exchange. They have been taught that in any transfer of goods or services between economically active adults, each participant is seeking to maximize their own personal gain. In fact, the core principles of mutual aid seem to be the exact opposite of those which drive market exchanges.

Mutual aid is often practiced by Native-American groups. One such system is described by 61-year-old Harold Grey, born and raised on a Canadian reservation in Saskatchewan:

> "Forty to forty-five years ago money was not the most important thing. What you were able to accomplish by yourself, and who needed you, were much more important. For the Indian there is always a question of whom you could do things for—a kind of socialist arrangement, no one is asking for help. You never ask for help. Help is offered.

> "Indians were quite prosperous prior to the 1940's. They depended upon themselves most of the time. Families grew up together. The first step was to be self-reliant and along with that to be able to give to others. For example, when you help someone with a job, you visit with him as you help. Each family farmed for themselves, but others came along and each donated so much work. That work was not returned to that particular person." He pointed out that it was not a reciprocal exchange between two parties. "The work was returned wherever it was needed, and to whomever needed help."[3]

Grey notes that when people began to use money to buy products to meet their needs, rather than relying on themselves and their neighbors, "this contributed to a feeling that 'no one needs me—why should I do anything'—a feeling of inadequacy!'"[4]

Mutual-aid systems still thrive in the U. S. heartland among the Amish, as described by Gene Logsdon:

> I first learned about the startlingly effective economy of Amish life when I was invited to a barn raising near Wooster, Ohio. A tornado had levelled four barns and acres of prime Amish timber. In just three weeks, the downed trees were sawed into girders, posts and beams and the four barns rebuilt and filled with livestock donated by neighbours to replace those killed by the storm. Three weeks! Nor were the barns the usual modern, one-storey metal boxes hung on poles. They were huge buildings, three and four storeys high, post-and-beam framed, and held together with hand-hewn mortises and tenons. I watched the raising of the last barn in open-mouthed awe. Some 400 Amish men and boys, acting and reacting like a hive of bees in absolute harmony of cooperation, started at sunrise with only a foundation and floor and by noon had the huge edifice far enough along that you could put hay in it.
>
> A contractor who was watching said it would have taken him and a beefed-up crew all summer to build the barn if, indeed, he could find anyone skilled enough at mortising to do it. He estimated the cost at $100,000. I asked the Amish farmer how much cash he would have in the barn. "About $30,000," he said. And some of that paid out by the Amish church's own insurance arrangements. "We give each other our labour," he explained. "We look forward to raisings. There are so many helping, no one has to work too hard. We get in a good visit."[5]

In many monetized cultures, poorer people help themselves through mutual aid capital creation.[6] In this form, a small group of people meet regularly to socialize, perhaps once a week or once a month. At every meeting, each member also donates a specified amount of money ($5, $150, or whatever) to the group. And each time the pooled total is given to a different member. If there are ten members, the group will meet ten times, until each participant has had the opportunity to receive their lump sum. The form varies in different cultures, with regard to membership size and criteria of membership, the order in which people receive their pots, and so on. But it is a widespread form of a cooperative financial institution.

Such mutual aid is found throughout Africa. Among the Yoruba people of Nigeria it is called "Esusu." Carried by West African slaves to the West Indies, it is now called "susu" in Trinidad, while in Jamaica and elsewhere it is called a "partner." Many West Indians have used money received through these partners to purchase real estate or start small businesses, first in the Islands and later as they moved to the United States or Great Britain. Due to differing patterns of slavery, it appears that the West Indians were able to maintain this African tradition, while it became lost among slaves taken directly to the United States.[7] Cooperative financial circles have also been common in southern China and rural Japan. The form was carried to the United States and used by many Chinese and Japanese immigrants to provide start-up capital for their own economic development.[8]

Many nonindustrial cultures practice formal, ritualized forms of mutual aid. For example, in the Kanak tribe of New Caledonia, an island in the Southern Pacific, the yam-farming clan and the fisherman clan regularly participate in a traditional ritual through which each group distributes part of their produce, or catch, to the other group. Although to Western observers this might look like a simple example of exchange—yams for fish—that's not what's going on, according to the French economist and activist Dominique Temple, who has written extensively on the role of the non-exchange economy in contemporary Third-World cultures.

More accurately, what's going on is a mutual relationship in which each group farms or fishes productively and abundantly, so that it can distribute its wealth not only within its own clan but also to the other clan. The self-identity and pride of each group is based on its ability to give abundantly to the other group. Temple calls this form of mutual aid "reciprocity economics" and notes that many cultures have used various kinds of mutual aid or reciprocity economics within their own communities but engage in barter or monetized exchanges "at their borders"—that is, with strangers or members of other cultures.[9]

The Benefits of Mutual Aid

From these examples we can conclude that mutual aid relationships are designed to ensure that any person who gives has enough both for themselves and for someone else, is able to give to the other adequately, and does not become depleted, but is able to keep on giving adequately in the future. Everyone in the society has the opportunity to both give to and receive from others. Thus, mutual aid can help create communities of abundance, where each individual's pride comes from being able to produce and share abundantly. But this means that mutual aid requires all participants to have a clear sense of how much is enough for them. Only when you know your own needs and limits will you feel secure about sharing your wealth with others, a perspective that contrasts sharply with a society where each individual is trained to look out only for him or herself and self-esteem is defined by how much you possess. It should not be surprising that in affluent modern societies, where there is no such thing as enough, and more is always better, that people are constantly plagued by fear of scarcity rather than being able to enjoy the abundance their work and technology have created.

It's also significant that in many societies that utilize mutual aid, the times of mutual giving are accompanied by a gala celebration, party, or fiesta. In effect, such societies are celebrating and reinforcing the ability of their members to be productive yet caring, powerful yet grateful, and self-reliant yet connected to each other.

The Commons

The commons refers not so much to a physical place as to the relationship between a resource and the human beings who use it. A commons could be described as a specific, local natural area adopted and protected by a specific local, human community. The commons provides resources for the community and its individual members—now and in the future—while in return the community and its individual members protect the continued productivity, diversity, and long-term integrity of this particular natural area.

Commons have existed worldwide throughout history. They can characterize people's relationship to a forest, pastureland, a body of water, or any other environment whose resources enhance human survival and well-being. Although the specifics vary widely, each community has developed a practical and adaptable set of rules or traditions about how their commons can be used in order to assure the continued protection of the three distinct interests: community, individual, and environmental well-being.

According to *Whose Common Future?*, an in-depth study of the economic and social role of the commons in today's world, this mode is constantly threatened by the modern paradigm. Commons of all kinds, everywhere, are taken away from their communities by private owners or a centralized government and turned into monocropped, money-producing ventures. The people who formerly derived their livelihoods and well-being from the commons are forcibly uprooted from the land, becoming landless wage earners or an unemployed underclass. And the products of these now privately owned lands are often exported to already affluent modern nations.[10]

Disruption of the commons is often most harmful to women. In many societies, women's economic self-sufficiency was due to their access to the resources of a commons. When the commons is stolen from a community to become the private property of a local elite, a government, or a multinational corporation, the men of the community may be assimilated into the new system as property owners or paid laborers. However, women most often lose their economic base and social status.[11] Reclaiming the commons is often essential to a more empowering economy.

The Sociable Market

Long before the market was a theoretical concept, it was a place set aside by the community for trade. Some marketplaces operate daily, but many are empty until the specially designated market day, when, as if by magic, a festive market appears. Such markets are characterized by dozens, perhaps hundreds, of independent entrepreneurs, such as family farmers or craftspeople, each operating their own booth or stall and conducting business directly with the public.

This form, which I call the sociable market, should not be confused with the modern shopping mall, a privately owned space whose purpose is to maximize the landlord's bottom line. Mall tenants are often large chains staffed by poorly paid employees. Rents are usually too high for small, local entrepreneurs. And security guards keep out undesirable people whose presence might distract customers from the rent-paying shops. By contrast, the purpose of the sociable market is to facilitate economic exchange while allowing everyone present—sellers, customers, and even onlookers—to create and enjoy a festive atmosphere.

Sociable markets have existed throughout the world, in ancient Greece and Rome, Egypt of the Pharaohs, ancient Babylon, classical China, across Africa and the Middle East, among the Aztecs, and throughout Europe.[12] This description, of an Indian market in Oaxaca, Mexico, in the 1950s, captures their characteristic flavor:

There is a section for flowers, another for fruits, a lane where nothing but rebozos are sold, an island where Oaxaca's fine cutlery gleams, a region of almost cathedral quiet where at least fifty varieties of chiles await the connoisseur, and near them, logically enough, are tomatoes, avocados, and onions. . . . [in the pottery and basketry section] during the afternoon lull, the small children are bathed in a great earthenware basin glazed in green, the most delectable sight in the market.

Domesticity of this kind belongs in the market; one sees courtships, gossip coteries, acts of neighborliness, political discussions, tribal and intertribal attitudes, the confiding of secrets, and many occasions for chuckling or laughter. This is home, this is the center. The market, with its strolling bands and mariachis, its masses of beautiful vegetables, fruits, flowers, arranged with tender artistry, its multiple smells, all pungent and most of them delightful, the gaily dressed people pushing and shoving and joking—what could be more jubilant than the market? This is abundance, heaped up and running over.[13]

Other examples include the time-honored bazaars of the Middle East and North Africa, and modern-day flea markets and farmers markets, where once again small, independent producers and entrepreneurs are able to do business directly with the public. Because they are also owners, each seller can adjust prices from moment to moment if necessary to meet changing market conditions or the financial capacity of individual customers. Bargaining—the ability of both buyer and seller to haggle over and renegotiate price—is another common feature of the sociable market. In numerous ways, the sociable market is perhaps the ultimate expression of truly free enterprise.

Participatory Planning

In the modern economic paradigm, planning often has a negative connotation, equated with a centralized government that makes top-down decisions that are out of touch with people's needs. However, people can also plan for themselves, in grassroots, democratic, or participatory planning. It can be applied to many economic activities, both within the workplace and in community-based economic development.

Some degree of participatory planning is increasingly found in new-paradigm businesses, and it is institutionalized by law in several European nations. In Germany, all factories and offices with more than five employees must have a works council, employee representatives who negotiate directly with management over such issues as work hours, health and safety, layoffs, and plant closings. In Sweden, employers are legally required to initiate discussions with their employees' unions before they decide on important workplace changes such as switching to a new line of business, reorganizing production methods, or selling the firm.[14]

Worker-owned businesses provide even more scope for participatory planning. In employee-owned firms of twenty people or less, it is feasible for all workers to participate directly in the ongoing process of shaping the enterprise. In larger worker-owned firms, large-scale decisions are usually delegated to a board of directors elected by the workers or to a manager hired by the board. But in order to assure democratic participation from the ground up, such firms can be organized into decentralized work units whose members make face-to-face decisions about issues relevant to their immediate work environment. Work units are also represented in larger decision-making bodies.[15]

Participatory planning for economic development was used by the Ulkatcho and Kluskus Indians of British Columbia in order to protect the forests on their lands from clear-cutting. They hired a forestry consultant to help them come up with a plan for use of the forest that would take into account diverse needs of tourists, tribal people, loggers, and the forest itself. Through this process the native community is now able to speak with a unified voice about their needs to loggers and the government.[16]

In the United States, the Rocky Mountain Institute's Economic Renewal Project facilitates participatory community economic planning. Through its community workshops, Project consultants bring together representatives from many different constituencies in a town, who jointly analyze their community's needs and resources, develop, and then help implement a plan for their community's economic improvement. Because of the Institute's commitment to sustainable resource and energy use, these community development plans emphasize energy efficiency and environmental sustainability.[17]

Restitution and Restoration

Restitution and restoration mean the redistribution of wealth, resources, or power in order to set things right. A donor gives not out of pity or compassion for the recipient but in order to right a wrong, to restore what is rightfully the recipient's. This ideal goes back at least as far as the Old Testament of the Bible. As described in Leviticus, poverty and hard times forced people to mortgage their homes or lands to others, or even to sell their relatives or themselves into slavery. But every forty-nine years came the Jubilee, when all mortgaged buildings and lands were to be returned to the original owners, and all enslaved people were to be given their freedom. The arrival of every Jubilee was announced by the blowing of the sacred ram's horn, proclaiming liberty throughout the land.[18]

Various activities today are inspired by this desire to restore justice or balance, sometimes for exploited people, sometimes in relation to the natural environment. Alternative trading organizations (ATOs) seek to reverse the pattern of Western exploitation of Third-World people. ATOs contact, and sometimes organize, worker-owned businesses in Third-World communities and make their agricultural products or handicrafts directly available to Western consumers through special catalogs and/or stores. The producers enjoy better working conditions, self-esteem, and earn considerably more than if they worked for conventional employers, and the customers have the satisfaction of knowing that their purchases are helping a community's economic empowerment.[19]

In order to acknowledge the environmental harm that our economic activities cause, and to support environmental restoration, some enterprises now include in their costs a "green tax"—a voluntary donation made by customers or an enterprise that goes to environmental projects. For example, New Society Publishers asks customers to include a voluntary green tax on their book purchases, in acknowledgment of the environmental damage caused in all publishing and printing processes. The money is disbursed to groups and organizations doing restoration, direct action, and education on ecological issues.

Planting Seeds for the Future

In the modern economic paradigm, the goal of all economic activities is to acquire more money, wealth, and power. Within that paradigm it's incomprehensible why anyone would voluntarily give up money or other resources or pleasures in the present, except in order to get back even more in the future. This is called "investing."

Consider, therefore, the tale of the old man who at the age of eighty began to plant seedlings that would one day become a fruit orchard. When onlookers asked him why he was doing this, since he would obviously be dead long before these trees matured, he replied, "I am planting them so that my children and grandchildren will be able to enjoy them."

Such investments in the future, in which the investor receives no material return at all, can be interpreted as a form of mutual aid, where wealth moves from generation to generation. Rather than the recipient repaying the original investor (who may no longer be alive by the time repayment is possible), the recipient is charged with passing the gift on to someone else. Meanwhile, the initiator has the satisfaction of knowing that they have set a new process of abundance in motion.

THE MEANING OF REAL ECONOMIC CHOICE

In the old paradigm, we can choose among different products or different brands, but we have only one option as to the form of economic activity: to buy or sell in the market. In the new economic paradigm, people can choose from among a variety of economic forms the ones most suitable for them. And as circumstances change, people are free to readjust their relationships with each other, and with the available resources, in order to continually maximize individual, community, and environmental well-being. When we are free to choose and put into practice whichever economic forms and relationships best meet our needs as whole people, then we are participating in a truly empowering economy.

NOTES

1. On self-interest, the market system, and the Invisible Hand, see Robert L. Heilbroner, *The Worldly Philosophers: The Lives, Times, and Ideas of the Great Economic Thinkers* (New York: Simon & Schuster, 1953), chap. 3; and Mark A. Lutz and Kenneth Lux, *Humanistic Economics: The New Challenge* (New York: Bootstrap Press, 1988) chaps. 3–5.

2. The Rocky Mountain Institute, 1739 Snowmass Creek Rd., Snowmass, CO 81654-9199, (303) 927-3851, has done much work on the concept of true-cost pricing. A few of their many publications on this topic, available from the Institute, include H. Richard Heede and Amory B. Lovins, "Hiding the True Costs of Energy Sources," *Wall Street Journal,* 17 September 1985, 28 ($1.50); Amory B. Lovins,

"Making Markets in Energy Efficiency," Rocky Mountain Instititute, June 1989 ($3.00); and H. Richard Heede and David Houghton, "Assembling a New National Energy Policy," Rocky Mountain Institute, 1991 ($4.00). See also Paul Hawken, *The Ecology of Commerce: A Declaration of Sustainability*, (New York: HarperBusiness, 1993), chaps. 5, 11, and pp. 167–175.

3. William M. Nichols and William A. Dyson, *The Informal Economy: Where People are the Bottom Line* (Ontario, Canada: Vanier Institute of the Family, 1983), 186.

4. Ibid.

5. Gene Logsdon, *At Nature's Pace* (New York: Pantheon, 1994), 130 ff.

6. A comprehensive discussion of mutual-aid capital creation is found in Ivan H. Light, *Ethnic Enterprise In America: Business And Welfare Among Chinese, Japanese, And Blacks* (Berkeley, Calif.: University of California Press, 1972), chap. 2. Like most Western observers, this book refers to this form as "rotating credit circles" or "loan associations," terms that I think miss the point because they focus on the monetary flow rather than on the essential characteristic: members' mutual participation in the group.

7. Ibid., 36–44.

8. Ibid., 23–30.

9. Dominique Temple has written passionately and widely on the economics of reciprocity, and how such systems have been misunderstood and destroyed by Westerners. A summary of his work, with a more complete bibliography, appears in Dominique Temple, "A Letter to the Kanak: The Policy of 'the Severed Flower,'" *Interculture*, English edition, 21 (January-March 1988), 10–35. *Interculture* is available from the Intercultural Institute of Montreal, 4917 St. Urbain St., Montreal, Quebec H2T 2W1, Canada.

10. The Ecologist, *Whose Common Future? Reclaiming the Commons* (Philadelphia: New Society Publishers, 1993), chaps. 2 and 3.

11. Ibid., 36–38.

12. Fernand Braudel, *The Wheels of Commerce: Civilization and Capitalism, 15th-18th Century*, vol. 2 (New York: Harper & Row, 1982), 29.

13. Helen Augur, *Zapotec* (Garden City, N.Y.: Doubleday, 1954), 84–87.

14. Bruce Stokes, *Helping Ourselves: Local Solutions to Global Problems* (New York.: W. W. Norton, 1981) 26–27.

15. Frank T. Adams and Gary B. Hansen, *Putting Democracy to Work: A Practical Guide for Starting Worker-Owned Businesses* (Eugene, Ore.: Hulogos'i, 1987), chaps. 8 and 9.

16. Bert Groenenberg, "Regaining the Forest, Land, and Dignity," in Christine Meyer and Faith Moosang, eds., *Living with the Land: Communities Restoring the Earth* (Philadelphia: New Society Publishers, 1992), 20–26.

17. Ecologically oriented community economic planning is being implemented by the Economic Renewal Project, Rocky Mountain Institute, 1739 Snowmass Creek Rd., Snowmass CO 81654-9199, (303) 927-3851.

18. See *Leviticus*, 25.

19. On alternative trading organizations (ATOs), see "Can Shopping Save the World?" *Utne Reader*, January–February 1993, 28–30.

Chapter 21

TINY STEPS, GIANT STEPS: BUILDING A MORE EMPOWERING ECONOMY

Modern industrial societies today are undergoing unprecedented changes. Powerful economic and social institutions are faltering, and long-held assumptions about everything from gender roles to international relationships to the shape of the future are being transformed. Times of immense change, such as we are now experiencing, can bring fear, uncertainty, and increased hardships. But difficult times also encourage people to reevaluate their goals and belief systems, to seek out and utilize new resources, and to develop more supportive relationships with others in order to get through the upheavals. As old institutions and assumptions come apart, the power of each individual to make a difference is increased.

By making even very small changes in our lives, you and I and the people around us can create a more empowering economy. The problem today is not that we are powerless but that each of us has so much potential to initiate change, in so many areas of life, that it may be difficult to know where to start. The following is offered as an action guide to those wondering what to do next.

AS A UNIQUE INDIVIDUAL

What do you need personally? What do you have to give? Begin by reflecting on how well your current life fulfills your own personal needs and dreams. Perhaps you need to bring in more income, or have more time for yourself, your family, and friends. Perhaps you need to change your paid or unpaid working conditions, learn new skills, find a different job, or start your own business. Perhaps you want to participate in new economic relationships and institutions that more fully permit you to express your values regarding justice, community, spirituality, or sustainability. Perhaps you want to cut down your spending, simplify your life, or become more self-reliant and resourceful. There are many possibilities for economic empowerment, and you can choose the direction(s) that make most sense for you.

To whom can you talk about such issues? What books or other informational resources can you take advantage of? What groups, classes, or other activities can help you in this process? Taking the time and energy to consider your own life, to reaffirm your own dreams and values, and to seek out others who can support you in achieving these more fully is a first step to greater empowerment.

AS A HOUSEHOLD AND FAMILY

Discuss these issues with other members of your family and household. Encourage them to conduct their own explorations. How can household members better achieve their own goals and assist each other, both individually and as a group? Discuss values that all household members support. How can you express these values in your daily lives—for example, in shopping, child-care arrangements, leisure-time activities, or holiday celebrations? Are there people and organizations around you that share these values and are also trying to realize them more fully? Reaching out to others with similar concerns is a second essential step to empowerment.

OTHER INSTITUTIONS AND ORGANIZATIONS

Consider the various social realms in which you participate: a workplace; an extended family or other social groups; a religious institution or spiritual community; a school; a labor union; neighborhood, community, civic, or professional associations; business or nonprofit affiliations; local or other government. Are people in these groups worried about changing times, values, and their future? Why not start discussion circles or task forces to explore new goals, activities, or policies for your group? Discovering the wealth of connections each of us has, and encouraging the people to whom you are connected to take a more active role in considering and shaping their circumstances, is another essential step to empowerment.

PARTICIPATING IN NEW ECONOMIC INSTITUTIONS

Which of the new economic models described in this book sparked your interest? Learn more about them. Read relevant publications and get in touch with the organizations mentioned. Are there any local examples you can visit, support, and/or participate in?

If the new economic activities that you want to become involved in do not exist locally, consider starting them. Possibilities range from meal sharing or reciprocal child care to more formal activities, such as establishing a barter network, neighborhood exchange, or community money system; initiating an environmental restoration program; or sponsoring a community economic development planning process. You and interested friends or colleagues can form study groups to research and share information about various aspects of economic empowerment. Research can include reading, field trips, and discussions with people already involved in new economic forms, and seeking out others in your community who can help implement new institutions. Putting your ideals into action is a crucial aspect of empowerment.

DEVELOPING NEW SKILLS

As the modern paradigm continues to come apart, we may find that large-scale institutions, corporations, and governments will be less able to provide us with the jobs, products, services, and guidance we have grown accustomed to expecting from them. Although this can be frightening, it also means that each one of us is now more important because of the unique individual contributions each of us has to offer

This means that now is a good time to learn new skills in order to diversify your abilities, so you will have more to give to yourself and others. This book includes numerous references to information and resources for achieving greater personal and community empowerment, and there are probably additional resources for learning in your local community. Consider new technical skills, community-building skills, creative skills and artistic self-expression, health-enhancing skills, skills in social change and political action, or skills in working with the natural world. Expanding and sharing your knowledge and abilities is another essential step to empowerment.

UNDERSTANDING THE LARGER CHANGES

Everything we do is connected, so thinking globally can enhance your ability to be effective locally. Be aware of the big picture. How do events in your community or region affect neighboring communities or regions? How do they influence—and how are they influenced by—communities and nations in other parts of the world? How can you make these connections more visible, and how can you and your community have a positive effect on emerging trends?

While reading and watching the news can provide information about the big picture, remember that many conventional news media are communicating through the filter of the old paradigm; they tend to promote old values and prevailing power relationships, and accept a passive, victimized, isolated view of life. To counter such distortions, seek out new-paradigm books, newsletters, and organizations that can provide a more constructive perspective on current events. Organize discussions, workshops, and conferences that explore new approaches and sponsor new-paradigm speakers in your community. Increasing your own and others' understanding of today's changes and possibilities is essential for greater empowerment.

AS A CITIZEN ACTIVIST

Through their control over resources and information, many powerful institutions in business, education, media, and other areas of life either consciously or unintentionally inhibit people's ability to become more empowered. And although the purpose of government is to serve the general good and protect citizens from harm and violence, many government programs and laws promote greater inequities of wealth, money, and power. Meanwhile, public officials often refuse to stop injustices and abuses perpetrated by powerful private institutions.

Recognizing and standing up to abuse and injustice against ourselves and others is a key source of empowerment. You can work with others to change unjust local, state, or federal laws or programs, challenge corporations that abuse their power, help protect poor people and poor communities from further degradation, eliminate institutional discrimination against disadvantaged groups, promote more equitable tax policies, stop the pollution of human communities and the natural environment, and make a difference with regard to many other issues. References throughout this book, and in the Resource List, cite many organizations doing such political and social-change work.

Use the concepts in this book to evaluate and challenge unjust corporate and government policies: Do proposed plans for economic development help already affluent people, at the expense of economically and socially disadvantaged groups? Do business or public policies promote economic addictions, ignore the contributions of the invisible economy, or increase its burdens? Most established institutions and experts justify their actions within the framework of the conventional economic paradigm. By applying the insights of whole life economics and the values of economic empowerment, balance, and mutuality, we can judge economic actions more accurately and develop more beneficial goals and outcomes.

HELPING TO EMPOWER OTHERS

As times become more difficult, the number of people in need will continue to increase. But many public and private programs designed to help people in need do not empower the recipients; they emphasize the wealth, power, or benevolence of the givers, and may help the recipients survive from day to day, but reinforce their helpless and dependent status.

If you want to assist people to become truly empowered, look for or help create programs that actively transfer skills, resources, and power to participants. Helping others in need not merely to survive but to gain more control over their lives is another crucial step toward empowerment.

AS AN INNOVATOR, LEARNER, AND TEACHER

As you explore new options, you will make unexpected discoveries and gain valuable experience. Take advantage of the numerous networks being developed, both face-to-face and through print or electronic media.[1] Let others know what you're trying, and how it's working out. Find out how others have dealt with the issues you're facing. Recognizing that we're all in this together, learning and helping each other learn how to create a more fulfilling way of life, is a vital basis of empowerment.

BUILDING A MORE EMPOWERING ECONOMY

This time of change and turmoil is also opening up numerous opportunities to build new institutions and relationships that can be more humane, more just, more personally, socially, and spiritually fulfilling, and more respectful of the natural environment than the institutions of the old paradigm. It is essential that we keep faith in the midst of uncertainty that our continuing efforts will help bring forth this emerging paradigm of a more empowering economy.

In the old economic paradigm, the economy is something "out there" that big, powerful corporations, or the government and experts, understand and create. But the first principle of the new paradigm is that the economy is everywhere, and that *we* create the economy. We can create the economy to meet all our needs, as whole people, not fragments separated mind from body from emotions from spirit. We don't have to be separated into artificial groups based on false categories of superiority or inferiority. We don't have to be driven by addictions, deny our limits, or give up our power and well-being to the irresponsible and destructive values of the addictive economy.

We can create the economy together with other people, with wisdom, communication, love, and caring to achieve win-win solutions from which all benefit. We can create the economy in cooperation with the natural world by becoming aware of and honoring its inherent richness and learning from its lessons of abundance, diversity, regeneration, appropriate limits, self-direction, and interdependence. We can learn from nature's generative and healing processes the constantly changing, cyclical rhythms of life, which exist not only outside of us but are also within us.

Our actions need not be enormous to have far-reaching effects. Your everyday actions, starting at the simplest level, as an individual and together with the people closest to you, then reaching out to others, can help change the economy within your community, your bioregion, and eventually the world. And there are many other people all around you who are seeking new ways and trying to build a more just, sustainable, and empowering economy. As we learn, act, and encourage each other, so the power of our actions grows.

NOTES

1. Many people interested in sustainable economics communicate electronically via Econet, an international computer network sponsored by the Institute for Global Communications (IGC). For more information about their services and affiliated networks, contact IGC, 18 De Boom St., San Francisco, CA 94107, (415) 442-0220; fax (415) 546-1794; e-mail: support@igc.apc.org., or info@igc.apc.org. There are also electronic discussions on many aspects of economics via Internet. Sam Houston State University in Huntsville, Texas has a gopher site that lists comprehensive resources on economics; contact their e-mail address: gopher-mgr@shsu.edu. You can also find listings of economics discussion groups in Eric Braun, *The Internet Directory* (New York: Fawcett Columbine, 1994); start with p. 60, 134 and 662.

SELECTED BIBLIOGRAPHY

AN INTRODUCTION TO THE NEW ECONOMIC PARADIGM

Many of these books, as well as others about the new economics, may be hard to find in mainstream bookstores, but can be obtained from distributors such as those named in parentheses.

Breton, Denise and Christopher Largent. *The Soul of Economies: Spiritual Evolution Goes to the Marketplace.* Wilmington, Del.: Idea House, 1991.

From an openly spiritual/religious perspective, the authors challenge conventional assumptions about economics and remind us that we create the economy out of our beliefs and values. (Knowledge Systems)

Daly, Herman E. and John B. Cobb, Jr. *For the Common Good: Redirecting the Economy Toward Community, the Environment, and a Sustainable Future.* Boston: Beacon Press, 1989.

An economist and a theologian critique mainstream economics and suggest new models and policies that value community and the environment. (But in my opinion, their solutions are too money-oriented, and they almost completely ignore women's issues.)

Dauncey, Guy. *After The Crash: The Emergence of the Rainbow Economy.* New York: Bootstrap Press, 1988.

A detailed survey of new economic institutions and activities through which individuals and communities in modern nations are reshaping their economic lives for greater justice, empowerment, and environmental responsibility. (Apex Press)

Dominguez, Joe and Vicki Robin. *Your Money or Your Life: Transforming Your Relationship with Money and Achieving Financial Independence.* New York: Penguin, 1992.

A practical approach to personal finances that allows the reader to lower the cost of living while increasing the quality of life and creating a more sustainable lifestyle.

Ekins, Paul, ed. *The Living Economy: A New Economics in the Making*. London: Routledge, 1986.

Economists and activists from around the world challenge mainstream economics and offer many examples of a more socially just and environmentally sustainable economics now emerging. (Apex Press)

Ekins, Paul, Mayer Hillman, and Robert Hutchison. *The Gaia Atlas of Green Economics*. New York: Doubleday, 1992.

A panoramic overview of the emerging economic paradigm, in theory and practice, locally and globally, in jargon-free language with full-color graphics and illustrations.

Ferber, Marianne A. and Julie A. Nelson, eds. *Beyond Economic Man: Feminist Theory and Economics*. Chicago: University of Chicago Press, 1993.

Feminist critiques of the mainstream economic paradigm, especially in an academic context.

Goodwin, Neva R. *Social Economics: An Alternative Theory, Vol. I. Building Anew on Marshall's Principles*. New York: St. Martin's Press, 1991.

An examination of the limitations of both neo-classical and Marxist economics, with proposals for more sustainable alternatives in both the academic and policy realms.

Hawken, Paul. *The Ecology Of Commerce: A Declaration of Sustainability*. New York: HarperCollins, 1993.

A radical reformulation of business goals and operations by a leading advocate of environmentally and socially responsible business.

Henderson, Hazel. *The Politics of the Solar Age: Alternatives to Economics* (1981). Indianapolis: Knowledge Systems, 1988.

One of Henderson's breathtaking and mind-expanding challenges to the mainstream paradigm, which explains why conventional economics no longer works.

Henderson, Hazel. *Paradigms in Progress: Life Beyond Economics*. Indianapolis: Knowledge Systems, 1991.

A breathtaking description of the current transition to a more sustainable economy, using systems theory and futurist perspectives, packed with examples and information from around the world.

hooks, bell. *Feminist Theory: From Margin to Center*. Boston: South End Press, 1984.

Perspectives on work, parenting, community, caring, gender, race, class, and social and economic justice, from an author-activist who speaks on behalf of three invisible categories: women, African-Americans, and the poor.

Lutz, Mark A. and Kenneth Lux. *Humanistic Economics: The New Challenge.* New York: Bootstrap Press, 1988.

An economist and a psychologist charge that mainstream economics is destroying ethics and a caring society. Includes a critical history of modern economic thought. (Apex Press)

Makhijani, Arjun. *From Global Capitalism to Economic Justice: An Inquiry into the Elimination of Systemic Poverty, Violence and Environmental Destruction in the World Economy.* New York: Apex Press, 1992.

An environmental scientist and peace activist describes how the Third World has always been the invisible source of wealth for industrialized nations and looks beyond both exploitative capitalism and centralized socialism for a sustainable global economy that integrates social justice with local initiative.

Meeker-Lowry, Susan. *Economics As If the Earth Really Mattered: A Catalyst Guide to Socially Conscious Investing.* Philadelphia: New Society Publishers, 1988.

A comprehensive overview of new institutions for a more sustainable, community-controlled economy.

Meeker-Lowry, Susan. *Invested in the Common Good: Economics as if the Earth Really Mattered.* Philadelphia: New Society Publishers, forthcoming 1995.

A comprehensive guide to investing one's time, skills, and money in new economic activities, relationships, and institutions in order to create more sustainable economies rooted in local ecosystems and cultures. Packed with case studies, contacts, and resources.

Mellor, Mary. *Breaking the Boundaries: Toward a Green, Feminist Socialism.* London: Virago Press, 1992.

A British scholar-activist explores why feminist, environmental, and anticolonialist perspectives must be integrated into contemporary socialism.

Mies, Maria and Vandana Shiva. *Ecofeminism.* London and New Jersey: Zed Books, 1993.

A German sociologist and an Indian physicist claim that modern capitalist/patriarchal policies and technologies are destroying nature and women's lives in both modern and Third-World nations; and propose more just models for the economy and human survival, relevant for both modern and not-yet industrialized societies.

Plant, Christopher and Judith Plant. *Green Business: Hope or Hoax? Toward an Authentic Strategy for Restoring the Earth.* Philadelphia: New Society Publishers, 1991.

An analysis and critique of the limitations of green business and green consumerism as a tool for restoring the Earth, with examples of more transformative, community-based, bioregional alternatives.

Polanyi, Karl. *The Great Transformation: The Political and Economic Origins of Our Time.* Boston: Beacon Press, 1957.

The classic study of how nonmarket economies and cultures around the world were uprooted in order to make way for the modern market economy.

Robertson, James. *The Sane Alternative: A Choice of Futures.* St. Paul, Minn.: River Basin Publishing Co., 1979.
A short, lively exploration of the possible economic futures we face, written to stimulate group discussion and empower participants. (Apex Press)

Ross, David P. and Peter J. Usher. *From the Roots Up: Economic Development as if Community Mattered.* Croton-On-Hudson, NY: Bootstrap Press, 1986.
A comprehensive study of the invisible community (informal) economy, its scope, unrecognized contributions to modern societies, and its role in economic development, with emphasis on Canadian examples. (Apex Press)

Schumacher, E. F. *Small Is Beautiful: Economics as if People Mattered.* San Francisco: Harper & Row, 1973.
A pioneering work that challenged the central values, practices, and underlying assumptions of modern economies.

Shiva, Vandana. *Staying Alive: Women, Ecology and Development.* London: Zed Books, 1989.
A physicist from India describes the sustainable economic practices of Third-World women, who are being destroyed by modern economic development policies.

Waring, Marilyn. *If Women Counted: A New Feminist Economics.* New York: Harper & Row, 1988. The classic work on the economic invisibility of women, which emphasizes that the natural environment is also economically invisible.

RESOURCE LIST

To learn more about, and connect with others developing a new economic paradigm.

BOOK PUBLISHERS/DISTRIBUTORS (ASK FOR THEIR CATALOGUES!)

APEX PRESS, c/o Council on International and Public Affairs, 777 UN Plaza, Suite 3C, New York, NY 10017, (212) 953-6920. Socially just, sustainable, and community economics from both Western and Third-World perspectives.

KNOWLEDGE SYSTEMS, INC., 7777 W. Morris St., Indianapolis, IN 46231, (800) 999-8517. Personal, social, and economic aspects of the new paradigm.

KUMARIAN PRESS, 630 Oakwood Ave., Suite 119, W. Hartford, CT 06110-1529, (800) 289-2664. New models, especially from the Third World.

MONTHLY REVIEW PRESS, 122 W. 27th St., New York, NY, (212) 691-2555. Economic and social change in the United States and the Third World, emphasizing the role of workers, women, and people of color.

NEW SOCIETY PUBLISHERS, 4527 Springfield Ave., Philadelphia, PA 19143, (800) 333-9093. Community economics, bioregionalism, and other aspects of sustainable living and nonviolent social change.

QUALITY TAPE SERVICES, P.O. Box 15352, Seattle, WA 98115. Recovering from overconsumption and money addiction; developing a more satisfying and sustainable way of life.

SOUTH END PRESS, 116 St. Botolph St., Boston, MA 02115, (617) 266-0629. Critical thinking and constructive action on economic, political, and ecological issues in the United States and the world.

WORLDWATCH INSTITUTE, 1776 Massachusetts Ave. NW, Washington, D.C. 20036-1904, (202) 452-1999. Economic and social policies for a more just and environmentally sustainable world.

ZED BOOKS, c/o Humanities Press International, 165 First Ave., Atlantic Highlands, NJ 07716, (908) 872-1441. International feminist and social justice perspectives on the environment and economic-development issues.

MAGAZINES

Business Ethics: The Magazine of Socially Responsible Business, 52 S. 10th St., Suite 110, Minneapolis, MN 55403-2001, (513) 890-9539. Practical and philosophical aspects of, and individuals and companies concerned about, environmentally and socially responsible business. $50/year (6 issues).

Co-Op America's National Green Pages, c/o Co-op America, 1612 K St., NW, Suite 600, Washington D.C., 20006, (800) 58-Green. Lists over one thousand U.S. enterprises committed to social and environmental responsibility, one hundred categories of goods and services—food, clothing, energy, toys, business consulting, travel, and more—with background articles and suggestions for further action. $5.95/year.

Dollars & Sense: What's Left in Economics, One Summer St., Somerville, MA 02143, (617) 628-8411. Down-to-earth analyses of current economic events from a socialist perspective. $22.95/year (6 issues). $42.00/year library subscriptions.

Equal Means: Women Organizing Economic Solutions, 2531 Ninth St., Suite 3, Berkeley, CA 94710, (510) 549-9931. Economic issues from a feminist perspective; women's strategies around economic justice, environmentally sustainable community and economic development, emphasizing multiracial, multicultural, and international linkages. $24/year (4 issues). Back issues $6 each.

GEO (Grassroots Economic Organizing Newsletter), P. O. Box 5065, New Haven, CT 06525, (203) 389-6194. Worker-owned enterprises, co-ops, community-based businesses, community-labor-environmental coalitions, and other initiatives for a participatory economy, in the United States and internationally. $15/year (6 issues). $3 sample copy. $30/year library and organization subscriptions.

Human Economy Newsletter, P. O. Box 28, W. Swanzey, NH 03469-0028, (603) 355-1250. Articles from a worldwide network of academicians and activists developing creative new approaches to economics as if people and the Earth mattered. Call or write for information about latest subscription rates and other publications.

In Context: A Quarterly of Humane Sustainable Culture c/o Context Institute, P. O. Box 11470, Bainbridge Island, WA 98110-9925, (800) 462-6683. Inspiring articles and real-life examples of the emerging paradigm in all its aspects. $24/year (4 issues). Back issues $6 each.

Utne Reader: The Best of the Alternative Press, 1624 Harmon Place, Suite 330, Minneapolis, MN 55403,(800) 736-UTNE. Reports and analyses of emerging social, economic, and cultural trends. $18/year (6 issues). Single issues $4 each.

Whole Earth Review: Access to Tools and Ideas, 27 Gate Five Rd., Sausalito, CA 94965, (415) 332-1716. New social, economic, and technological developments, emphasizing practical information for individual and community empowerment and environmental sustainability. $27/year (4 issues). Back issues $7 each.

ORGANIZATIONS

This is a highly selective list. For more groups, see specific chapters within the book itself.

BUSINESSES FOR SOCIAL RESPONSIBILITY, 1030 15 St. NW, Suite 1010, Washington D.C., 20005, (202) 842-5400. An alliance of socially responsible businesses promoting social, environmental, and worker-friendly practices in corporate and government policy.

CENTER FOR ETHICS AND ECONOMIC POLICY, 2512 9th St. #3, Berkeley, CA 94710-2342, (310) 349-9931; and CENTER FOR POPULAR ECONOMICS, P.O. Box 785, Amherst, MA 01004, (413) 545-0743. Two separate organizations, both demystify economics and relate it to current problems through their publications for laypeople and workshops for activists and community groups.

CENTER FOR NEIGHBORHOOD TECHNOLOGY, 2126 W. North Ave., Chicago, IL 60647, (312) 278-4800. Promotes urban-oriented community empowerment, appropriate technology, and environmentally sustainable community-based economic development. Publications include practical handbooks and the national magazine *The Neighborhood Works: Building Alternative Visions for the City* ($30/year, 6 issues).

CENTER FOR RURAL AFFAIRS, P. O. Box 406, Walthill, NE 68067-0406, (402) 846-5428. Promotes rural community empowerment through sustainable agriculture, locally controlled economic development, aid to established and new farmers, local and national policy work, and coalition building with nonfarm groups.

CO-OP AMERICA, 1612 K St. NW, Suite 600, Washington, D.C. 20006, (202) 872-5307. A nonprofit membership organization promoting a sustainable economy based on values of peace, cooperation, and environmental sustainability, its publications and outreach programs promote new economic models, connect consumers and investors with socially responsible businesses and community development initiatives, and challenge old-paradigm businesses.

E. F. SCHUMACHER SOCIETY, Box 76, RD 3, Great Barrington, MA 01230, (413) 528-1737. Promotes sustainable community economies through educational programs, publications, and a resource library. Affiliated demonstration projects include a land trust, community-supported enterprise development, and locally issued money.

FEDERATION FOR INDUSTRIAL RETENTION AND RENEWAL, 3411 W. Diversey Ave., #10, Chicago, IL 60647, (312) 278-5918. A nationwide alliance of community/labor/environmental/religious coalitions working for socially just, sustainable, community-based economic development in regions that have lost their industrial base.

FOOD FIRST (INSTITUTE FOR FOOD AND DEVELOPMENT POLICY), 398 60th St., Oakland, CA 94618, (510) 654-4400. An educational and activist organization that empowers citizens to understand and address the roots of hunger and other economic and political inequities between industrialized and Third-World nations.

THE FUNDING EXCHANGE, 666 Broadway, #500, New York, NY 10025, (212) 529-5300. A national network of alternative foundations dedicated to social change, not charity. Receives donations from private individuals and sponsors workshops on wealth redistribution for personal empowerment and social change.

INSTITUTE FOR LOCAL SELF-RELIANCE, 2425 18th St., NW, Washington, D.C. 20009, (202) 232-4108. Conducts research, policy analysis, offers publications, and provides technical assistance to citizens' groups, local government, and small business to promote and implement sustainable materials use.

INSTITUTE FOR WOMEN'S POLICY RESEARCH, 1400 20th St., NW, Suite 104, Washington, D.C. 20036, (202) 785-5100. Through its research projects, publications, and conferences, IWPR examines the realities of women's economic life in the United States and advocates for women's economic and social empowerment.

INTERCULTURAL INSTITUTE OF MONTREAL, 4917 St. Urbain St., Montreal, Quebec, Canada H2T 2W1, (514) 288-7229. An educational institute whose programs and journal *Interculture* promote alternatives to mainstream Western economic and cultural paradigms.

INTERNATIONAL ASSOCIATION FOR FEMINIST ECONOMICS, c/o Department of Economics, Bucknell University, Lewisburg, PA 17837. Its educational programs, networking, and publications develop and promote the theory and practice of feminist economics.

THE MEDIA FOUNDATION, 1243 West 7th Ave., Vancouver, B. C. V6H 1B7, Canada, (604) 736-9401 or (800) 663-1243. An in-your-face media literacy and activist group that challenges the North American advertising/consumerist life-style through television uncommercials, guerrilla anti-advertisements, and demarketing campaigns. Publishes *Adbusters Quarterly* (4 issues/$18).

REDEFINING PROGRESS, 116 New Montgomery St., Suite 209, San Francisco, CA 94105, (415) 543-6511. Uses public education and organizing to advocate for new economic and social indicators of real well-being, and for more socially and environmentally sustainable policies in business and government.

ROCKY MOUNTAIN INSTITUTE, 1739 Snowmass Creek Rd., Snowmass, CO 81654-9199, (303) 927-3851. A resource-policy organization that studies and advocates more sustainable energy, water, agriculture, transportation, and community economic-development policies. Activities include research projects, publications, and consulting on utility and community programs. RMI emphasizes a "true-cost" approach to market economics.

SOCIETY FOR THE ADVANCEMENT OF SOCIO-ECONOMICS, University of New Mexico, 2808 Central Ave. SE, Albuquerque, NM 87106, (505) 277-5081. An international organization of academicians, policy makers and businesspeople who through conferences and publications seek to integrate economics within philosophical, psychological, societal, historical, institutional, and ethical contexts.

SOUTHERN ORGANIZING COMMITTEE FOR ECONOMIC AND SOCIAL JUSTICE (SOC), P. O. Box 12602, Birmingham, AL 35202, (205) 781-1781. A multiracial network of African-American, white, Native-American, Latino, and Asian-American individuals and organizations fighting environmental racism, pollution, and toxic dumping in poor communities throughout the South and Southwest, and working for democracy and a better quality of life for all the South's poor and working-class people.

VOLUNTARY SIMPLICITY ASSOCIATION, c/o Phinney Neighborhood Association, 6532 Phinney Ave. N., Seattle, WA 98103, (206) 783-2244. Send a self-addressed stamped envelope to receive information on how to organize your own voluntary simplicity study circles and support groups.

WOMEN'S ENVIRONMENT AND DEVELOPMENT ORGANIZATION (WEDO), 854 Third Ave., 15th floor, New York, NY 10022, (212) 759-7982. An international organization and network that empowers women to work at the local and larger levels for a healthy environment and economic and political development that enhances women's lives.

WORKWELL NETWORK, Box 3483, Courtenay, B. C., Canada V9N 6Z8, (604) 334-0998. An education and activist network that combats work addiction and promotes shorter work-time policies in Canada.

For the names and addresses of many more organizations, see *Organizing For Social Change: A Manual for Activists in the 1990s* (Arlington, Va.: Seven Locks Press, 1991), available from the publisher, at (800) 354-5348.

Index

A

B

(

D

E

F

G

H

I

J

K

L

M

N

O

P

Q

R

∫

Sustainable materials, 161
Swann, Bob, 170, 176(n5)

Sweden, 128, 189
Synergies, 190-191, 194(n12)

T

Taylorism, 28
Technical assistance, 123
Telecommuting, 128
Temple, Dominique, 207
Temporary work, 43
Theorell, Töres, 26
Third World
    alternative trading organiza-
        tions, 210
    and economic addiction, 81
    economic forms from, 109-110
    economic invisibility, 19, 20,
        21(n8), 34, 41-42, 44(n20)
    and economism, 99
    environmental destruction in,
        53, 143
    invisible economy, 49

plant relocations in, 12, 43, 88
poverty of, 74
See also U.S. foreign relations
Thurow, Lester C., 18
The Tightwad Gazette, 151
Time Dollar model, 172-173
"A Time for Men to Pull
    Together" (Kimbrell),
    140-141
Tortoriello, Frank, 170
*Toward a New Psychology of
    Women* (Miller), 101
Traditional economies, 106, 107,
    109-110
Transfer payments, 47
True-cost pricing, 203
The Turning Point (Capra), 7

U

Ulkatcho Indians, 210
Underground economy, 49
Unemployment, 12, 88-89, 130
United Autoworkers, 93-94
United Nations, 82, 129. *See also*
    International Labor
    Organization

U.S. foreign relations
    and economic addiction, 74-75
    in postmodern paradigm, 13,
        159
    See also Third World
Unremunerated Work Act, 129
Usher, Peter J., 50

V

Values, 69-71, 79-80, 84(n3)
Vanier Institute of the Family, 50

Visible economy
    definition of, 53

W

Y

ABOUT THE AUTHOR

After publication, Barbara Brandt will continue to track and provide information about the emerging postmodern economic paradigm. She is also available for lectures, workshops, and consulting. Please send your comments, news about new-economic activities, and requests for more information (include self-addressed stamped envelope) to: Whole Life Economics Network, P. O. Box 44-1615, West Somerville, MA 02144-0013.

Photograph by Don Davis.

BARBARA BRANDT is a long-time organizer and social-change activist from the Boston area who integrates environmental, community, economic, and gender issues with personal and societal concerns. She founded the community-gardening program in the town where she lives and the Boston-area Urban Solar Energy Association, has worked with Environmentalists for Full Employment and the Shorter Work-Time Group of Boston/Women for Economic Justice, and helped organize international conferences for The Other Economic Summit (TOES) in Toronto (1988) and Houston (1990). She also studies and teaches women's sacred dance.

NEW SOCIETY PUBLISHERS

New Society Publishers is a not-for-profit, worker-controlled publishing house. We are proud to be the only publishing house in the United States committed to fundamental social change through nonviolent action.

We are connected to a growing worldwide network of peace, feminist, religious, environmental, and human rights activists, of which we are an active part. We are proud to offer powerful nonviolent alternatives to the harsh and violent industrial and social systems in which we all participate. And we deeply appreciate that so many of you continue to look to us for resources in these challenging and promising times.

New Society Publishers is a project of the New Society Educational Foundation and the Catalyst Education Society. We are not the subsidiary of any transnational corporation; we are not beholden to any other organization; and we have neither stockholders nor owners in any traditional business sense. We hold this publishing house in trust for you, our readers and supporters, and we appreciate your contributions and feedback.

New Society Publishers
4527 Springfield Avenue
Philadelphia, Pennsylvania
19143

New Society Publishers
P.O. Box 189
Gabriola Island, British Columbia
V0R 1X0